Understanding Islamic Sciences

The Department of Research and Publications at the Islamic College for Advanced Studies (ICAS) is an academic and cultural centre, concerned with general issues of Islamic thought. The idea of an Islamic institution of higher learning grounded on Islamic normative values and historical heritage, yet fully capable of responding to, and guiding Muslims in meeting the demands of modern Western epistemological, cultural, socio-political and economic ideas, are based on years of experience and contemplation, all of which now form conceptual history of ICAS. The Department provides a meeting point for the Western and Islamic worlds of learning. At ICAS it contributes to the multi-disciplinary and cross-disciplinary study of the contemporary world. Beyond ICAS, its role is strengthened by developing international academic contacts. It is an intellectual forum working from an Islamic perspective to promote and support research projects, organise intellectual and cultural seminars and publish scholarly works. It tries to establish a distinct intellectual trend in Islamic thought which relates to the vivid legacy of the Muslim nation and its continuous efforts for intellectual and methodological reform. This involves a large number of researchers and scholars from various parts of the world.

ICAS' publications fall into the following categories: *Theology, Philosophy, Mysticism, Islamic Legal Theory and Islamic Law, hermeneutics and Qur'anic studies, Hadith methodology, Social Sciences, and Languages.*

Since ICAS is an academic college promoting intellectual debate, and scholarship, the views expressed in the books published will always reflect independent views and diverse approaches to the problems being dealt with.

ICAS Press

Murtada Mutahhari

Understanding Islamic Sciences

Philosophy • Theology • Mysticism • Morality • Jurisprudence

ICAS Press

British Library Cataloguing-in-Publication Data
A catalogue record for this book is available from the
British Library

ISBN 1 904063 03 9 (pb)

This edition first published 2002

Published by
Islamic College for Advanced Studies Press (ICAS)
133 High Road, Willesden, London NW10 2SW

Distributed by
Saqi Books
26 Westbourne Grove, London W2 5RH

Contents

Preface

This book is a collection of martyr Murtaḍā Muṭahharī's essential papers and articles on (1) philosophy (2) theology (*al-kalām*) (3) *'irfān* (Islamic mysticism) (4) *uṣūl al-fiqh* (the principles of jurisprudence) (5) *fiqh* (Islamic law) and (6) morality (*ḥikmat-e-'amali'*). The six parts together serve both as a comprehensive survey of the essentials of different branches of Islamic studies and a general guide to understanding the basic teachings of Islam, along with the main points of difference among various sects of Muslims. Martyr Muṭahharī's important work is probably the most thorough of all introductions to Islamic studies and deserves to be prescribed reading for all students of Islam. It is also very useful for non-specialists who wish to acquaint themselves with Islamic knowledge. All introductory books that have been published to date in this field are written either by Orientalists or by Muslim scholars. Orientalists are naturally biased and fail to give a true picture of the development of the different Islamic sciences. Muslim scholars consciously or subconsciously incorporate in their writings certain misleading notions propagated by Orientalist scholars about Islamic studies and its various branches. It is also true to say that no other introductory text covers all Muslim schools of thought and their specific views. Martyr Murtaḍā Muṭahharī's exposition and evaluation of various theories are objective and unbiased, which makes them uniquely suitable for students looking for a fair, clear and comprehensive introduction.

Murtaḍā Muṭahharī was born in a village some forty kilometres from Mashhad in 1338/1919–20. He received his earliest education mostly at the hands of his father and while still a child entered the *hawza-yi 'ilmiya*, the traditional educational establishment, of Mashhad, but soon afterwards left for Qum, the centre for religious education in Iran. While he was pursuing elementary studies there he was greatly affected by the lessons in *akhlāq* (Islamic ethics) given by Ayatullah Khumaynī, which Muṭahharī himself described as being, in reality, lessons in *ma'ārif wa sayr-u-sulūk* (the theoretical and practical approaches to mysticism). He later studied metaphysics (*falsafa*) with him, as well as jurisprudence (*uṣūl al-fiqh*). He was especially attracted by *falsafa*, theoretical mysticism (*'irfān*) and theology (*kalām*), known as 'intellectual knowledge', and he went on to study these subjects with 'Allama Tabataba'i. His teachers in law (*fiqh*) were all important figures of the time, especially Ayatullah Burūjirdī, who became the authoritative jurisconsult (*marja' al-taqlīd*), as well as head of the *hawza-yi 'ilmiya* of Qum, in 1945. Murtaḍā Muṭahharī studied both *fiqh* and *uṣūl al-fiqh* in the classes of Ayatullah Burūjirdī for ten years. He was also deeply affected at about this time by lessons on *Nahj al-Balāghah* given by Mirzā 'Alī Aqā Shīrāzī Isfahānī, whom he had met in Isfahan. He later said that, although he had been reading this work since his childhood, he now felt that he had discovered a 'new world'. Subsequently, Muṭahharī became a well-known teacher in Qum, first in Arabic language and literature, and later in logic (*mantiq*), *uṣūl al-fiqh*, *falsafa* and *mysticism*.

In 1952 Murtaḍā Muṭahharī moved to Tehran, where, two years later, he began teaching in the Theology Faculty of the University. Not only did he make a strong impression on students, but his move to Tehran also meant that he could become involved with organizations for political and social change. These Islamic associations were groups of students, engineers, doctors, merchants, etc., set up during the 1950s and 1960s; they formed the nucleus of the movement that was eventually to become the revolution. He was also a founder member of the Husayniya-yi Irshād, which played a central role in the religious life of the capital during the four years of its existence until its closure by the authorities in 1973. At the same time he maintained his contact with traditional religious activities, teaching first in the Madrasa-yi Marvi in Tehran and later back in Qum, and also preaching in mosques in Tehran and elsewhere in the country. Through his lectures, articles and books he became a famous and much-respected figure throughout Iran, but it was mainly among the students and teachers of the schools and universities that he was most influential, setting an example and inspiring them as a committed and socially aware Muslim with a traditional education who could make an intellectually appropriate and exciting response to modern secularizing tendencies.

His wide-ranging knowledge and scholarship are reflected in the scope of his writings, which cover the fields of law, philosophy, theology, history and literature. He was also one of the few high-ranking *'ulamā'* to be in continuous contact with Ayatullah Khumaynī during the fifteen or so years in which the movement that led to the revolution was developing. He was actively engaged in all the stages of this movement.

His life came to an abrupt and untimely end when he was shot in the street by an assassin after a meeting of the Revolutionary Council on the evening of

1 May 1979. Many mourners accompanied his funeral cortege from Tehran to Qum, where he was buried near the shrine of the sister of the eighth Shi'i Imām. Shahīd Mutahharī contributed a great deal to Islamic scholarship through his many publications, most of which have been translated into English. They include: *Islamic Modest Dress* (Macmillan Publishing Company, Inc., 1990); *Universal Prototype*, translated by Laleh Bakhtiar (Abjad Book Designers & Builders, 1989); *Hijab*, translated by Laleh Bakhtiar (Abjad Book Designers & Builders, 1993); *Iqbal* (Abjad Book Designers & Builders, 1993); *Reviving Islamic Ethos; Master and Mastership; Jurisprudence and Its Principles; Spiritual Discourses; The Awaited Saviour; Light within Me; The Goal of Life; Man and Universe; Polarization Around the Character of 'Ali ibn Abi Talib; Woman and Her Rights;* and *Anecdotes of Pious Men.*

Apart from the above-mentioned books, there are many other published works in Arabic and Persian and we hope to be able to publish some, if not all of them, in English translation. The Department of Research at the Islamic College for Advanced Studies in London is happy to publish this present work in the hope of introducing some of his most important writings in one volume to the English-speaking world.

Some of his other books in Persian are as follows:

Nizām Huquq zan dar Islām; Sireyeh Nabavi; Jādbibeh va dāfi'et Ali; Sayri dar nahjul balāghah; Sireyeh A'imat al-at-haar; Ashna-i-ba ulum islami; Imamah va rahbari; Mas'alet al-riba; Ta'lim va tarbiyat dar islam; Islam va muqtaẓayāt ẓamān; Jihād; Guftār haye ma'navi; Irfān ḥāfiẓ; Dah Guftār; Khātimiyyat; Insān kāmil; Mas'alet ḥijāb; Haq va bāṭil; Takāmule ijtimā' insāne; Uṣūl falsafah va ravesh realism; Sharḥ manẓūmah; Falsafah tārikh; Insān va imān; Jahan biniye tawḥidi; Jāmi'ah va tarikh; Vahy va nubuvat; Ḥamāsah al-ḥusaini; Pirāmon Jumhori Islāmi; 'Ilale Garayesh be Mādigrī; Mas'alat shenākht; Akhlāq Ḥussein; Qiyām va inqilāb Māhdi; Insān va sarvenesht; Fiṭrah; and *Nizām Iqtisād Islami.*

Part One

Islamic Philosophy

Literal and Semantic Definitions

Logicians say that when one asks about the 'whatness' of a thing, one is actually asking various things. Sometimes the question refers to the conceptual meaning of a word. When we ask what a thing is, we are asking about the word itself. In asking about its whatness, we seek to know the lexical or idiomatic meaning of the word. Suppose in a book we run across the word *pupak* (hoopoe) and do not know its meaning. We may ask someone, 'What is a *pupak*?' and may receive the answer, '*Pupak is* the name of a bird'. Or suppose we run across the word *kalimah* (word) in the terminology of logicians and we ask someone, 'What does *kalimah* mean in the terminology of logicians?' '*Kalimah*,' we may be told, 'in the terminology of logicians is equivalent to *fi'l* (verb) in the language of grammarians.' Plainly, the relation between word and meaning is conventional and terminological, whether the terminology is restricted or general.

In answering such a question, one must search out instances of usage or consult a dictionary. The question may have numerous answers, all of them correct, because it is possible for a single word to have various meanings in various contexts. For instance, a word may have a special meaning in the usage of logicians and philosophers and another in that of grammarians. The word *kalimah* has one meaning in common usage and in the usage of grammarians, and another meaning in the usage of logicians. Similarly, the word *qiyās* (analogy, syllogism) has one meaning in the usage of logicians and another in the usage of jurists and legists. When a word has two or more meanings within a single body of usages, we may have to specify that it has one meaning in this expression, and another in that. Answers given to such questions are called verbal definitions.

Sometimes a question about the whatness of a thing requires for an answer not the meaning of the word, which we know, but the reality of its referent. For instance, if we ask, 'What is a man?', we do not seek to know the coinage attached to the word 'man'. We all know that the word is applied to a bipedal, speaking, sentient being. Instead, we seek to know the identity and the reality of man. Plainly, in this case there can be only one correct answer, called the real definition.

The verbal definition is prior to the real definition. That is, one must ascertain first the conceptual meaning of the word and then the real definition of the referent so defined. Otherwise, fallacies and disputes may arise because a word has numerous lexical and idiomatic meanings, and this multiplicity of meanings is easily overlooked. One person may give a special meaning or an idiomatic definition of a word, unaware that to another person the word connotes something different. Consequently they may engage in pointless disputes.

The failure to distinguish the meaning of the word from the reality of its referent sometimes results in a transformation as a result of which the meaning of the word is ascribed to the reality of its referent. For instance, a certain word may at first be applied to a whole and then, through changes in usage, to a part of that whole. If one fails to distinguish the meaning of the word from the reality of its referent, one may suppose that that whole has been fragmented, whereas in fact no change has occurred in the whole, but rather the word applying to it has been displaced in meaning to apply to a part of that whole.

An error of precisely this type has arisen in regard to the word 'philosophy' as used in all Western philosophy and its imitators in the East. 'Philosophy' is an idiomatic word with numerous and varied meanings. Different philosophers have defined philosophy, each in a special way, but this discrepancy in definition does not bear on any reality. Each party has used the word in a special sense, which it has defined as its object. What one person calls philosophy, another does not call philosophy but calls it something else or regards it as part of another science. So neither party regards the other as philosophers. I shall take these various usages into account.

The Word 'Philosophy'

Falsafa has a Greek origin. The word is an Arabic verbal noun derived from the Greek word *philosophia,* which is a compound of *philos* and *sophia*, the former meaning 'love', the latter 'wisdom'. Thus *philosophia* means 'love of wisdom'. Plato called Socrates a *philosophos*, meaning that he was a lover of wisdom.[1] The word *falsafa is* an Arabicization, which means 'the work or pursuit of philosophers'.

Before Socrates, a group appeared calling themselves Sophists, or scholars. They made human perception the measure of reality and used fallacious arguments in their deductions. Accordingly, 'sophist' (*sophistes*) lost its original meaning and came to mean one who makes use of fallacious arguments. Thus we have the word 'sophistry', which has a cognate in the Arabic *safsafa,* with the same meaning.

Socrates, out of humility and also perhaps a desire to avoid being identified with the Sophists, forbade people to call him a *sophistes,* or 'scholar',[2] and instead called himself a *philosophos*, a 'lover of wisdom'. Gradually, the word *philosophos,* with its original sense, displaced *sophistes,* and the latter was downgraded to its modern sense of 'one who uses fallacious reasoning'. *Philosophia* became synonymous with wisdom. Therefore, *philosophos* as a technical term had been applied to no one before Socrates, nor was it applied to anyone immediately after him. The term *philosophia*, too, had no definite meaning in those days; it is said that not even Aristotle used it. Later, use of the terms *philosophia* and *philosophos* became widespread.

Muslim Usage

Having taken the word 'philosophy' from the Greeks, Muslims gave it an Arabic form and an Eastern nuance, using it to mean pure rational knowledge. Philosophy in the common Muslim usage did not refer to a special discipline or science; it embraced all rational sciences, as opposed to transmitted sciences, such as etymology, syntax, declension, rhetoric, stylistics, prosody, exegesis, tradition and jurisprudence. Because the word had a generic meaning, only someone who comprehended all the rational sciences of his time, including theology, mathematics, the natural sciences, politics, ethics and domestic economy, would be called a philosopher. Thus it was said that, 'Whoever is a philosopher becomes a world of knowledge, analogous to the objective world'.

When Muslims sought to reproduce Aristotle's classification of the sciences, they used the words *falsafah* or *ḥikmah.* In their eyes, philosophy was the rational science, which had two branches: the theoretical and the practical.

Theoretical philosophy addresses things as they are; practical philosophy addresses human actions as they ought to be. Theoretical philosophy is threefold: theology or high philosophy, mathematics or middle philosophy and natural science or low philosophy. High philosophy, or theology, in turn comprehends two disciplines, general phenomenology and theology per se. Mathematics is fourfold, each of its areas being a science in itself: arithmetic, geometry, astronomy and music. Natural science has numerous divisions.

Practical philosophy is divisible into ethics, domestic economy and civics. The complete philosopher comprehends all these sciences.

True Philosophy

In the philosophers' view, one area enjoys special prominence among the numerous areas of philosophy. It is called first philosophy, high philosophy, the supreme science, the universal science, theology or metaphysics. The ancients believed that one of the features distinguishing this science from all others is its firmer foundation in demonstration and certainty. Another is that it presides over all other sciences; it is in truth the queen of the sciences because the others depend on it totally, but it has no such dependence on them. A third distinguishing feature is that it is more general and universal than any other science.[3] According to these philosophers, this science is the true philosophy. The word 'philosophy' is therefore sometimes applied exclusively to this science, but this usage is rare.

In the view of the ancient philosophers, the word 'philosophy' had two meanings: one, the prevalent meaning of rational knowledge as such, including all but the transmitted sciences, and the other the rare meaning of theology, or first philosophy, one of the three divisions of theoretical philosophy.

Thus there are two possibilities if we choose to define philosophy according to the usage of the ancients. First, if we adopt the common usage, in which philosophy is a generic term applying to no special science or discipline, it will have no special definition. It will mean all non-transmitted sciences. To be a philosopher will mean to comprehend all such sciences. It was in accordance with such a generalized conception of philosophy that it was said that, 'Philosophy is the perfection of the soul of man from both a theoretical standpoint and a practical one'.

Second, if we adopt the uncommon usage, defining philosophy as that activity the ancients called true philosophy, first philosophy or the supreme science, this will constitute a special definition for philosophy. The answer to the question 'What is philosophy?' will then be that philosophy is a science of the states of being from the standpoint that is being, not from the standpoint of its having a special individuation, for instance, of its being body, quantity, quality, man, vegetable or any other tangible thing.

Our knowledge of things is of two kinds. It may be restricted to a certain species or genus; it may apply to the special states, determinations (*aḥkām*) and accidents (*'awāriḍ*) of a certain species or a certain genus, as does, for instance, our knowledge constituting the science of the determinations of numbers (arithmetic), of quantities (geometry), of the states and properties of plants (botany) or of the states, properties and determinations of the human body (medicine or physiology).[4] This sort of knowledge embraces the rest of the sciences, such as meteorology, geology, mineralogy, zoology, psychology, sociology and atomic theory.

Or our knowledge may not be restricted to a certain species; rather, we may say that being has these determinations, states and properties, not from the standpoint that it is of a certain species but from the standpoint that it is being. The universe may be studied in terms of plurality and as a series of discrete subjects, or it may be studied in terms of its unity; that is, we may regard being as a unity and this unity that embraces all things will underlie our assumptions.

If we liken the universe to a body, we see that our studies of that body will be of two kinds. Some of our studies will pertain to the members of that body (for instance, its head, hands, feet or eyes); others will pertain to the whole of that body, as, for instance, when we consider when this body came into being and how long it will persist.

Or is it at all meaningful to look at the body as an aggregate? Does this body have a real unity, the multiplicity of the members being an apparent, not a real, multiplicity? Or is its unity nominal, on the level of a mechanical interrelationship; that is, does it have no more unity than a manufactured device? Has this body a source member from which the other members have sprung? For instance, has this body a head, which is the source for the other members? Or is it a body without a head? If it has a head, does this head have a sensible and perceiving mind, or is it hollow and empty? Does the whole of the body down to the nails and bones enjoy a kind of life, or is the intelligence and perception of this body confined to some entities that have appeared by chance, like worms on a corpse – these worms being what we call the animals of the world, including humans? Does this body as a whole pursue an end, a perfection and a reality or is it aimless? Are the appearance and disappearance of the members an accident or does the law of causation govern them, no phenomenon being without cause and every particular effect arising from a particular cause? Is the system governing this body certain and inescapable? Or does no necessity or certainty govern this body? Are the order and priority of the members of this body real or not? How many basic organs does this body have?

Inquiry that pertains to an organology of the universe of being is science, and inquiry that pertains to a physiology of the universe as a whole is philosophy.

There is thus a special class of questions that resemble those of none of the world's sciences, which investigate particular beings but which compose a class of their own. When we consider this class of questions as an exploration of the parts of the sciences, and try to understand in what respect questions of this class are, technically speaking, accidents, we see that they are accidents of being *qua* being.

Whenever we inquire into the identities (*māhiyat*, essences) of things – as, for instance, when we ask what is the identity, the whatness, the true definition of a body or of man – or whenever we inquire into the being of things – as, for instance, to ask whether a real circle or line exists – the same discipline is involved, because to inquire into these phenomena is to inquire into the accidents of being *qua* being. These identities are, so to speak, among the accidents and determinants of being *qua* being.

Before answering the question, 'What is philosophy?', we must recognize that the word tends to have a usage peculiar to the user. Among Muslims, it is most commonly a generic noun representing all the rational sciences, not the name of a particular science and less commonly a name for first philosophy, a science of the most universal aspects of being, pertaining to no particular subject but to all subjects. This is a science that investigates all of being as a unified subject.

Metaphysics

Aristotle was the first to devise a series of questions that belong to none of the natural, mathematical, ethical, social or logical sciences and must be seen as belonging to a separate science. He may have been the first to discern the pivot on which all these questions turn as accidents and states, which is being *qua* being. He may also have been the first to discover the factor that connects the questions of any one science and the standard by which they are to be distinguished from the questions of another science – in other words, what it is that is called the subject of a science.

The questions of this science, like those of any other, were later to be greatly expanded and augmented. This fact becomes clear if one compares the metaphysics of Aristotle with the metaphysics of Ibn Sīnā, not to mention the metaphysics of Mullā Ṣadrā. But Aristotle was the first to elaborate this science as an independent field, to give it a special place among the sciences.

Aristotle gave this science no name. His works were posthumously compiled into an encyclopedia. The section in question followed that on natural philosophy and, having no special name, came to be known as *metaphusika*, meaning 'after physics'. It was translated into Arabic as *mā ba'd al-tabī'a.*

The prosaic derivation of the name was eventually forgotten. Students of Aristotle's work instead supposed that the name had been applied because at least some of the questions this science addresses, such as God and the pure intelligences, are external to nature. Accordingly, it occurred to some, including Ibn Sīnā, that this science should be called not 'metaphysics' but 'pro-physics' because it includes the subject of God, who is prior to nature, not posterior to it.[5]

This error in translation later led to an error in meaning among some modern students of philosophy. Many Europeans supposed that metaphysics is equivalent to hyper-physics and that the subject of this science consists of phenomena external to nature. They erroneously defined metaphysics as the science that deals solely with God and phenomena separate from nature. In fact, the science includes the natural and the supernatural, in sum, everything that exists.

Philosophy in Modern Times

The watershed between the modern era (beginning in the sixteenth Christian century) and the ancient was marked by the displacement of the syllogistic and rational method of science by the experimental and empirical method, a change instituted by a group foremost among whom were the Frenchman Descartes and the Englishman Bacon. The natural sciences *en bloc* departed the domain of syllogistic reasoning and entered that of the experimental method. Mathematics took on a semi-syllogistic, semi-experimental character.

After this course of events, some decided that the syllogistic method was unreliable. So, if a science is beyond the reach of concrete experiment, if it calls exclusively for syllogistic reasoning, it is groundless. Since this is the case with metaphysics, that is, concrete experiment has no place in it, this science must be groundless. Its questions are beyond confirmation or refutation through research. People who thought in this way drew a line through the science that once stood above all others and had been called the most noble, the queen of sciences. According to them, the science of metaphysics or first philosophy did not and could not exist. They thus deprived human beings of the opportunity to pose those questions that matter most to them.

Others maintained that the syllogistic method was not in all cases unreliable and must be employed in metaphysics and ethics. They created a new terminology. What could take the form of research based on the experimental method they called science, and what had to be approached through the syllogistic method, including metaphysics, ethics and logic, they called philosophy. Philosophy consists of those sciences that conduct research through the syllogistic method only and in which concrete experiment plays no part.

In this view, as in the view of the ancient scholars, philosophy is generic, not specific, in meaning. It is not the name of one science, but comprehends several sciences. But philosophy in this sense encompasses less than it did according to ancient usage. It includes metaphysics, ethics, logic, law and perhaps a few other disciplines, but mathematics and the natural sciences are outside its compass.

Members of the first group totally denied the validity of metaphysics and the syllogistic method, trusting in the empirical and experimental sciences. In time, they realized that if everything that exists falls into the domain of the experimental sciences, and if the questions they pose are restricted to particular subjects, then we are going to be wholly deprived of an overall understanding of the universe, such as philosophy or metaphysics can provide. Thus, they founded a scientific philosophy, a philosophy based completely on the sciences. Through comparative study of the sciences, inquiry into the way in which their questions connect with other questions and discovery of the kind of relationships among the laws and questions of the sciences and the totality they compose, a range of more general questions would evolve. They called these more general questions 'philosophy'. The Frenchman Auguste Comte and the Englishman Herbert Spencer took up this method.

Philosophy was no longer an autonomous science either in its subject-matter or in its sources, since such an autonomous science had for its subject being *qua* being and had its sources – at least its chief source – in first axioms. Philosophy had become a science whose function was to study the products of the other sciences, to interrelate them and to derive general questions from their more limited questions. Auguste Comte's philosophy of positivism and Herbert Spencer's synthetic philosophy are of this sort. According to this view, philosophy is not a science apart from the other sciences, but constitutes a broader and fuller view of things seen and learnt through the sciences.

Some others, such as Kant, thought it necessary first to study knowledge itself, along with the faculty that is its source, that is, reason. They made a critique of human reason and designated their researches 'philosophy' or 'critical philosophy'. However, this too has nothing but the word in common with what the ancients called philosophy or with Comte's positivism or Spencer's synthetic philosophy. Kant's philosophy has more to do with logic, which is a special form of ideology in the strict sense (*fikr shināsī*), than with philosophy in its original meaning, which is cosmology.

In the European cultural sphere, whatever was not science, that is, whatever did not fit into any of the natural or mathematical sciences but was a theory of the universe, man, or society gradually came to be known as 'philosophy'. If someone were to collect all the 'isms' that have been called philosophy in Europe and America and list all their definitions, one would see that they have nothing in common except that they are not science.

The difference between ancient and modern philosophies is dissimilar in kind to the difference between ancient and modern sciences. Compare ancient and modern medicine, geometry, psychology or botany. Ancient science is not different in identity from modern science (for example, the word 'medicine' did not refer to one science in ancient times and another in modern times). Ancient and modern medicine share a single definition; medicine has always consisted in knowledge of the states and symptomatic conditions of the human body. But ancient and modern medicine differ in how they approach questions. Modern medicine is the more empirical; ancient medicine is the more deductive and syllogistic. Modern medicine is also the more developed. This sort of difference holds for all other sciences.

The term 'philosophy', however, has had various referents and a separate definition for each referent in the course of the ancient and modern periods. In ancient times, philosophy sometimes designated rational science as such and sometimes had a specialized meaning applying to one of the branches of this science (such as metaphysics or first philosophy). In modern times, the word has been applied to numerous referents, having a different definition in accordance with each.

Divorce of the Sciences from Philosophy

An egregious but prevalent error of our time that arose in the West and has spread widely among Eastern imitators of Western thinkers is the myth of the divorce of the sciences from philosophy.

A linguistic change pertaining to a convention of usage has been mistaken for a change of meaning pertaining to a real referent. In the language of the ancients, the words 'philosophy' and '*ḥikmah*' were generally used to mean rational, as opposed to transmitted knowledge. Thus, these words comprehended all of man's rational and intellectual ideas in their meanings. In this usage, philosophy was a generic, not a proper noun.

In modern times, the word became restricted to metaphysics, logic, aesthetics and the like. This change in the name has led some to suppose that in ancient times philosophy was a single science embracing theology and the natural, mathematical and other sciences and that later the natural and mathematical sciences were divorced from philosophy and grew independent of it. It is as if the word 'body' once meant the human frame, as opposed to the spirit, and included the whole human form from head to foot and later acquired the secondary sense of the trunk and limbs, minus the head. Suppose one were to imagine that the head of a person had become separated from his body. A linguistic change would have been mistaken for a change in meaning. Consider also the word 'Fars', which once referred to the whole of Iran but today refers only to one of its southern provinces. An observer may might think the province of Fars had seceded from Iran. This is the status of the divorce of the sciences from philosophy. The sciences were once lumped together under the name 'philosophy', but today this name is applied to one of the sciences only.

This change in name has nothing to do with a divorce of the sciences from philosophy. The sciences have never been part of philosophy proper; so they could not be divorced from it.

Illuminationism and Peripateticism

Islamic philosophers are divisible into two groups: illuminationists and peripateticists. Foremost among the illuminationist philosophers of Islam is the sixth-century scholar Shaykh Shihāb ad-Dīn Suhrawardī (otherwise known as Shaykh-i Ishrāq, but to whom I shall refer as Suhrawardī), and foremost among the peripatetic philosophers of Islam is Shaykh ar-Ra'īs Abū 'Alī ibn Sīnā (Ibn Sīnā). The illuminationists are considered to be followers of Plato and the peripatetic followers of Aristotle. The principal and essential difference between the two methods is that the illuminationists consider deduction and rational thought insufficient for study of philosophical questions, especially of divine wisdom (*ḥikmat-i ilāhi*), and the path of the heart, asceticism and purification of the soul as incumbent on anyone wishing to realize inner realities. Peripatetics rely solely on deduction.

The word *ishrāq*, meaning 'illumination', aptly conveys a sense of the illuminationist method, but the word *mashshā'*, which means 'peripatetic' or 'ambulant', is purely arbitrary and conveys nothing of the peripatetic method. Aristotle and his followers were called the *mashshā'īn*, the peripatetics, because Aristotle held forth while taking walks. 'Deductionist' would more actually describe the peripatetics' method, but I shall continue to use the more common term, peripatetic.

The major questions over which illuminationists and peripatetics differ in Islam today generally pertain to Islam and not to Plato or Aristotle. They include the questions of essentialism (*aṣālat-i māhiya*) versus existentialism (*aṣālat-i wujūd*), the unity versus the multiplicity of being, the question of fabrication (*ja'l*), the question of whether a body is compounded of matter and form, the question of ideas (*muthūl*) and archetypes (*arbāb-i anvā'*), and the question of the principle of the more noble possibility (*imkān-i ashrāf*).[6]

Did Plato and Aristotle actually have two different methods? Did such a difference in outlook exist between the master, Plato, and the pupil, Aristotle? Was Suhrawardī's method, propounded in the Islamic era, actually Plato's method? Did Plato follow the way of the heart, asceticism and the discipline of the soul, or the illumination and witness of the heart? Was he an exponent of what Suhravardi later called experiential wisdom (*ḥikmat-i dhawqī*)? Do the questions that have differentiated illuminationists and peripatetics since the time of Suhravardi (questions of essence and existence, of fabrication, of the compoundedness or simplicity of the body, of the formula of the more noble possibility and of the unity or multiplicity of being) actually date back to differences of opinion between Plato and Aristotle? Or are the questions, at least some of them, later developments unknown to Plato or Aristotle? There were certainly differences of opinion between the two; Aristotle refuted many of Plato's theories and countered them with different ones.

In the Alexandrian period, which was the watershed between the Hellenic and Islamic eras, the followers of Plato and Aristotle formed two opposed ranks. Farabi, in *al-Jam' bayn Ra'yay al-Ḥakīmayn* ('The Reconciliation of the Views of the Two Sages'), discusses the disagreements between the two philosophers and strives to resolve them. There are three basic questions on which Plato and Aristotle differed, questions different from those discussed during the Islamic era.

It is highly doubtful that Plato advocated a spiritual way, with asceticism and discipline of the soul and witness of the heart. Thus, the notion that Plato and Aristotle had two distinct methods, the illuminationist and the peripatetic, becomes highly debatable. It is by no means clear that Plato was recognized as an illuminationist, an exponent of inner illumination, in his own time or any time soon thereafter. It is not even clear that the term peripatetic was applied exclusively to Aristotle and his followers in his own time. As Shahristani says, 'Now the strict peripatetics are the members of the Lyceum. Plato, honoured for his wisdom, always taught them while taking walks. Aristotle followed his example, and accordingly he [apparently Aristotle] and his followers were called peripatetics.'[7] Aristotle and his followers were certainly called peripatetics, and this usage was simply continued in Islamic times.

Prior to Suhrawardī, we never find any of the philosophers, such as Fārābī and Ibn Sīnā, or any of the historians of philosophy, such as Shahristani, speaking of Plato as a sage who advocated experiential or illuminationist wisdom.[8] It was Suhrawardī who gave this term currency, and it was he who, in his *Ḥikmat al-Ishrāq* ('Wisdom of Illumination'), designated some of the ancient sages, including Pythagoras and Plato, exponents of experiential and illuminationist wisdom and called Plato chief of the illuminationists.

I believe Suhrawardī adopted the illuminationist method under the influence of the *'urafā'* and the *ṣūfis*; the combination of illumination and deduction is his own invention. But he, perhaps in order to improve acceptance of his theory, spoke of a group of ancient philosophers who had the same method. Suhravardi offers no sort of documentation on this subject, just as he offers none on the matter of the ancient Iranian sages. Certainly, if he possessed such documentation, he would have presented it and so avoided leaving an idea to which he was so devoted in ambiguity and doubt.

Some writers on the history of philosophy, in discussing Plato's beliefs and ideas, have not mentioned his supposed illuminationist method. Shahristani's *Al-Milal wa'n-Niḥal*, Dr Human's *Tārikh-i Falsafa*, Will Durant's *History of Philosophy* and Muḥammad 'Alī Furūghi's *Sayr-i Ḥikmat dār Urupa* omit any reference to this method in the sense in which Suhrawardī understands it. Furughi mentions Platonic love, a love of the beautiful, which in Plato's belief – at least as expressed in the Symposium – is rooted in divinity. It bears no relation to what Suhravardi has said about the purification of the psyche and the gnostic way to God. Plato's position is said to be: 'Before coming to the world, the spirit beheld absolute beauty; when in this world it sees outward beauty, it remembers absolute beauty and feels pain at its exile. Physical love, like formal beauty, is metaphysical. But true love is something else; it is the basis for illuminating perception and realization of eternal life.'[9]

In his *History of Western Philosophy*, Bertrand Russell repeatedly mentions the admixture of ratiocination and illumination in the philosophy of Plato. However, he offers no documentation or quotations that would clarify whether Plato's illumination arises from discipline and purification of the soul or is just that experience born of love of the beautiful.[10] Further investigation of this question must include direct study of Plato's entire corpus.

Pythagoras may have employed the illuminationist method, apparently under the inspiration of Oriental teachings. Russell, who regards Plato's method as illuminationistic, maintains that Plato came under the influence of Pythagoras in this regard.[11]

Whether or not we see Plato as an illuminationist in method, there are pivotal ideas among his beliefs that define his philosophy, all of which Aristotle opposed. One such concept is the theory of ideas, according to which all we witness in this world, substances and accidents alike, have their origin and reality in the other world. The individual beings of this world amount to shadows or reflections of other-worldly realities. For instance, all the human individuals who dwell in this world have a principle and reality in the other world; the real and substantive man is that man of the other world.

Plato called these realities ideas. In Islamic times, the Greek word for idea was translated as *mithāl* ('likeness', 'idea'), and these realities were called collectively the *muthūl-i aflātūni* ('Platonic ideas'). Ibn Sīnā strenuously opposed the theory of Platonic ideas, and Suhravardi just as strenuously advocated it. Among later philosophers holding to the theory of ideas are Mir Damad and Mullā Ṣadrā. However, these two sages' definitions of idea, especially Mir Damad's, differ from Plato's and even from Suhrawardī's.

Mir Findiriski is another advocate of the theory of ideas from the Safavid era. He has a well-known *qaṣīda* in Persian in which he propounds his own views on this theory. Here is how it begins:

> Lo! The star-studded wheel, so beauteous and splendid! What is above has a correspondent form here below. Should this lower form scale the ladder of gnosis, it will ever find union above with its origin. The intelligible form that is endless, eternal, is compendious and single with all or without all. No external prehension will grasp this discussion, be it Bu Naṣr Farābī or Bu 'Āli Sīnā.[12]

Another of Plato's pivotal theories concerns the human spirit. He believes that, prior to being attached to bodies, spirits were created and dwelt in a world above and beyond this, which is the world of ideas (or of similitudes, *'ālam-i muthūl*).

The third of Plato's theories is based on the first two and amounts to a corollary of them. It holds that knowledge comes through recollection, not through actual learning. Everything we learn in this world, although we presume it to be something of which we were previously ignorant and have learnt for the first time, is in reality a recollection of those things we knew before, in that, prior to being attached to the body in this world, the spirit dwelt in a higher world in which it witnessed ideas. Because the realities of all things are the ideas of those things, which the spirits perceived earlier, these spirits knew realities before coming to this world and finding attachment to bodies. After finding this attachment, we forgot these things.

For the spirit, the body is like a curtain hung across a mirror that prevents the transmission of light and the reflection of forms from the surface of the mirror. Through dialectics (discussion, argument and rational method), through love or, as Suhrawardī and like-minded people imply, through asceticism, discipline of the soul and the spiritual way, the curtain is lifted, the light shines through and the forms are revealed.

Aristotle parts company with Plato on all three of these ideas. First, he denies the existence of ideal, abstract and celestial universals; he regards the universal or, more properly speaking, the universality of the universal as a purely subjective phenomenon. Second, he believes that the spirit is created after the body, that is, at the same time as the creation of the body is completed and perfected. Third, Aristotle considers the body in no way a hindrance or curtain to the spirit; on the contrary, it is the means and instrument by which the spirit acquires new learning. The spirit acquires its learning by means of these senses and bodily instruments; it had no prior existence in another world in which to have learnt anything.

Plato's and Aristotle's differences of opinion over these basic questions, as well as over some less important ones, were kept alive after their deaths. They each had their followers in the Alexandrian school. Plato's followers there became known as neo-Platonists. This school was founded by the Egyptian Ammonius Saccas. Its most celebrated and outstanding exponent was an Egyptian of Greek descent, Plotinus, whom the Islamic historians called the Greek master (AshShaykh al-Yunāni). The neo-Platonists introduced new topics, perhaps borrowing from ancient Oriental sources. Aristotle's Alexandrian followers and expositors were numerous. The most famous were Themistius and Alexander of Aphrodisias.

Islamic Methods of Thought

There have been other methods of thought in the Islamic world, at variance with the illuminationist and peripatetic methods, which have played genuine and basic roles in the development of Islamic culture. Two such methods are *'irfān* (gnosis) and *kalām* (scholastic theology).

Neither the *'urafā'* nor the *mutakallimīn* have regarded themselves as followers of the philosophers, whether illuminationists or peripatetics. Indeed, they have opposed and clashed with these philosophers and the clashes have had an appreciable effect on the fate of Islamic philosophy. *'Irfān* and *kalām* have both moved Islamic philosophy forward as a result of conflict and opened up new horizons for philosophy.

Four Islamic Approaches

Many of the questions contained within Islamic philosophy were first addressed by the *mutakallimīn* or the *'urafā'*, although they express themselves in ways that differ from those of the philosophers. Islam comprehends four methods of thought and Islamic thinkers may adhere to any one of these methods. I am discussing methods of thought having a philosophical character in the most general sense, that is, constituting an ontology and a cosmology. I am dealing with the universals of philosophy and not the methods of thought of jurisprudence, exegesis, tradition, letters, politics or ethics, which are another matter entirely. Each of these methods has taken on a special character under the influence of Islamic teachings and differs from its counterparts outside the Islamic sphere. Each is governed by the particular spirit of Islamic culture.

One method is the deductive method of peripatetic philosophy. It has numerous adherents in history. Most Islamic philosophers, including al-Kindī, Fārābī, Ibn Sīnā, Khwāja Nāṣir ad-Dīn Ṭūsī, Mir Damad, Ibn Rushd of Andalusia, Ibn Baja of Andalusia and Ibn as-Sa'igh of Andalusia have followed this method. The perfect exemplar of this school is Ibn Sinā. Such philosophical works of his as the *Kitāb ash-Shifā'* ('The Book of Healing', the so-called *Sufficientia*), *Ishārāt va Tanbihāt* ('Allusions and Admonitions'), *Najāt* ('Deliverance'), *Danishnama yi 'Alā'i* ('The Book of Knowledge', dedicated to 'alā ad-Dawla), *Mabda' va Ma'ād* ('The Source and the Destination'), *Ta'ligāt-i Mubāḥāthāt* ('Annotations to the Discussions') and *'Uyūn al-Ḥikma* ('Wellsprings of Wisdom') are all works of peripateticism. This method relies exclusively on rational deduction and demonstration.

A second method is the illuminationist method. This has fewer adherents than the first method. It was revived by Shihāb ad-Dīn Suhrawardī and followed by Qutb ad-Dīn Shīrāzi, Shahrazūri and a number of others. Suhravardi is considered the perfect exemplar of this school. He wrote numerous books, including the *Ḥikmat al-Ishrāq* ('Wisdom of Illumination'), *Talwihāt* ('Intimations'), *Muṭarahāt* ('Conversations'), *Muqāwamāt* ('Oppositions') and *Hayākil an-Nūr* (Temples of Light'). The best-known of them is the *Ḥikmat al-Ishrāq*; this is the only work wholly devoted to the illuminationist method. Suhravardi has written some treatises in Persian, among them *Avaz-i Par-i, Gabra'il* ('The Song of Gabriel's Wing') and *'Aql-i Surkh* ('The Red Intelligence').

The illuminationist method rests on rational deduction and demonstration and on endeavour and purification of the soul. According to this method, one cannot discover the underlying realities of the universe by means of rational deduction and demonstration alone.

The wayfaring method of *'irfān,* or Sufism, is the third method. It relies exclusively on a purification of the soul based on a concept of making one's way to God and drawing near to the Truth. This way is said to culminate in the attainment of Reality. The method of *'irfān* places no confidence at all in rational deduction. The *'urafā'* say that the deductionists stand on wooden legs. According to the method of *'irfān,* the goal is not just to uncover reality, but to reach it.

The method of *'irfān* has numerous adherents, some of whom have grown famous in the Islamic world, including Bayāzid Bastāmi, Ḥallāj, Shibli, Junayd of Baghdād, Dhū'n-Nūn Miṣrī, Abū Saīd-i Abi'l-Khayr, Khwaja Abdullah Anṣāri, Abū Tālib Makki, Abū Naṣr Sarrāj, Abū'l-Qāsim Qushayri, Muḥyi'd-Dīn Ibn 'Arabi of Andalūsia, Ibn Faridh of Egypt and Mawlānā Rūmi. The supreme exponent of Islamic *'irfān,* who codified it as a science and had a compelling influence on all who followed him, is Muḥyi 'd-Dīn Ibn 'Arabi.

The wayfaring method of *'irfān* has one feature in common with the illuminationist method and two features at variance with it. Their shared feature is reliance on reform, refinement and purification of the soul. The distinguishing features of each are as follows: The *'ārif* wholly rejects deduction; the illuminationist upholds it and uses thought and purification to aid each other. The illuminationist, like any other philosopher, seeks to discover reality; the *'ārif* seeks to attain it.

Fourth is the deductive method of *kalām.* Like the peripatetics, the *mutakallimīn* rely on rational deduction, but with two differences. First, the principles on which the *mutakallimīn* base their reasoning are different from those on which the philosophers base theirs. The most important convention used by the *mutakallimīn,* especially by the Mu'tazilites, is that of beauty and ugliness. However, they differ among themselves as to the meaning of this convention: the Mu'tazilites regard the concept of beauty and ugliness as rational, but the Ash'arites regard it as canonical. The Mu'tazilites have derived a series of principles and formulae from this principle, such as the formula of grace (*qā'ida yi lutf*) and the incumbency of the optimal (*wujūb-i aṣlaḥ*) upon God Most High.

The philosophers, however, regard the principle of beauty and ugliness as a nominal and human principle, like the pragmatic premises and intelligibles propounded in logic, which are useful only in polemics, not in demonstration. Accordingly, the philosophers call *kalām* 'polemical wisdom', as opposed to 'demonstrational wisdom'.

Second, the *mutakallimīn*, unlike the philosophers, regard themselves as committed to the defence of the bounds of Islam. Philosophical discussion is free; that is, the philosopher does not have the predetermined object of defending a particular belief. The *mutakallīm* does have such an object.

The method of *kalām is* subdivided into three methods: the Mu'tazilites, the Ash'arite and the Shiite.

Mu'tazilites are numerous in history. There are Abū'l Hudhayl Allaf, Naẓẓām, Jāhiẓ, Abū 'Ubayda and Mu'ammar ibn Muthannā, all of whom lived in the second or third centuries of the Hijrah. Qāḍi 'Abd al-Jabbar in the fourth century and Zamakhshari around the turn of the sixth century also exemplify this school.

Shaykh Abū'l-Ḥaṣan Ash'ari (d. 330) perfectly exemplifies the Ash'arite school. Qāḍi Abū Bakr Bāqillāni, Imām al-Ḥaramayn Juwayni, Ghazzāli and Fakhr ad-Dīn Rāzi all followed the Ash'ari method.

Shī'ī *mutakallimīn* are also numerous. Hishām ibn al-Ḥikam, a companion of Imām Ja'far Ṣādiq (peace be upon him) was a Shī'ī *mutakallīm.* The Nawbakhti family, an Iranian Shī'ī family, produced some outstanding *mutakallimīn.* Shaykh Mufīd and Sayyid Murtaḍā 'Alam al-Hudā are also ranked among Shī'ī *mutakallimīn.* The perfect exemplar of Shī'ī *kalām* is Khwaja Nasir ad-Dīn Ṭūsī. His *Tajrīd al-'Aqā'id* ('Refinement of Beliefs') is one of the most famous works of *kalām.* He was also a philosopher and mathematician. After him, *kalām* took a wholly different course and assumed a more philosophical character.

Among the Sunnis' works of *kalām,* the most famous is the *Sharḥ Mavāqif* ('Elucidation of the Stations'), with text by Qāẓi 'Azud ad-Dīn Iji (a contemporary of Ḥāfiẓ, who praised him in his poetry) and annotations by Sharif Jurjani. This work was deeply influenced by the *Tajrīd al-'Aqā'id.*

Sublime Wisdom

The four streams of thought continued in the Islamic world until they reached a point of confluence called 'sublime wisdom' (*ḥikmat-i muta 'āliya*). The science of sublime wisdom was founded by Ṣadr al-Muta'allihin Shīrāzi (or Mullā Ṣadrā; d. 1050/1640).[13] The term 'sublime wisdom' occurs in Ibn Sīnā's *Ishārāt*, but Ibn Sīnā's philosophy never became known by this name.

Mullā Ṣadrā, however, formally designated his philosophy 'sublime wisdom', and it became so known. His school resembles Suhrawardī's in method in that it seeks to combine demonstration with mystic vision and direct witness, but it differs in its principles and conclusions.

In Mullā Ṣadrā's school, many of the points of disagreement between peripateticism and illuminationism, between philosophy and *'irfān*, or between philosophy and *kalām* have been definitively resolved. Mullā Ṣadrā's philosophy is not a syncretism, however, but a unique philosophical system, which one must regard as autonomous, even though the various Islamic methods of thought had an impact on its formation.

Mullā Ṣadrā has written numerous works, among them the *Asfār-i Arba 'a* ('The Four Journeys' or 'Books'), *Ash-Shavāhid ar-Rubūbiya* ('Witnesses to Lordship'), *Mabda' wa Ma'ād* ('The Source and the Destination'), *'Arshiya* ('On the Empyrean'), *Mashā'ir* ('The Perceptual Faculties') and *Sharḥ-i Hidāya yi Athir ad-Dīn Abhari* ('An Elucidation of Athir ad-Dīn Abhari's Guidance').

Among Mullā Ṣadrā's followers is Ḥajj Mullā Hādi Sabzavari (1212/1798–1289/1878), author of the *Kitab-i Manẓūma* ('The Rhymed Book') and the *Sharh-i Manẓūma* ('The Elucidation of the Rhymed Book'). A typical basic library for study of the ancient sciences might consist of Sabzavari's *Sharh-i Manẓūma*, Mullā Ṣadrā's *Asfār*, Ibn Sīnā's *Ishārāt* and *Shifā* and Suhrawardī's *Ḥikmat al-Ishrāq*.

Mullā Ṣadrā's organization of the philosophical topics concerning the intellectual and rational way paralleled the manner in which the *'urafā'* had propounded the way of the heart and spirit. The *'urafā'* hold that the wayfarer accomplishes four journeys in carrying through the method of the *'ārif*.

1. The journey from creation to God. At this stage, the wayfarer attempts to transcend nature as well as certain supernatural worlds in order to reach the Divine Essence, leaving no veil between himself and God.
2. The journey by God in God. After the wayfarer attains proximate knowledge of God, with His help the wayfarer journeys through His phases, perfections, names and attributes.
3. The journey from God to Creation by God. In this journey, the wayfarer returns to Creation and rejoins people, but this return does not mean separation and remoteness from the Divine Essence. Rather, the wayfarer sees the Divine Essence with all things and in all things.
4. The journey in Creation by God. In this journey, the wayfarer undertakes to guide the people and lead them to the Truth.

Mullā Ṣadrā, considering that philosophical questions constitute a 'way', if an intellectual one, sorted them into four sets.

1. Topics that constitute a foundation or preliminary to the study of *tawḥīd*. These (the ordinary matter of philosophy) constitute our mental journey from Creation to God.

2. Topics of *tawḥīd*, theology, and divine attributes – the journey with God in God.
3. Topics of the divine acts, the universal worlds of being – the journey with God from God to Creation.
4. Topics of the soul and the Destination (*ma'ād)* – the journey in Creation with God.

The Asfār-i Arba'a, which means 'the four journeys', is organized on this basis.

Mullā Ṣadrā distinguished between his own philosophical system of 'sublime wisdom' and what he called common or conventional philosophy, whether illuminationist and peripatetic.

Overview of Philosophies and Wisdoms

Philosophy and wisdom, in the widest sense, are variously classified from different perspectives; but if we consider them from the standpoint of method, they fall under four headings: deductive wisdom, experiential wisdom, experimental wisdom and polemical wisdom.

Deductive wisdom rests on syllogism and demonstration. It has to do only with greater and lesser, result and concomitant, contradictory and contrary, and the like.

Experiential wisdom pertains not only to deduction but also to experience, inspiration and illumination. It takes its inspiration more from the heart than from the reason.

Experimental wisdom pertains neither to a priori reasoning and deduction nor to the heart and its inspirations. It pertains to sense, trial and experiment. It takes the products of the sciences, the fruits of trial and experiment and, by interrelating them, welds them into wisdom and philosophy.

Polemical wisdom is deductive, but the premises for its deductions are what logicians call common knowledge (*mashhūrāt*) and accepted facts (*maqbūlāt*). There are several kinds of premises to deduction, including first axioms (*badīhiyāt*) and common knowledge. For instance, the idea that two things each equal to a third are equal to each other, which is expressed in the phrase 'the equal to the equal are equal', and the idea that it is impossible for both a proposition and its contradictory to hold true at the same time are considered axiomatic.

The idea that it is ugly to yawn in the presence of others is considered common knowledge.

Deduction on the basis of axioms is called demonstration, and deduction on the basis of common knowledge is considered an element of polemics. Therefore, polemical wisdom means a wisdom that deduces global and universal ideas from common knowledge.

The *mutakallimīn* generally base their deductions on the beauty or the ugliness of a thing, on rational beauty and ugliness, as it were. The *ḥukamā'* hold that all beauty and ugliness relate to the sphere of human life; one cannot evaluate God, the universe and being by these criteria. Thus, the *ḥukamā'* call *kalām* polemical wisdom.

The *ḥukamā'* believe that the central principles of religion may be better deduced from the premises of demonstration and from first axioms than from the premises of common knowledge and polemics. In Islamic times, especially among the Shīʿa, philosophy, without departing from its mission of free inquiry or committing itself in advance, gradually proved the best source of support for Islamic principles. Accordingly, polemical wisdom, in the hands of such persons as Khwāja Nāṣir ad-Dīn Tūsī, gradually took on a demonstrational and illuminationistic character. Thus, *kalām* came to be overshadowed by philosophy.

Although experimental wisdom is extraordinarily valuable, it has two shortcomings. One is that its compass is confined to the experimental sciences and the experimental sciences are confined to what is sensible and palpable. Man's philosophical needs extend beyond what is in the domain of sense experience. For instance, when we discuss the possibility of a beginning of time, an end to space or an origin for causes, how are we to find what we seek in the laboratory or under the microscope? Thus, experimental wisdom cannot satisfy man's philosophical instinct and must remain silent on basic philosophical questions.

The other shortcoming lies in the fact that the value of experimental questions is rendered precarious by their confinement to and dependence upon nature. Questions of experimental science are time-bound and may become obsolete at any moment. A wisdom based on experiment is naturally precarious and so does not meet a basic human need, the need for certainty. Certainty arises in questions having mathematical abstraction or philosophical abstraction and the meanings of mathematical and philosophical abstractions can be clarified only by philosophy.

There remain deductive wisdom and experiential wisdom. The questions discussed in the following sections should elucidate these two wisdoms and demonstrate their value.

Problems in Philosophy: Being

Being *qua* being is the subject of philosophy and all philosophical topics turn on it. Being – or existence – is to philosophy what the body is to medicine, number is to mathematics or quantity is to geometry.

Several kinds of questions turn on being. One group of questions pertains to being or existence and to its opposites in the two respective senses: non-being and essence (*māhiya*).[14] There is nothing but being in the objective world. Being has no opposite outside the mind. But the conceptualizing mind of man has formed two concepts vis-à-vis being or existence: non-being and essence (strictly, essences). A range of philosophical questions, especially in sublime wisdom, pertains to existence and essence, and another range pertains to being and non-being.

A second group of questions pertains to divisions of being. Being in its turn has divisions that are regarded as amounting to species of being; in other words, being is divisible (for instance, into the objective and the subjective, the necessary and the possible, the eternal and the created in time, the stable and the changing, the singular and the plural, the potential and the act and the substance and the accident). Of course, these are the primary divisions of being, that is, the divisions that enter into being by virtue of the fact that it is being.

To illustrate, divisions into black and white, large and small, equal and unequal, odd and even or long and short are divisions not in being *qua* being but in being *qua* body or in being *qua* quantifiable. Corporeality in being corporeality or quantity in being quantity admit of such division. However, division into singular and plural or division into necessary and possible is division of being *qua* being.

Intensive research has been done in philosophy as to the criteria for these divisions, what distinguishes the divisions of being *qua* being from other divisions. Some philosophers have regarded certain divisions as applying to body *qua* body and thus falling outside the scope of first philosophy, but other philosophers for various reasons have regarded these divisions as applying to being *qua* being and thus falling under this same domain.

A third group of questions pertains to the universal laws governing being, such as causality, the correspondence of cause and effect, the necessity governing the system of cause and effect and priority versus synchronism among the levels of being.

A fourth group of questions pertains to demonstration of the planes of being or worlds of being. Being has particular planes or worlds. The *ḥukamā'* of Islam believe that there are four general worlds or four emergences (*nash'a*):

- The world of nature, or the *nāṣūt*
- The world of ideas, or the *malakūt*
- The world of [separate] intelligences, or the *jabarūt*
- The world of divinity, or the *lahūt.*

The world of *nāṣūt* is the world of matter, motion and space-time. It is the world of nature and sense objects, this world.

The world of [Platonic] ideas [similitudes], or the *malakūt,* is a world superior to nature, having forms and dimensions, but lacking motion, time and change.

The world of *jabarūt* is the world of the [separate] intelligences or the world of the [abstract] idea (*ma'nā*), free of forms and images and thus superior to the world of *malakūt.*

The world of *lāhūt* is the world of divinity and unity.

A fifth group of questions pertains to the relations between the world of nature and the worlds above it, the descent of being from *lāhūt* to nature and the ascent from nature to the higher worlds. With special reference to man, these are called questions of the destination (*ma'ād*) and figure very prominently in sublime wisdom.

Existence and Essence

Is existence substantive, or is essence? We always distinguish two valid senses in which things may be spoken of: the 'isness' of a thing and the 'whatness' of a thing. For instance, we know that a person is, a tree is, number is and quantity is, but number has one whatness, one essence, and a person has another.[15] If we ask, 'What is number?', we receive one answer. If we ask, 'What is man?', we receive another.

Many things have a patent isness; that is, we know that they are. But we may not know what they are. For instance, we know that life is or that electricity is, but we may not know what life is or what electricity is. We know what many things are – for instance, we have a clear definition of a circle and so know what a circle is – but we do not know whether the circle exists in objective nature. Thus, isness is something other than whatness.

This plurality, this dichotomy of essence and existence, is purely subjective. In extensional reality, no thing is twofold. Therefore, one of these two is objectively so and substantive, and the other is nominal and not substantive.

The whole question of existentialism versus essentialism has no ancient historical antecedents. This topic originated in the Islamic world. None of the early philosophers, Fārābī, Ibn Sīnā, Khwāja Nāṣir ad-Dīn Ṭūsī or even

Suhravardi, discussed anything under this heading. The topic made its debut in philosophy in the time of Mir Damad (the beginning of the eleventh century of the Hijrah). Mir Damad was an essentialist. However, his famous pupil, Mullā Ṣadrā, made a compelling case for existentialism, and from then on every philosopher of note has been an existentialist.[16] In the third volume of *Uṣūl-e Falsafah va Rawishe Riyalism*, I have discussed the respective ideas of the *'urafā'*, the *mutakallimīn* and the philosophers as precursors to this philosophical conception of Mullā Ṣadrā's.

Another philosophy sometimes known as existentialism has flourished in our own time. This form of existentialism pertains to man and has reference to the idea that man, by contrast with all other beings, has no definite, preassigned essence and no form determined by nature. Man designs and builds his own whatness. This idea is largely correct and supported by Islamic philosophy, except that, first, what in Islamic philosophy is called existentialism does not apply to man alone but to the whole universe and, second, when we speak of existentialism, or *aṣālat al-wujūd*, in an Islamic context, we are using the term *aṣālat* (-ism) in its sense of substantive reality or objective being, as opposed to nominal or mental existence. When we use it in the Western context of modern existentialism, we are using it in its sense of primacy or priority. One should by no means conflate the two senses.

The Objective and the Subjective

A thing is either objective or subjective. Objective being means being external to and independent of the human mind. We know, for instance, that mountain, sea and plain have being external to our minds and independent of them. Whether our minds conceive of them or not, indeed, whether we ourselves and our minds exist or not, mountain, sea and plain exist.

But that mountain, sea and plain have an existence in our minds as well. When we imagine them, we give them being in our minds. The being things find in our minds is called subjective being or mental being.

Two questions arise here. One is why the images of things appearing in our minds should be conceived of as a kind of being for those things in our minds. If they are, one might say that the image of a thing painted on a wall or printed on a sheet of paper deserves to be called another kind of being, a parietal being or a papyraceous being. If we term mental images a form of being for the thing imagined, to be just, we have employed a metaphor and not spoken the literal truth, but philosophy ought to deal with the literal truth.

The relation of a mental form to an external object (for instance, the relation of a mental mountain or sea to an external mountain or sea) is far more profound than the relation of the picture of a mountain or a sea on a sheet of paper or a wall to that external mountain or sea. If what appears in the mind were only a simple image, it would never give rise to consciousness, just as the image on the wall does not give rise to consciousness in the wall. Rather, the mental image is consciousness itself.

The other question is whether mental being, as a concept actually relating to man and the human psyche, belongs to the realm of psychology. Philosophy deals with general questions, and such particular questions pertain to the sciences.

Philosophers have demonstrated that we are conscious of external objects because our mental images, far from being simple, are a kind of realization of existence in our minds for the essences (*māhiya*) of the objects. Although, from one standpoint, the question of mental images is a question of the human psyche and so belongs to the field of psychology, from another standpoint, that man's mind is in fact another emergence (*nash'a*) of being and that being in its essence consequently takes two forms, subjective and objective, it is a question for philosophy.

Ibn Sīnā and Mullā Ṣadrā have said (the former allusively, near the beginning of the 'Ilahiyat' of his *Shifā*; and the latter explicitly and at length in his commentary to the same work) that at times a question may pertain to two different disciplines from two standpoints; for instance, a question may pertain to philosophy from one standpoint and to the natural sciences from another.

Truth and Error

Another angle of the question of mental being has been studied: it has to do with the validity of perceptions, the extent to which our perceptions, sensations and conceptions of the external world are valid. From ancient times, philosophers have asked whether what we perceive by means of our senses or our reason corresponds to actuality, the thing in itself.

Some postulate that some of our sense perceptions or rational perceptions do correspond to actuality, the thing in itself, and some do not. Those that correspond to actuality are termed 'truth', and those that do not are termed 'error'. Sight, hearing, taste, touch and smell are all subject to error. But most of our sense perceptions correspond fully to reality. Through these same senses, we accurately distinguish night from day, far from near, large from small in volume, tough from smooth and cold from hot.

Our reason is likewise subject to error. Logic was compiled to avert errors of reason in its deductions. But most of our rational deductions are valid. When we add up all the debits and all the credits in a ledger and subtract the former from the latter, we are performing a mental and rational procedure that we are perfectly assured will hold true if we are sufficiently careful and exact.

However, the Sophists of Greece denied the distinction between truth and error. They said that whatever a person feels and thinks is for that person the truth. They said that man is the measure of all things. They radically denied reality and, having denied it, left no standard by which human perceptions and sensations could be true, in corresponding to it, or erroneous, in failing to correspond to it.

The Sophists were contemporaries of Socrates (Socrates came along near the close of the Sophist period). Protagoras and Gorgias were two famous Sophists. Socrates, Plato and Aristotle rebelled against them.

After Aristotle's time, another group appeared in Alexandria, called the Sceptics, the most famous of whom is Pyrrho. The Sceptics did not deny actuality in principle but denied that human perceptions correspond to it. They said that one perceives an object in a certain way under the influence of internal states and certain external conditions. Sometimes two people experiencing different states or viewing from different angles will see the same event in two different ways. A thing may appear ugly in the eyes of one and beautiful in those of another or single in the eyes of one and double in those of another. The air may feel warm to one and cold to another. A flavour may taste sweet to one and bitter to another. The Sceptics, like the Sophists, denied the validity of knowledge.

Bishop Berkeley wholly rejects external reality. No one has been able to refute his reasons for his position, although everyone knows they are fallacious.

Those who have sought a reply to the ancient Sophists exemplified by Berkeley have not taken the approach that could resolve the sophism. The philosophers of Islam have held that the basic approach to resolving this sophism consists in our perceiving the reality of mental being. Only thus is the puzzle solved.

In approaching mental being, the *ḥukamā'* of Islam first define knowledge, or perception, as consisting in a kind of being for the object perceived within the being of the perceiver. They go on to cite certain demonstrations in support of this position, and then they recount and reply to certain objections to mental being or allegations of problems in it.

This topic did not exist in this form early in the Islamic period and *a fortiori* did not exist in Hellenic times. Nāṣir ad-Dīn Ṭūsī was the first to speak of the objective and the subjective in his works of philosophy and *kalām*. Thereafter, it came to occupy a major place in the works of such comparatively recent philosophers as Mullā Ṣadrā and Mullā Hadi Sabzavari. Fārābī, Ibn Sīnā and even Suhravardi, as well as their followers, never broached the subject of mental being or even used the term in their works. The term first appeared after Ibn Sīnā's time.

However, what Fārābī and Ibn Sīnā said on other subjects shows that they believed perception to consist of a simulacrum of the reality of the object perceived within the being of the perceiver. But they neither sought to demonstrate this point nor conceived of it as an independent question of being, an independent division of being.

The Created in Time and the Eternal

The Arabic word *ḥadīth* has the lexical and customary meaning of new, whereas *qadīm* means old. However, these words have other meanings in the terminologies of philosophy and *kalām*. Like other people, when philosophers speak of the *ḥadīth* and the *qadīm,* they seek to know what is new and what is old, but in describing a thing as new, they mean that before it was, it was not – that is, first it was not, then it was. In describing a thing as old, they mean that it always has been and never was not. Suppose there is a tree that has lived for billions of years. In common usage, it would be spoken of as old, indeed very old, but according to the terminologies of philosophy and *kalām,* it is *ḥadīth* (new) because there was a time billions of years ago when it was not.

Philosophers define createdness in time (*ḥudūth*) as the precedence of a thing's non-being to its being, and they define eternality (*qidām*) as the non-precedence of a thing's non-being to its being. Therefore, an entity is created in time whose non-being precedes its being, and an entity is eternal for which no non-being prior to its being can be conceived.

Discussion of the question of the created in time and the eternal turns on this point: is everything in the universe created in time and nothing eternal, such that whatever we consider first was not and then was? Or is everything eternal and nothing created in time, such that everything has always been? Or are some things created in time and some eternal, such that, for instance, shapes, forms and externals are created in time, but matter, subjects and invisible things are eternal? Or are individuals and parts created in time, whereas species and wholes are eternal? Or are natural and material phenomena created in time, whereas abstract and supramaterial phenomena are eternal? Or is only God, the Creator of the whole and Cause of causes, eternal, whereas all else is created in time? Overall, is the universe created in time or is it eternal?

The *mutakallimīn* of Islam believe that only God is eternal. All else – matter and form, individuals and species, parts and wholes, abstract and material – constitutes what is called the world or 'other' (*masiva*) and is created in time. The philosophers of Islam, however, believe that createdness in time is a property of the material world, whereas the supernatural worlds are abstract and eternal. In the world of nature, too, principles and universals are eternal, whereas the phenomena and particulars are created in time. Therefore, the universe is created in time with respect to its phenomena and particulars but eternal with respect to its principles and universals.

The issue of createdness in time and eternality has excited acrimonious disputes between the philosophers and the *mutakallimīn*. Abū Ḥāmid Ghazzālī, who, although leaning to *'irfān* and Sufism in most of his works, leans to *kalām* in some, declares Ibn Sīnā an unbeliever for his stand on several questions, among them his belief in the eternality of the world. In his famous *Tahāfut al-Falsafa* ('The Incoherence of the Philosophers'), Ghazzālī has criticized philosophers on twenty points and exposed what he believes to be the incoherencies in their thought. Ibn Rushd of Andalūsia has rebutted Ghazzālī in *Tahāfut at-Tahāfut* ('The Incoherence of the "Incoherence"').

The *mutakallimīn* say that if a thing is not created in time but eternal – if it has always been and never not been – then that thing has no need of a creator and cause. Therefore, if we suppose that eternal things exist other than the Essence of the Truth, it follows that they will have no need of a creator and so in reality will be necessary beings in their essence, like God; and the demonstrations that show the Necessary Being in Essence to be singular do not permit us to profess more than one such Necessary Being. Accordingly, no more than one Eternal Being exists, and all else is created in time. Therefore, the universe is created in time, including the abstract and the material, principles and phenomena, species and individuals, wholes and parts, matter and form, visible and invisible.

The philosophers have rebutted the arguments of the *mutakallimīn* decisively, saying that all the confusion turns on one point, which consists in supposing that, if a thing has a continuous existence into the indefinite past, it has no need of a cause, whereas this is not so. A thing's need or lack of need for a cause pertains to its essence, which makes it a necessary being or a possible being; it has nothing to do with its createdness in time or eternality.[17] By analogy, the sun's radiance stems from the sun and cannot exist apart from it. Its existence depends on the sun's existence. It issues from the sun whether we suppose there was a time this radiance did not exist or we suppose it has always existed, along with the sun. If we suppose that the sun's radiance has coexisted with the sun itself from pre-eternity to post-eternity, this does not entail its having no need of the sun.

Philosophers maintain that the relation of the universe to God is as the relation of the radiance to the sun, with this difference: the sun is not conscious of itself or of its action and does not perform its function as an act of will; the contrary is true of God.

At times we encounter expressions in the primary texts of Islam that compare the relation of the universe and God to the relation of radiance and the sun. The noble verse of the Qur'ān states, 'God is the Light of the heavens and the earth' (24:35). Exegetes have interpreted this verse to mean that God is the light-giver of the heavens and the earth (that the being of heaven and earth is a ray of God).

Philosophers do not adduce any evidence for the eternality of the universe from the universe itself; rather, they approach this argument from the position that God is the Absolutely Effulgent and the Eternally Beneficent – we cannot possibly conceive of His effulgence (emanation) and beneficence as limited, as terminating somewhere. In other words, the theistic philosophers have arrived at the eternality of the universe through an a priori demonstration, that is, by making the being and attributes of God the premise to the eternality of the universe. Generally, those who disbelieve in God advance the position of the eternality of the universe, but the theistic philosophers say that the very thing non-believers adduce as a reason for God's non-existence is what in their view implies God's existence. The eternality of the universe is a hypothesis to non-believers, but it is an established fact to theistic philosophers.

The Mutable and the Constant

Change means transformation and constancy means uniformity. We continually witness changes in the universe. We ourselves continually make transitions from state to state, from period to period, beginning when we are born and ending when we die. The same holds for earth and sea, for mountains, trees, animals, stars, solar systems and galaxies. Are these changes outward, pertaining to the configuration, form and accidents of the universe, or are they profound and fundamental, such that no constant phenomenon exists in the universe? Are the changes that occur in the universe transient and instantaneous, or are they gradual and protracted?

These questions, too, date from remote times; they were discussed in ancient Greece. Democritus, known as the father of atomic theory and also as 'the laughing philosopher', maintained that all change or transformation is superficial because natural being is based on atomic particles, which are forever in one state and unchangeable. The changes we witness are like those in a heap of gravel, massed sometimes in one shape, sometimes in another, but never changing in identity or real nature. This is the mechanistic outlook and constitutes a kind of mechanistic philosophy.

Another Greek philosopher, Heraclitus, maintained that nothing remains in the same state for two successive instants. You cannot, for example, set foot twice in the same river because at the second instant you are not who you were before and that river is not the same river. This philosophy is opposed to Democritus' in seeing everything in a state of flux and inconstancy, but it says nothing contrary to mechanism; that is, it advances no idea of dynamics.

Aristotle's philosophy has no quarrel with the idea that all the parts of nature change, but it undertakes to determine which changes are gradual and protracted and which are transient and instantaneous. It terms the gradual changes 'motion' and the transient changes 'generation' and 'corruption' (a transient coming into being is called generation, and a transient extinction is called corruption). Because Aristotle and his followers considered the basic changes occurring in this world, especially those that appear in substances, as transient, they termed this 'the world of generation and corruption'.

At other moments, constancy obtains. If we regard changes as transient, because they occur in an instant, although at other instants or through time things are constant, such mutable things have a relative mutability and a relative constancy. Therefore, if change is in the mode of motion, it is absolute change. If it is in the mode of generation and corruption – if it is in an instantaneous mode – it is relative.

According to the Aristotelians, although nothing absolutely constant and uniform exists in nature, but everything is mutable (contrary to the view of the Democriteans), because substances are basic to nature and changes in substances are transient, the world has a relative constancy along with relative change. But constancy governs the world to a greater extent than does change.

Aristotle and the Aristotelians regard all things as falling under ten basic generic classes, which they call the ten categories: substance, quantity, quality, determination in space, position, determination in time, relation, condition, action and passion.

Motion occurs only in the categories of quantity, quality and determination in space. In all other categories change is transient; in other words, all other categories enjoy a relative constancy. Even those three categories in which motion occurs, because the motion is intermittent, are governed by a relative constancy. Therefore, in Aristotle's philosophy, one encounters more constancy than change, more uniformity than transformation.

Ibn Sīnā believed that motion occurs in the category of position as well. He demonstrated that certain motions, such as the rotation of the earth about its axis, constitute a positional motion, not a motion in spatial determination. Thus, after Ibn Sīnā, motion in spatial determination was restricted to transferential motion. Ibn Sīnā did not demonstrate the existence of a new sort of motion, but reclassified as positional what had previously been categorized as a motion in spatial determination. His reclassification is generally accepted.

Mullā Ṣadrā effected a major transformation in Islamic philosophy by demonstrating substantial motion. He demonstrated that, even on the basis of the Aristotelian principles of matter and form, we must accept that the substances of the world are in continuous motion; there is never so much as an instant of constancy and uniformity in the substances of the world. The accidents (that is, the nine other categories), as functions of the substances, are also in motion. According to Mullā Ṣadrā, nature equals motion, and motion equals continuous, uninterrupted creation and extinction.

Through the principle of substantial motion, the visage of the Aristotelian universe is wholly transformed. According to this principle, nature, or matter, equals motion. Time consists in the measure or tensile force of this substantial motion, and constancy equals supernatural being. What exists consists of, on the one hand, absolute change (nature) and, on the other, absolute constancy (the supernatural). The constancy of nature is the constancy of order, not the constancy of being; that is, a definite, immutable system governs the universe, and the contents of the system are all mutable (they are change itself). Both the being and the system of this universe stem from the supernal. Were it not for the governance of the other world, this world, which is wholly flux and mutation, would be cut off from its past and future. 'Many times has the water exchanged in this stream,/Still the moon's and the stars' reflections remain.'[18]

Prior to Mullā Ṣadrā, the topic of the mutable and the constant was felt to belong to the natural sciences, in that any determination or any division that applies to a body *qua* body belongs to the natural sciences. It was said that it is such-and-such a body that is either constant or mutable, or that is either still or in motion. In other words, motion and stasis are among the accidents of a body. Therefore, the topic of the constant and the mutable ought to fall wholly within the domain of the natural sciences.

This all changed with Mullā Ṣadrā's realization of existentialism (the substantive reality of being), his realization of substantial motion and his demonstration that the natures of the universe constitute the mobile *qua* mobile and the mutable *qua* mutable (that is, that a body is not something to which motion is merely added as an accident, whereby at times this motion can be annulled, leaving the motionless state we call stasis). Rather, the natures of the universe are motion itself, and the contrary of this substantial motion is constancy, not stasis. Stasis holds for the accidental motions the state of whose absence we call stasis but is inconceivable in the case of essential, substantial motion. The contrary of this substantial motion that is the substance itself consists of substances for which constancy is the very essence. These are entities beyond space and time, devoid of spatio-temporal forces, potentialities or dimensions. Therefore, it is not the body that is either constant or mutable. Rather, it is being *qua* being that appears either as constancy itself (as supramaterial beings) or as continuous flux/becoming/creation itself (the world of nature). Therefore, just as being is in its essence divisible into necessary and possible, so is it also in its essence divisible into the constant and the fluid.

Thus, according to Mullā Ṣadrā, only certain kinds of motions – the accidental motions of a body having stasis for their opposite – ought to be studied under the heading of the natural sciences. Other motions, or indeed these very motions when not regarded from the standpoint of their being accidents of natural bodies, ought to be discussed and studied in first philosophy. Mullā Ṣadrā himself brought in his discussions of motion under 'general phenomena' in the *Asfār* in the course of discussing potentials and acts, although it warranted a chapter to itself.

Among the key conclusions arising from this great realization – basically, that being in its essence is divisible into the constant and the fluid and that constant being is one modality of being, while fluid being is another – is that becoming is precisely a plane of being. Although, nominally speaking, we may regard becoming as a synthesis of being and non-being, this synthesis is actually a kind of notion or metaphor.'[19]

In truth it is the realization of the substantive reality of being and of the nominal status of essences (*māhīya*) that permits us to perceive this key reality. Without a grasp of the substantive reality of being, neither a conception of substantial motion nor a conception that flux and becoming are precisely a plane of being would be possible.

Motion has recovered its proper place in the modern philosophy of Europe by other avenues. Some philosophers came to believe that motion is the cornerstone of nature, that nature equals becoming. However, because this idea was not based on existentialism (the substantive reality of being) and the primary division of being into the constant and the fluid, these philosophers supposed that becoming was the same union of opposites that the ancients had deemed absurd. They likewise supposed that becoming falsified the principle of identity (*huhuya*), which the ancients had taken for granted.

These philosophers said that the presiding principle in the thought of the ancients was the principle of constancy and that, in deeming beings constant, the ancients had supposed that either being or non-being must hold sway over things. Therefore, one alone of these holds true (the principle of the impossibility of union and the cancellation of opposites). That is, either there is always being or there is always non-being; no third alternative obtains.

Similarly, because the ancients thought things constant, they supposed of everything that is itself (the principle of identity). But with the realization of the principle of motion and change in nature, the realization that nature is continually in a state of becoming, the two principles are groundless because becoming is a union of being and non-being; where a thing is both being and non-being, becoming has been demonstrated. A thing in a state of becoming both is and is not; at every instant, its self is its not-self; its self is at once its self and not its self; the self of its self is progressively negated. Therefore, if the principle governing things were that of being and non-being, both the principle of the impossibility of the union of opposites and the principle of identity would hold true. Because the principle governing things is the principle of becoming, neither of these other principles holds true.

The principle of the impossibility of the union of opposites and the principle of identity, which held unrivalled sway over the minds of the ancients, arose from a further principle that they also accepted implicitly: the principle of constancy. As the natural sciences showed the invalidity of the principle of constancy, these two principles, too, lost their credibility. This development represents the conception of many modern philosophers, from Hegel onward.

Mullā Ṣadrā invalidated the principle of constancy by other means. Motion, according to his realization, implies that nature equals inconstancy and constancy equals abstraction. Unlike the modern philosophers, however, he never concludes that because nature equals flux and becoming, the principle of the impossibility of the union and cancellation of opposites is falsified. Although Mullā Ṣadrā regards becoming as a kind of union of being and non-being, he does not treat this as a union of opposites because he has realized a more important principle: that being is divisible in its essence into the constant and the fluid. Constant being is a plane of being, not a synthesis of being and non-being. The synthesis of becoming from being and non-being is not a union of two opposites just as it is not the negation of the self of a thing.

The modern philosophers' confusion has two roots: their failure to perceive the division of being into the constant and the fluid and their inadequate conception of the principles of contradiction and contrariety.

Cause and Effect

The most ancient of philosophical questions is that of cause and effect. The concept of cause and effect appears in every philosophical system, unlike such concepts as existentialism and subjective being, which have a prominent place in some philosophies and pass unnoted in others, the concept of potential and act, which plays an important role in Aristotelianism, or the concept of the constant and the mutable, which has a deservedly prominent position in the philosophy of Mullā Ṣadrā.

Causation is a kind of relation between two things, one of which we call the cause and the other, the effect. This is the most profound of relations. The relation of cause and effect consists in the cause's giving being to the effect. What the effect realizes from the cause is its whole being, its whole reality; therefore, if the cause were not, the effect would not be. We find such a relation nowhere else. Therefore, the effect's need of the cause is the keenest of needs, a need at the root of being. Accordingly, if we would define cause, we must say, A cause is that thing an effect needs in its essence and being'.

Every phenomenon is an effect, and every effect needs a cause; therefore, every phenomenon needs a cause. That is, if a thing is not being itself in its essence – if it has appeared as an accident, a phenomenon – it must have arisen through the intervention of a factor we call a cause. Therefore, no phenomenon is without a cause. The hypothesis contrary to this theory is that a phenomenon may appear without a cause. This hypothesis is called coincidence (*ṣudfa*) or chance (*ittifāq*). The philosophy of causality radically rejects this hypothesis.

Philosophers and *mutakallimīn* concur that every phenomenon is an effect and needs a cause, but the *mutakallimīn* define such a phenomenon as created in time (*ḥadīth*), and the philosophers define it as possible (*mumkin*). That is, the *mutakallimīn* say that whatever is created in time is an effect and needs a cause, and the philosophers say that whatever is possible is an effect and needs a cause. These two definitions lead to the different conclusions previously discussed in *The Created in Time and the Eternal* above.

A certain cause produces only a certain effect, and a certain effect proceeds only from a certain cause. There are special relations of dependence among the beings of the universe such that any one thing cannot necessarily give rise to any other thing and any one thing cannot necessarily arise from any other thing. We rely on this truth in our everyday experience. For instance, eating is the cause of satiety, drinking water is the cause of quenching of thirst and study is the cause of literacy. Therefore, if we wish to realize any of these qualities, we have resort to the appropriate cause. For instance, we never drink water or study for the sake of satiety, nor do we consider eating sufficient for the attainment of literacy.

Philosophy demonstrates that such a clear relation obtains among all the processes in the universe. It makes this point through this definition: a unique correspondence and symmetry govern every single cause-and-effect relation and appear in no other such relation. This is the single most important principle in giving order to our thought and in presenting the universe to our thought not as a chaotic aggregate in which nothing is conditional upon anything else but as an ordered, systematic cosmos in which every part has a special place, in which no one thing can displace another.

There are four kinds of cause in the philosophy of Aristotle: the efficient cause, the final cause, the material cause and the formal cause. These four causes are well illustrated in human industry: if we build a house, the builder or workman is the efficient cause; to dwell in that house is the final cause; the building materials are the material cause; and the configuration of the house, in being appropriate to a dwelling and not, say, to a granary, a bathhouse or a mosque, is the formal cause. In Aristotle's view, every natural phenomenon, whether a stone, a plant or a human being, has these same four causes.

Cause as defined by natural scientists differs somewhat from cause as defined by theologians. In theology, or what we now call philosophy, cause means 'giver of existence'. Philosophers call what brings something into existence its cause. Otherwise they do not call it cause, although they may at times call it contributory (*mu'idd*). Natural scientists, however, use the word 'cause' even where the relation between two things is simply one of transfer of momentum. Therefore, in natural scientists' terminology, the builder is the cause of the house in being the point of issue for its construction, through a series of transfers of materials. The theologians, however, never call the builder the cause of the house, in that he does not bring the house into being. Rather, the materials for the house existed beforehand, and the builder's work has been confined to organizing them. Likewise, according to natural scientists, the relation of mother and father to child is causal; but according to philosophy, it is that of an antecedent, a contributory factor or a channel, not that of a cause.

The sequence of causes (causes in the terminology of the philosophers, not that of the natural scientists, that is, causes of being, not causes of motion) terminates. It is absurd that it should be interminable. If the being of a thing proceeds from a cause, arises from a cause, and if the being of that cause arises from a further cause, and if the being of that cause arises from a yet further cause, this process could go on through thousands, millions, billions of causes and more. However, it must finally terminate in a cause that arises through its own essence and not through another cause. Philosophers have often demonstrated that an endless regress of causes is absurd, which phrase they shorten to 'a regress of causes is absurd' or usually even further to 'regress is absurd'.

The word *tasalsul* (regress) is derived from the word *silsila* (sequence, series, range), with the root meaning of chain. Therefore, *tasalsul* means an endless chain of causes. Philosophers thus liken the ordered system of causes and effects to a chain whose links interlock in sequence.

The Necessary, the Possible and the Impossible

Logicians say that if we attribute a predicate to a subject, if, for instance, we say *a is b*, the relation of *b* to *a* will have one of three qualities. First, it may be necessary, that is, certain, inevitable and inviolable; in other words, reason may refuse to accept anything contrary to it. Second, the opposite may be true. That is, the relation may be impossible, meaning it is absurd that the predicate should be an accident of the subject. In other words, reason refuses to accept that it should be one. Third, the relation may be such that it may be affirmed or negated; that is, it is susceptible both to affirmation and to negation. In other words, reason refuses to accept neither this relation nor its contrary.

For instance, if we consider the relation of the number four to evenness, we see that it is necessary and certain. Reason refuses to accept its contrary. Reason says that the number four is certainly and necessarily even. Therefore, necessity governs this relation.

But if we say that the number five is even, this relation is impossible. The number five has no possibility of being even, and our reason in perceiving this relation rejects it. Therefore, impossibility and inconceivability govern this relation.

But if we say that today the weather is sunny, this is a possible relation. That is, the nature of the day does not require that the weather be sunny or that it be cloudy. Either may accord with the nature of the day. Possibility governs this relation.

It follows that, whatever subject and whatever predicate we consider, their relation will not be devoid of these three qualities, which at times from a certain standpoint we term the three modalities. I have described the logicians' approach.

The philosophers, who study being, say that any idea or concept we consider, take as a subject and of which we predicate being will fall into one of these three categories. The relation of being to that idea or concept may be necessary; that is, that thing must necessarily exist. We then call that thing a necessary being.

God is discussed in philosophy under the heading of proofs for necessary being. Philosophical demonstrations show that there is a Being for which nonexistence is absurd and existence is necessary.

If the relation of being to that idea is impossible, that is, if it is absurd that it should exist, we call it an impossible being. An example is a body that is at once spherical and cubical.

If the relation of being to that idea is possible, that is, if that idea is an essence for which reason rejects neither the existence nor the nonexistence, we call it a possible being. All the beings in the universe, in appearing and then disappearing according to a sequence of causes, are possible beings.

Every possible being in itself becomes a necessary being through its cause, but a being necessary through other, not a being necessary in itself. That is, whenever all the causes and preconditions for a possible being exist, it must exist and so becomes a being necessary through other. If it does not come into existence – if so much as one of its preconditions or one of the elements of its causal nexus is lacking – it becomes a being impossible through other.

The philosophers accordingly say that as long as a thing is not necessary, it does not exist. That is, until the existence of a thing reaches the stage of necessity, it will not come into being. Therefore, whatever comes into being does so according to necessity, within a definite and inviolable system. Thus, the system governing the universe and all that is in it is a necessary, certain and inviolable system. In the language of modern philosophers, it is a determinate system.[20]

In discussing cause and effect, I said that the principle of correspondence between cause and effect imparts a special order to our thought and marks out a special connection between principles and ramifications, between causes and effects, in our minds. This principle-that every possible being gains necessity from its cause – which, from one standpoint, pertains to cause and effect and, from another, to necessity and possibility – imparts a special character to the system of our cosmology in making it a necessary, certain and inviolable system. Philosophy succinctly terms this the principle of cause-and-effect necessity. If we accept the principle of the final cause in reference to nature (if we accept that nature pursues ends in its evolutionary journey and that all these ends revert to one primary end that is the end of ends), the system of our cosmology takes on a further special character.

Notes

1. See Muḥammad Shahristani, *Kitāb-i Milal va Niḥal* ('Nations and Sects') vol. 2, p. 231, and Dr Human, *Tārikh-i Falsafa* ('History of Philosophy'), vol. 1, p. 20.
2. Human, *Tārikh-i Falsafa*, vol. 1, p. 69.
3. To explicate or demonstrate these three features is beyond the scope of these brief discussions. See Ibn Sīnā, *Danishnama yi A 'la'i: Ilāhiyāt*, the first three chapters, and Mullā Ṣadrā, *Al-Asfār al-Arba'a*, the first few sections.
4. *Ahkam:* the plural of *ḥukm*, a term in logic, meaning conformity to the affirmative or negative relation between subject and predicate.
5. See the *Ilāhiyat* of *ash-Shifa'* (old edition), p. 15.
6. Existentialists are said to hold that what is 'fabricated in itself' (*maj'ūl bi'dh-dhat*) is being, but essences are nominal. Essentialists are said to hold the contrary.

   That 'more base' (i.e. natural) possible beings should arise directly from the Essence of the Truth is said to violate the law of correspondence between cause and effect. Thus, 'more noble' possible beings, such as intelligences and souls, must exist as intermediate causes. Suhravardi is said to have originated this idea, and Mullā Ṣadrā to have endorsed it.
7. *Kitāb-i Milal va Nihal*, vol. 2.
8. Henry Corbin believes that this word was used for the first time in the Islamic world near the turn of the fourth century by Ibn Wahshiya. See Seyyed Hossein Nasr, *Three Muslim Sages* (Cambridge, MA, 1964), pp. 63 and 151, no. 22. [Nasr cites for his source H. Corbin, *Les Motifs Zoroastriens dans la philosophie de Suhrawardi* (Tehran, 1946), p. 18. See also Henri [sic] Corbin, *Histoire de la philosophie islamique* (Paris, 1964), p. 285.

   Sayyid Hasan Taqizada, in his Yad Dashtha-yi Tarikh-i 'Ulum dar Islam' ('Notes on the History of the Sciences in Islam'), in *Majallayi Maqālat va Barrasiha* (Monographs and Researches Bulletin), 3 and 4 (Tehran, Publications Group of the College of Theology and Islamic Sciences), p. 213, after mentioning an unknown book attributed to this Ibn Wahshiya, says:

   Another book by Ibn Wahshiya the Nabataean has occasioned much discussion, titled *Al-Falāḥat an-Nabatiya* ('Nabataean Agriculture'), which has also been attributed to a sage of Babul named Quthami and which quotes older books from Babul, such as the writings of Zagrith and Yanbu Shad. Even Ibn Khaldūn, with his flair for research, attributed this book to the Nabataean scholars and saw it as an Arabic translation from the Greek. But finally, through the researches of the German scholars Gutschmid and Noldeke and especially of the Italian Nallino it grew clear that this book is a fabrication and full of balderdash; Nallino goes so far as to hold that no Ibn Wahshiya ever existed and that Abū Ṭālib Zayyat compiled all these fantasies and attributed them to an imaginary person. Researchers believe that such books are works of the Shu'ubiya, who sought to prove that the sciences belonged to non-Arab peoples and that the Arabs had no part in them.

   It is not unlikely that the source of Suhravardi's error was *Al Falāḥat an-Nabatiya* or some similar work of the Shu'ubiya. This book is not available to us at present, so we cannot compare its contents with what Suhravardi has said on the subject.

9. Muḥammad 'Alī Furūghi, *Sayr-i Ḥikmat dar Urupa*, *3* vols (n.p., n.d.), vol. 1, p. 20.
10. Bertrand Russell, *A History of Western Philosophy* (New York, 1945). See especially pp. 119–43.
11. For further study of Pythagoras, see ibid., pp. 105, 120, 126, and Shahristani, *Kitāb-i Milal va Niḥal*, vol. 2.
12. *Tafsīr al-Mizān* (Arabic text), vol. 7, under the *sūra An'am*, verse 59.
13. For a detailed study of Mullā Ṣadrā's thought, see Fazlur Rahman, *The Philosophy of Mullā Ṣadrā* (Albany, NY, 1975).
14. There is no question here of a systematic distinction between being and existence. I have merely used the two English words to correspond to the two contexts in which being is discussed here. *Māhiya* has appeared throughout this work as 'identity', but here only 'essence' serves the context.
15. *Māhiya is* an Arabic word, a contraction of *mā huwiya*. The phrase *mā huwa* means 'what is it?'. With the final letters *ya'* and *ta' marbuta,* it becomes the verbal noun *mahuwiya,* which is contracted to *māhiya*. Thus, *māhiya* means 'what-is-it-ness', or 'whatness'.
16. See Rahman, *The Philosophy of Mullā Ṣadrā*, pp. 27–34.
17. Here is how the *ḥukamā'* have expressed this point: 'A thing's need of cause hinges on possibility, not on createdness in time.' For detailed discussion of this point, see my *'Ilal-i Girayish bi Maddigari* ('Causes of the Turn to Materialism'; Mashhad, 1350 Sh./1971; also many subsequent editions).
18. Unknown.
19. See 'Asl-i Tazadd dar Falsafa-yi Islami' ('The Principle of Contradiction in Islamic Philosophy') in my *Magalati-Falsafī* ('Philosophic Essays').
20. This determinism is not opposed to free will in the case of man, and should not be confused with the form of determinism that is. The necessity of the system of the universe is not inimical to man's free will.

PART TWO

'Ilm al-Kalām: Islamic Theology

'Ilm al-kalām is one of the Islamic sciences. It treats of the fundamental Islamic beliefs and doctrines in which it is necessary for a Muslim to believe. It explains them, argues about them and defends them.

The scholars of Islam divide Islamic teachings into three parts:

1. Doctrines (*'aqā'id*): These constitute the issues that must be understood and believed in, such as the Unity of God, the Divine Attributes, universal and restricted prophethood, etc. However, there are certain differences between Muslim sects as to what constitutes the basic articles of faith (*uṣūl al-Dīn*) in which belief is necessary.
2. Morals (*akhlāq*): These consist of the commands and teachings relating to the spiritual and moral characteristics of human beings, such as justice, fear of God (*taqwā*), courage, chastity, wisdom, endurance, loyalty, truthfulness, trustworthiness, etc., and prescribe 'how' a human being should be.
3. The Law (*aḥkām*): Under this heading are discussed the issues relating to practice and the correct manner of performing acts, such as, prayers (*ṣalāt*), fasting (*ṣawm*), *ḥajj*, *jihād*, *al-amr bil ma'ruf wa al-nahy 'an al-munkar*, buying, renting, marriage, divorce and division of inheritance.

The science that deals with the first of the above-mentioned is *'ilm al-kalām*. The study of the second is *'ilm al-akhlāq* (ethics). The study of the third is called *'ilm al-fiqh* (the science of jurisprudence). What is subjected to division in this classification is the corpus of Islamic teachings; that is, those things that constitute the content of Islam. It does not include all those Islamic studies that form the preliminaries for the study of Islamic teachings, such as literature, logic and occasionally philosophy.

In this classification the criterion behind division is the relationship of Islamic teachings to the human being: things that relate to human reason and intellect are called *'aqā'id*; things that relate to human qualities are called *akhlāq*; and things that relate to human action and practice are included in *fiqh*.

Although *fiqh* is a single discipline from the viewpoint of its subject, it consists of numerous disciplines from other viewpoints.

In any case, *'ilm al-kalām* is the study of Islamic doctrines and beliefs. In the past, it was also called *uṣūl al-Dīn* or *'Ilm al-tawḥīd wa al-ṣifāt.*

The Beginnings of Kalām

Although nothing definite can be said about the beginnings of *'ilm al-kalām* among Muslims, what is certain is that discussion of some of the problems of *kalām*, such as the issue of predestination (*jabr*) and free will (*ikhtiyār*) and that of Divine Justice, became current among Muslims during the first half of the second century of Hijrah. Perhaps the first formal centre of such discussions was the circle of al-Haṣan al-Baṣri (d. 110/728–29). Among the Muslim personalities of the latter half of the first century, the names of Ma'bad al-Juhani (d. 80/699) and Ghaylan ibn Muslim al-Dimashqi (d. 105/723) have been mentioned, adamant defenders of the ideas of free will (*ikhtiyār*) and human freedom. There were others who opposed them and supported predestination (*jabr*). The believers in free will were called *qadariyyah* and their opponents were known as *jabriyyah*.

Gradually the points of difference between the two groups extended to a series of other issues in theology, physics, sociology and other problems relating to man and the Resurrection, of which the problem of *jabr* and *ikhtiyār* was only one. During this period, the *qadariyyah* came to be called *Mu'tazilites* and the *jabriyyah* became known as *Ash'arites*. The Orientalists and their followers insist on considering the beginnings of discursive discussions in the Islamic world from this point or thereabouts.

However, the truth is that rational argumentation about Islamic doctrines starts with the Holy Qur'ān itself, and has been followed up in the utterances of the Holy Prophet (S) and especially in the sermons of Amīr al-Mu'minīn 'Alī (A) – despite the fact that their style and approach are different from those of the Muslim *mutakallimīn*.[1]

Inquiry or Imitation?

The Holy Qur'ān has laid the foundation of faith and belief on thought and reasoning. Throughout, the Qur'ān insists that men should attain faith through the agency of thought. In the view of the Qur'ān, intellectual servitude is not sufficient for believing and understanding its basic doctrines. Accordingly, one should take up a rational inquiry of the basic principles and doctrines of the faith. For example, the belief that God is One should be arrived at rationally. The same is true of the prophethood of Muḥammad (S). This requirement resulted in the establishment of *'ilm al-'uṣūl* during the first century.

Many factors gave rise to the unprecedented realization among Muslims of the need to study the fundamentals of the Islamic faith and to undertake the task of defending them, a realization that led to the emergence of prominent *mutakallimīn* during the second, third and fourth centuries. These were: the embracing of Islam by various nations who brought with them a series of (alien) ideas and notions; the mixing and coexistence of the Muslims with peoples of various religions, such as Jews, Christians, Magians and Sabaeans, and the ensuing religious debates and disputes between the Muslims and those peoples; the emergence in the Islamic world of the Zanādiqah[2] – who were totally against religion – as a result of general freedom during the rule of the 'Abbāsid Caliphs (as long as it did not interfere in matters of state politics); and the birth of philosophy in the Muslim world – which itself gave birth to doubts and scepticism.

The First Problem

Apparently, the first problem that was discussed and debated by the Muslims was that of predestination and free will. This was natural, since it is a primary problem that is linked with human destiny and attracts the interest of every thinking adult. It is arguably impossible to find a society that has reached intellectual maturity in which this problem has not been raised. Moreover, the Holy Qur'ān has a large number of verses on this subject, which inevitably instigate thought about it.[3]

Accordingly, there is no reason to try to seek another source for the origin of this problem in the Islamic world.

Orientalists, in order to negate the originality of Islamic teachings, habitually try at any cost to trace the roots of all sciences that originated among Muslims to the world outside the domains of Islam, in particular the Christian world. They insist that the roots of *'ilm al-kalām* should be acknowledged to lie outside Islam, and they make similar attempts and claims with regard to the study of grammar, prosody (and perhaps semantics, rhetoric and studies of literary and poetic devices) and Islamic *'irfān*.

The problem of determinism and free will (*jabr wa ikhtiyār*) is the same as the problem of predestination and Divine Providence (*qaḍā' wa qadar*); the first formulation relates to man and his free will, while the second one relates to God. This problem also raises the issue of Divine Justice, because there is an explicit connection between determinism and injustice, on the one hand, and free will and justice, on the other.

The problem of justice raises the issue of the essential good and evil of actions, and the latter in its turn brings in its train the problem of the validity of reason and purely rational judgements. These problems together lead to the discussion of Divine Wisdom (that is the notion that there is a judicious purpose and aim behind Divine Acts),[4] and thereby, gradually, to the debate about the unity of Divine Acts and the unity of the Attributes, as we shall explain later.

The formation of opposite camps in the debates of *kalām* later acquired a great scope and extended to many philosophical problems, such as substance and accident, nature of indivisible particles that constitute physical bodies, the problem of space, etc. This was because, in the view of the *mutakallimīn*, discussion of such issues was considered a prelude to the debate about theological matters, particularly those related to *mabda'* (primeval origin) and *ma'ād* (resurrection). In this way many of the problems of philosophy entered *'ilm al-kalām*, and now there are many problems common to both.

If one were to study the books on *kalām*, especially those written after the 7th/13th century, one would see that most of them deal with the same problems as those discussed by philosophers – especially Muslim philosophers – in their books.

Islamic philosophy and *kalām* have greatly influenced each other. One of the results was that *kalām* raised new problems for philosophy, and philosophy helped to widen the scope of *kalām*, in the sense that dealing with many philosophical problems came to be considered necessary in *kalām*. With God's help, we hope to give an example of each of these two results of reciprocal influence between philosophy and *kalām*.

Al-Kalām al-'Aqli *and* al-Kalām al-Naqli

Although *'ilm al-kalām* is a rational and discursive discipline, it consists of two parts in terms of the preliminaries and fundamentals it uses in arguments:

1. *'aqli* (rational);
2. *naqli* (transmitted, traditional).

The *'aqli* part of *kalām* consists of the material that is purely rational, and if there is any reference to *naqli* (tradition), it is for the sake of illumination and confirmation of a rational judgement. But in problems such as those related to Divine Unity, prophethood and some issues of Resurrection, reference to *naql* – the Book and the Prophet's Sunnah – is not sufficient; the argument must be purely rational.

The *naqli* part of *kalām* consists of issues related to the doctrines of the faith – and it is necessary to believe in them – but since these issues are subordinate to the issue of prophethood, it is enough to quote evidence from the Divine Revelation or the definite *aḥādīth* of the Prophet (S), e.g. in issues linked with *imāmah* (of course, in the Shī'ī faith belief in *imāmah* is considered a part of *uṣūl al-Dīn*) and most of the issues related with the Resurrection.

Definition and Subject Matter of 'Ilm Al-kalām

For a definition of *'ilm al-kalām*, it is sufficient to say that, 'It is a science that studies the basic doctrines of the Islamic faith (*uṣūl al-Dīn*). It identifies the basic doctrines, seeks to prove their validity and answers any doubts that may be cast upon them.'

In texts on logic and philosophy it is mentioned that every science has a special subject of its own, and that the various sciences are distinguished from one another by virtue of their separate subject matter. This is certainly true, and those sciences whose subject matter has a real unity are such. However, there is nothing wrong with forming a discipline whose unity of subject matter and the problems covered by it are arbitrary and conventional, in the sense that it covers diverse, mutually exclusive subjects, which are given an arbitrary unity because they serve a single purpose and objective. In sciences whose subject has an essential unity, there is no possibility of overlapping of problems. But in sciences in which there is a conventional unity among the issues, there is no reason why issues should not overlap. The commonness of the problems between philosophy and *kalām*, psychology and *kalām* or sociology and *kalām* is a result of this.

Some Islamic scholars have sought to define and outline the subject matter of *'ilm al-kalām*, and have expressed various opinions. But this is a mistake, because a clear-cut delineation of the subject of study is possible for only those sciences that have an essential unity among the problems dealt with. But in those sciences in which there is a conventional unity of problems dealt with, there can be no unity of subject. This issue cannot be discussed further here.

The Term 'ilm al-Kalām

Why has this discipline been called *'ilm al-kalām* and when was this name given to it? Some have said that it was called *kalām* (literally, 'speech') because it gives an added power of speech and argument to one who is well versed in it. Some say that the reason lies in the fact that experts in this science habitually began their own statements in their books with the expression *al-kalāmu fī kadhā*. Others explain that it was called *kalām* because it discussed issues regarding which the *Ahl al-Ḥadīth* preferred to maintain complete silence. Yet according to others this name came to prominence when the issue as to whether the Holy Qur'ān (called *kalamullāhi*, the Divine Utterance)[5] is created (*makhlūq*) or not became a matter for hot debate among Muslims – a controversy that led to animosity between the two opposite camps and to much bloodshed. This is also the reason why that period is remembered as a 'time of severe hardship' – *miḥnah*. That is, since most of the debates about the doctrines of the faith revolved around the *ḥudūth* (createdness, temporality) or the *qidām* (pre-eternity) of the 'Utterance' or *kalām* of God, the discipline that discussed the principal doctrines of the faith came to be called *'ilm al-kalām* (literally, 'the science of the Utterance'). These are the various theories about the origin of the name *'ilm al-kalām*.

The Various Schools of Kalām

Muslims differed with one another in matters of the Law (*fiqh*), following differing paths and dividing into various sects, such as Ja'fari, Zaydi, Ḥanafi, Shāfi'i, Māliki and Ḥanbali, each of which has a *fiqh* of its own. Similarly, from the point of view of doctrine, they divided into various schools, each with its own set of principal doctrines. The most important of these schools are the Shī'ites, the Mu'tazilites, the 'Ash'arites and the Murji'ah.

Some may regret the division of Muslims into sects in matters dealing with *kalām* and *fiqh* and wonder why they could not maintain their unity in these spheres. The difference in matters of *kalām* causes disunity in their Islamic outlook, and the disagreement in the matter of *fiqh* deprives them of the unity of action.

Both the question and the regret are justified. But it is important to note the two following points:

1. The disagreement in issues of *fiqh* among Muslims is not so great as to shatter the foundations of their unity of doctrinal outlook and mode of

practice, which have so much in common that the points of difference are not capable of inflicting any serious damage.

2. Theoretical differences and divergences of views are inevitable in societies in spite of their unity and agreement in principles; and as long as the roots of the differences lie in methods of inference, and not in vested interests, they are even beneficial; because they cause mobility, dynamism, discussion, curiosity and progress. Only when the differences are accompanied by prejudices and emotional and illogical alignments and lead individuals to slander, defame and treat one another with contempt, instead of motivating them to endeavour to reforming themselves, that they are a cause of misfortune.

In the Shīʿī faith, the people are obliged to imitate a living *mujtahid*, and the *mujtahidūn* are obliged to ponder the issues and form their opinions independently and not to be content with what has been handed down by the ancestors. *Ijtihād* and independence of thought inherently lead to difference of views; but this divergence of opinions has given life and dynamism to the Shīʿī *fiqh*. Therefore, difference in itself cannot be condemned. What is to be condemned is difference that originates in evil intentions and selfish interests, or difference on issues that drive Muslims on separate paths, such as the issue of *imāmah* and leadership; not difference in secondary and non-basic matters.

To examine the intellectual history of the Muslims in an attempt to find which differences originated in evil intentions, vested interests and prejudices, and which were a natural product of their intellectual life, whether all points of difference in the sphere of *kalām* should be regarded as fundamental, or whether all problems in *fiqh* should be regarded as secondary, or if it is possible that a difference in *kalām* may not be of fundamental significance whereas one in *fiqh* may have such importance – these are questions that lie outside the brief scope of this discussion.

Before we turn to the schools of *kalām*, it is essential to point out that there has been a group of scholars in the Islamic world who were basically opposed to the very idea of *ʿilm al-kalām* and rational debate about Islamic doctrines, considering it a taboo and an innovation in the faith (*bidʿah*). They are known as Ahl al-Ḥadīth. Aḥmad ibn Ḥanbal, one of the imams of jurisprudence of the Ahl al-Sunnah, stands foremost among them.

The Ḥanbalis are totally against *kalām*, Muʿtazilites or Ashʿarite, not to speak of the Shīʿī *kalām*. In fact, they are basically opposed to logic and philosophy. Ibn Taymiyyah, who was one of the eminent scholars of the Sunni world, gave a verdict declaring *kalām* and logic 'unlawful'. Jalāl al-Dīn al-Suyuṭi, another figure among the Ahl al-Ḥadīth, has written a book called *Ṣawn al-*

mantiq wa al-kalām 'an al-mantiq wa al-kalām ('Protecting Speech and Logic from [the Evil of] *'ilm al-kalām* and the Science of Logic').

Mālik ibn Anas is another Sunni Imām who considers any debate or inquiry about doctrinal matters to be unlawful. I have explained the Shī'ī viewpoint in this matter in the introduction to Vol. V of *Uṣūl-e falsafah wa rawishe riyalism.*[6]

The important schools of *kalām*, as mentioned earlier, are Shī'ī, Mu'tazilah, Ash'arite and Murji'ah. Some sects of the Khawārij and the Batinis, such as the Isma'ilis, have also been considered as schools of Islamic *kalām.*[7]

However, in my view, none of these two sects can be considered as belonging to the schools of Islamic *kalām*. The Khawārija held specific beliefs in matters of doctrine and perhaps were the first to raise doctrinal problems by expressing certain beliefs about *imāmah*, the *kufr* (apostasy) of the *fāsiq* (evil-doer, one who commits major sins) and considered the disbelievers in these beliefs to be apostates. But, first, they did not create a rationalist school of thought in the Muslim world and, second, their thinking deviated so much from the viewpoint of the Shī'ites that it is difficult to count them among Muslims. What makes things easy is that the Khawārij ultimately became extinct and only one of their sects, called 'Abādiyyah, has some followers today. The 'Abādiyyah were the most moderate of all the Khawārij, and that is the reason why they have survived.

The Bātinis, too, have so liberally interfered in Islamic ideas on the basis of esotericism that it is possible to say that they have twisted Islam out of shape. For this reason the Muslim world is not prepared to consider them as one of the sects of Islam.

About thirty years ago when the Dār al-Taqrīb Bayna al-Madhāhib al-'Islāmiyyah was established in Cairo, the Imāmiyyah Shī'ā, the Zaydiyyah, the Ḥanafi, the Shafi'i, the Māliki and the Ḥanbali sects each had a representative. The Isma'ilis tried hard to send a representative of their own; but no such representative was accepted by other Muslims. Contrary to the Khawārij, who did not create a system of thought, the Bātinis, despite their serious deviations, do have a significant school of *kalām* and philosophy. There have emerged among them important thinkers who have left behind a considerable number of works. Lately, Orientalists have been showering great attention on Bātini thought and works.

One of the prominent Isma'ili figures is Nāṣir Khusrow al-'Alawi (d. 841/1437–38), the well-known Persian poet and author of such famous works as *Jāmi' al-ḥikmatayn*, *Kitāb wajh al-Dīn* and *Khuwan al-'ikwān*. Another is Abū Hatam al-Razi (d. 332/943–44), the author of *A'lām al-nubuwwah*. Others are Abū Ya'qub al-Sijistani, the author of *Kashf al-mahjūb* (its Persian translation has been recently published), who died during the second half of the 4th/loth century; Ḥāmid al-Dīn al-Kirmani, a pupil of Abū Ya'qub al-Sijistani, who has written a large number of books about the Isma'ili faith; Abū Hanifah Nu'man ibn Thabit, well known as Qāḍī Nu'man or 'the Shī'ī Abū Hanifah' (i.e. Isma'ili); his knowledge of *fiqh* and *ḥadīth* is good, and his well-known book *Da'a'im al-'Islam* was printed by lithotype several years ago.

Mu'tazilites

We shall begin our discussion – and we shall explain later why – with the Mu'tazilites. The emergence of this sect took place during the latter part of the first century or at the beginning of the second. Obviously *'ilm al-kalām*, like any other field of study, developed gradually and attained maturity slowly.

First we shall enumerate the principal Mu'tazilite beliefs, or rather, the basic and salient points of their school of thought. Second, we shall mention well-known Mu'tazilite figures and their role in history. Then we shall outline the transitions and changes in their thought and beliefs.

The Mu'tazilites hold many, not all confined to religious matters or to matters that they believe form an essential part of faith. They cover a number of physical, social, anthropological and philosophical issues, which are not directly related to the faith. However, there is a certain relevance of these problems to religion, and Mu'tazilites believe that any inquiry about the matters of religion is not possible without studying them.

There are five principal doctrines that, according to the Mu'tazilites themselves, constitute their basic tenets:

1. *Tawhid*, i.e. absence of plurality and attributes.
2. Justice (*'adl*), i.e. God is just and that He does not oppress His creatures.
3. Divine retribution (*al-wa'ed wa al-wa'id*), i.e. God has determined a reward for the obedient and a punishment for the disobedient, and there can be no uncertainty about it. Therefore, Divine pardon is possible only if the sinner repents, for forgiveness without repentance (*tawbah*) is not possible.
4. *Manzilah bayna al-manzilatayn* (a position between the two positions). This means that a *fāsiq* (i.e. one who commits one of the 'greater sins', such as a wine drinker, adulterer or liar) is neither a believer (*mu'min*) nor an infidel (*kāfir*); *fisq* is an intermediary state between belief and infidelity.
5. *Al-amr bil ma'rūf wa al-nahy 'an al-munkar* (bidding to do what is right and lawful, and forbidding what is wrong and unlawful). The opinion of the Mu'tazilites about this Islamic duty is, first, that the Sharī'ah is not the exclusive means of identifying the *ma'rūf* and the *munkar*; human reason

can, at least partially, independently identify the various kinds of *ma'rūf* and *munkar*. Second, the implementation of this duty does not necessitate the presence of the Imām, and is a universal obligation of all Muslims, whether the Imām or leader is present or not. Only some categories of it are the obligation of the Imām or ruler of Muslims, such as implementation of the punishments (*ḥudūd*) prescribed by the Sharī'ah, guarding of the frontiers of Islamic countries and other such matters relating to the Islamic government.

Occasionally, the Mu'tazilite *mutakallimīn* have devoted independent volumes to discussion of their five doctrines, such as the famous *al-Uṣūl al-khamsah* of al-Qāḍi 'Abd al-Jabbār al-Astarabādi (d. 415/ 1025), a Mu'tazilite contemporary of al-Sayyid al-Murtaḍā 'Alam al-Hudā and al-Ṣāhib ibn 'Abbād (d. 100/995).

As can be seen, only the principles of *tawḥīd* and justice can be considered parts of the essential doctrine. The other three principles are significant only because they characterize the Mu'tazilites. Even Divine Justice – although the notion of it is definitely supported by the Qur'ān, and belief in it is a necessary part of the Islamic faith and doctrine – has been made one of the five major doctrines because it characterizes the Mu'tazilites. Belief in Divine Knowledge and Power are as much an essential part of the Islamic faith and principal doctrine.

In the Shī'ī faith also the principle of Divine Justice is considered one of the five essential doctrines. The question thus naturally arises: what is particular about Divine Justice that it should be counted among the essential doctrines, whereas justice is only one of the Divine Attributes? Is not God just in the same manner as He is the Omniscient, the Mighty, the Living, the Perceiver, the Hearer and the Seer? All those Divine Attributes are essential to the faith. Then why is justice is given so much prominence among the Divine Attributes?

The answer is that justice has no advantage over other Attributes. The Shī'ī *mutakallimīn* have specially mentioned justice among the principal Shī'ī doctrines because the Ash'arites – who form the majority of the Ahl al-Sunnah – implicitly deny that it is an Attribute, whereas they do not reject the Attributes of knowledge, life, will, etc. Accordingly, justice is counted among the specific doctrines of the Shī'ites, as also of the Mu'tazilites. The abovementioned five doctrines constitute the basic position of the Mu'tazilites from the viewpoint of *kalām*. But, as was said earlier, the Mu'tazilite beliefs are not confined to these five and cover a broad range from theology, physics and sociology to anthropology, in all of which they hold specific beliefs. Discussion of these lies outside the scope of this text.

The Doctrine of al-Tawḥīd

Tawḥīd has various kinds and levels: *al-tawḥīd al-dhāti* (Unity of the Essence), *al-tawḥīd al-ṣifāti* (Unity of the Attributes, i.e. with the Essence), *al-tawḥīd al-af'āli* (Unity of the Acts), *al-tawḥīd al-'ibādi* (monotheism in worship).

Al-Tawḥīd al-dhāti means that the Divine Essence is one and unique; it does not have a like or match. All other beings are God's creations and inferior to Him in station and in degree of perfection. In fact, they cannot be compared with Him. The idea of *al-tawḥīd al-dhāti* is made clear by the following two [Qur'ānic] verses:

> Nothing is like Him. (42:11)
> He has no match [whatsoever]. (112:4)

Al-Tawḥīd al-ṣifāti means that the Divine Attributes such as Knowledge, Power, Life, Will, Perception, Hearing, Vision, etc. are not realities separate from God's Essence. They are identical with the Essence, in the sense that the Divine Essence is such that the Attributes are true of It, or is such that It manifests these Attributes.

Al-Tawḥīd al-af'āli means that all beings, or rather all acts (even human acts) exist by the Will of God, and are in some way willed by His sacred Essence.

Al-Tawḥīd al-'ibādi means that no other being except God deserves worship and devotion. Worship of anything besides God is *shirk* (polytheism) and puts the worshipper outside the limits of Islamic *tawḥīd* or monotheism.

In a sense *al-tawḥīd al-'ibādi* (*tawḥīd* in worship) is different from other kinds of *tawḥīdi*, because the first three relate to God and this kind relates to creatures. In other words, the Unity of Divine Essence, His Uniqueness and the identity of the Essence and Attributes, the unity of the origin of everything – all these are matters that relate to God. But *tawḥīd* in worship, i.e. the necessity of worshipping the One God, relates to the behaviour of creatures. In reality, of course, *tawḥīd* in worship is also related to God, because it means Uniqueness of God as the only deserving object of worship, and that He is in truth the One Deity Worthy of Worship. The statement '*lā ilāha illallāh*' encompasses all aspects of *tawḥīd*, although its first signification is monotheism in worship.

Al-tawḥīd al-dhāti and *al-tawḥīd al-'ibādi* are part of the basic doctrines of Islam. Any failure to adhere wholly to belief in these two principles would put one outside the pale of Islam. No Muslim has ever opposed these two basic beliefs.

Lately, the Wahhabis, who are followers of Muḥammad ibn 'Abd al-Wahhab, who in turn was a follower of Ibn Taymiyyah, a Ḥanbali from Syria, have claimed that some common beliefs of the Muslims, such as a belief in intercession (*shafā'ah*), and some of their practices, such as invoking the assistance of the prophets (A) and holy saints (R), are opposed to the doctrine of *al-tawḥīd al-'ibādi*. But these are not considered by other Muslims to conflict with. The point of difference between the Wahhabis and other Muslims is not whether anyone besides God – for instance the prophets or saints – is worthy of worship. There is no debate on this point. The debate is about whether the invoking of intercession and assistance can be considered a form of worship or not. Therefore, the difference is a secondary, not a primary one. Islamic scholars have rejected the viewpoint of the Wahhabis in elaborate, well-reasoned answers.

Al-tawḥīd al-ṣifāti (the Unity of Divine Essence and Attributes) is a point of debate between the Mu'tazilites and the Ash'arites. The latter deny it while the former affirm it. *Al-tawḥīd al-af'āli* is also another point of difference between them, only in this instance it is the Ash'arites who affirm it and the Mu'tazilites who deny it.

When the Mu'tazilites call themselves *'ahl al-tawḥīd'*, and count it among their doctrines, they mean thereby *al-tawḥīd al-ṣifāti*, not *al-tawḥīd al-dhāti* nor *al-tawḥīd al-'ibādi* (which are not disputed) nor *al-tawḥīd al-af'āli*. This is because, first, they negate *al-tawḥīd al-af'āli* and, second, they expound their own viewpoint about it under the doctrine of justice, their second article.

The Ash'arites and the Mu'tazilites formed two radically opposed camps on the issues of *al-tawḥīd al-ṣifāti* and *al-tawḥīd al-af'āli*. To repeat, the Mu'tazilites affirm *al-tawḥīd al-ṣifāti* and reject *al-tawḥīd al-af'āli*, while the Ash'arite position is the reverse. Both have advanced arguments in support of their positions. We shall discuss the Shī'ī position regarding these two aspects of *tawḥīd* in the relevant chapter.

The Doctrine of Divine Justice

I have mentioned above the five fundamental Mu'tazilite principles and explained the first issue, i.e. their doctrine of *tawḥīd*. Here we shall take up their doctrine of Divine Justice.

Of course, it is evident that none of the Islamic sects denied justice as one of the Divine Attributes. No one has ever claimed that God is not just. The difference between the Mu'tazilites and their opponents is in the interpretation of justice. In the view of the Mu'tazilites, the interpretation of the Ash'arites amounts to a denial of the Attribute of justice. The Ashʿarites themselves naturally have no desire to be considered the opponents of justice.

The Muʿtazilites believe that some acts are essentially 'just' and some intrinsically 'unjust.' For instance, rewarding the obedient and punishing the sinners is justice; and God is Just, i.e. He rewards the obedient and punishes the sinners, and it is impossible for Him to act otherwise. Rewarding the sinners and punishing the obedient is essentially and intrinsically unjust, and it is impossible for God to do such a thing. Similarly, compelling His creatures to commit a sin or creating them without any power of free will, then putting sinful acts into their hands and punishing them on account of those sins – this is injustice, an ugly thing for God to do; it is unjustifiable and unGodly. But the Ashʿarites believe that no act is intrinsically or essentially just or unjust. Justice is essentially whatever God does. If, supposedly, God were to punish the obedient and reward the sinners, it would be as just. Similarly, if God creates His creatures without any free will or freedom of action, then causes them to commit sins and punishes them – it is not essential injustice. If we suppose that God acts in this manner, it must be justice:

> Whatever Khusrow does is sweet (*shirin*).

For the same reason that the Muʿtazilites emphasize justice, they deny *al-tawḥīd al-afʿāli*. They say that *al-tawḥīd al-afʿāli* implies that God, not human beings, is the maker of human deeds. Since it is accepted that man attains reward and punishment in the hereafter, if God is the creator of human actions and yet punishes them for their evil deeds – which not they but God Himself has brought about – that would be injustice (*ẓulm*) and contrary to Divine Justice. Accordingly, the Muʿtazilites consider *al-tawḥīd al-afʿāli* to be contrary to the doctrine of justice.

Moreover, the Muʿtazilites are staunch believers in and defenders of human freedom and free will, unlike the Ashʿarites who deny human freedom and free will.

Under the doctrine of justice – in the sense that some deeds are inherently just and some inherently unjust, and that human reason dictates that justice is good and must be practised, whereas injustice is evil and must be abstained from – they advance another general, more comprehensive doctrine, which is that 'beauty' (*ḥusn*) and 'ugliness' (*qubḥ*) or good and evil are inherent properties of acts. For instance, truthfulness, trustworthiness, chastity and fear of God are intrinsically good qualities, and falsehood, treachery, indecency and neglectfulness are intrinsically evil. Therefore, deeds in essence possess inherent goodness or evil, even before they come before the judgement of God.

This leads them to another doctrine about reason, namely, that human reason can independently judge (or perceive) the good or evil in things. The good or evil of some deeds can be judged by human reason independently of the commands of the Sharīʿah. The Ashʿarites oppose this view too.

The belief in the inherent good or evil of acts and the capacity of reason to judge them, upheld by the Muʿtazilites and rejected by the Ashʿarites, brought many other problems in its wake, some of which were related to theology, some to human predicament; such as whether the Divine Acts or, rather, the creation of things has purpose or not. The Muʿtazilites claimed that absence of a purpose in the creation is *qabīḥ* (an ugly thing) and so rationally impossible. What about a duty that is beyond one's power to fulfil? Is it possible that God may burden someone with a duty that is beyond his capability? The Muʿtazilites considered this, too, to be *qabīḥ* and so impossible.

Is it within the power of a believer (*mu'min*) to turn apostate? Does the infidel (*kāfir*) have any power over his own infidelity (*kufr*)? The answer of the Muʿtazilites is in the affirmative; for if the believer and the infidel had no power over their belief and infidelity, it would be wrong (*qabīḥ*) to reward and punish them. The Ashʿarites rejected Muʿtazilite doctrines entirely.

*Retribution (*al-waʿd wa al-waʿīd*)*

Wa'd means the promise of reward and *waʿīd* means the threat of punishment. The Muʿtazilites believe that God does not break His own promises (all Muslims unanimously accept this) or renounce His threats, as the Qur'ānic verse regarding Divine promise confirms:

> Indeed God does not break the promise. (13:31)

Accordingly (the Muʿtazilites say), all threats addressed to sinners and the wicked, such as the punishments declared for an oppressor, a liar or an imbiber of wine, will all be carried out without fail, except when the sinner repents before death. Therefore, pardon without repentance is not possible.

From the viewpoint of the Muʿtazilites, pardon without repentance implies failure to carry out the threats (*waʿid*), and such an act, like the breaking of a promise (*khalf al-waʿd*), is *qabīḥ*, and thus impossible. Thus the Muʿtazilite beliefs regarding Divine retribution and Divine forgiveness are interrelated, and both arise from their belief in the inherent good and evil of deeds determinable by reason.

Manzilah Bayna al-Manzilatayn

The Muʿtazilite belief in this matter emerged in the wake of two opposite beliefs in the Muslim world about the faith (*imān*) or infidelity (*kufr*) of the *fāsiq*. For the first time the Khawārij maintained that committing any of the capital sins (*kabā'ir*) was contrary to faith (*imān*) and equal to infidelity. Therefore, the perpetrator of a major sin is a *kāfir*.

As we know, the Khawārij emerged after the incident of arbitration (*taḥkīm*) during the Battle of Ṣiffīn about the year 37/657–58 under the caliphate of Amir al-Mu'minīn ʿAlī (A). As the Nahj al-Balāgha tells us, Amir al-Mu'minīn (A) argued with them on this issue and refuted their viewpoint by numerous arguments. The Khawārij, even after ʿAlī (A), were against the caliphs of the period, and staunchly espoused the cause of *al-amr bi al-maʿrūf wa al-nahy ʿan al-munkar*, denouncing others for their evil and calling them apostates and infidels. Since most of the caliphs indulged in the capital sins, they were naturally regarded as infidels by the Khawārij. Accordingly, they were adversaries of the current politics.

Another group that emerged (or was produced by the hands of vested political interests) was that of the Murjiʿah, whose position with regard to the effect of capital sins was precisely opposite to that of the Khawārij. They held that faith and belief are a matter of the heart. One would remain a Muslim if one's faith – which is an inner affair of the heart – were intact; evil deeds cannot do any harm. Faith compensates for all wickedness.

The opinions of the Murjiʿah were to the benefit of the rulers, and tended to make the people regard their wickedness and indecencies as unimportant, and even to consider them, despite their destructive character, as men worthy of paradise. The Murjiʿah stated in unequivocal terms, 'The respectability of the station of the ruler is secure, no matter how much he may sin. Obedience to him is obligatory and prayers performed in his leadership are correct.' The tyrannical caliphs therefore backed them. For the Murjiʿah, sin and wickedness, no matter how serious, are no detriment to one's faith; the perpetrator of the major sins is a *mu'min*, not a *kāfir*.

The Muʿtazilites took a middle path in this matter. They maintained that the perpetrator of a major sin is neither a *mu'min* nor a *kāfir*, but occupies a position in between, which they termed *manzilah bayna al-manzilatayn*.

It is said that the first to express this belief was Wāsil ibn 'Ata', a pupil of al-Ḥaṣan al-Baṣrī. One day Wāsil was sitting with his teacher, who was asked his opinion about the difference between the Khawārij and the Murjiʿah on this issue. Before al-Ḥaṣan could say anything, Wāsil declared, 'In my opinion a perpetrator of the major sins is a *fāsiq*, not a *kāfir*. After this, he left the company or perhaps was expelled by al-Ḥaṣan al-Baṣrī – and as he went his own way he started propagating his own views. His pupil and brother-in-law ʿAmr ibn 'Ubayd joined him. At this point Ḥaṣan declared, '*I'tazala 'annā*' ('He [Wāsil] has departed from us'). According to another version, people said of Wāsil and 'Amr, '*'I'tazala qawl al-'ummah*' ('They have departed from the doctrines held by the *ummah*'), and that they had invented a third path.

Al-Amr bi al-Ma'rūf wa al-Nahy 'an al-Munkar

Al-amr bi al-ma'rūf wa al-nahy 'an al-munkar is an essential Islamic duty, unanimously accepted by all Muslims. Differences occur only in the limits and conditions related to it.

For instance, the Khawārij believed in it without any limits and conditions whatsoever. They believed that this twofold duty must be performed in all circumstances. Others believed that the conditions of probability of effectiveness (*al-ma'rūf*) and absence of any dangerous consequences were necessary for this obligation to be applicable, whereas the Khawārij did not believe in any such restrictions. Some believed that it is sufficient to fulfil the duty of *al-amr wa al-nahy* with the heart and the tongue, i.e. one should support *al-ma'rūf* and oppose *al-munkar* in one's heart and use one's tongue to speak up for *al-ma'rūf* and against *al-munkar*. But the Khawārij considered that the only right way to fulfil this duty was to take up arms and to unsheathe one's sword.

Opposed to them was a group who considered *al-amr wa al-nahy* to be subject to the above conditions and, moreover, that there was no need to go beyond the confines of the heart and the tongue to satisfy them. Ahmad ibn Ḥanbal is counted among them. According to this group, a bloody uprising is not justified or permitted as a means of struggling against unlawful activities.

The Mu'tazilites accepted the conditions for *al-amr wa al-nahy*, but, not limiting it to the heart and the tongue, maintained that, if unlawful practices become common or if the state is oppressive and unjust, it is obligatory for Muslims to rise in armed revolt.

Thus the belief special to the Mu'tazilites in regard to *al-amr bi al-ma'rūf wa al-nahy 'an al-munkar* – which contrasts with the position of the Ahl al-Ḥadīth and the Ahl al-Sunnah – is the belief in the necessity to rise up in arms to confront corruption. The Khawārij too shared this view, with the difference pointed out above.

Other Mu'tazilite Notions and Beliefs

Hitherto we have looked at the basic doctrines of the Mu'tazilites. But as we mentioned before, the Mu'tazilites raised many an issue and defended their opinions about them. Some of them related to theology, some to physics, some to sociology and some to the human situation. Of the theological issues, some related to general metaphysics (*umūr 'āmmah*) and some to theology proper (*ilāhiyyāt bi al-ma'na al-'akhāṣṣ*).[8] Like all other *mutakallimīn*, the Mu'tazilites raised metaphysical questions so as to use them to prepare the ground for the discussion of theological issues, which are their ultimate objectives. Similarly discussions in the natural sciences were intended to serve an introductory purpose, that is, to prove some religious doctrines or to find answers to objections. Here we shall enumerate some of these beliefs, beginning with theology.

Theology

(i) *Al-tawḥīd al-ṣifāti* (i.e. unity of the Divine Attributes)
(ii) *'Adl* (Divine Justice).
(iii) *The Holy Qur'ān* (kalām Allāh) is created (kalām, or speech, is an attribute of Act, not of the Essence).
(iv) The Divine Acts are caused and controlled by purposes (i.e. every Divine Act is for the sake of some beneficial outcome).
(v) Forgiveness without repentance is not possible (the doctrine of retribution, or *wa'd wa wa'īd*).
(vi) Pre-eternity (*qidām*) is limited to God (in this belief, they are challenged only by the philosophers).
(vii) Delegation of a duty beyond the powers of the *mukallaf* (*al-taklīf bimā lā yuṭāq*) is impossible.
(viii) The acts of creatures are not created by God for five reasons; the exercise of Divine Will does not apply to the acts of men.[9]
(ix) The world is created and is not pre-eternal (only philosophers are opposed to this view).
(x) God cannot be seen with the eyes, either in this world or in the Hereafter.

Physics

(i) Physical bodies are made up of indivisible particles.
(ii) Smell relates to particles scattered in air.
(iii) Taste is nothing but the effect of particles.
(iv) Light is made up of particles scattered in space.

(v) Interpenetration of bodies is not impossible (this belief is attributed to some Muʿtazilites).

(vi) The leaping of particles (*tafrah*)[10] is not impossible (this belief, too, is attributed to some Muʿtazilites).

Human Problems

(i) Man is free, endowed with free will; not predetermined (this question, the problem of the nature of human acts [whether created by God or man] and the problem of Divine Justice are all interrelated).

(ii) Ability (*istiṭāʿah*); that is, man has power over his own acts, before he performs them or desists from them.

(iii) The believer (*mu'min*) has the power to become an infidel and the infidel (*kāfir*) is able to become a believer.

(iv) A *fāsiq* is neither a *mu'min* nor a *kāfir*.

(v) Human reason can understand and judge some matters independently (without the prior need of guidance from the Sharīʿah).

(vi) In the case of conflict between reason and Ḥadīth, reason is to be preferred.

(vii) It is possible to interpret the Qur'ān with the help of reason.

Political and Social Problems

(i) *Al-amr bi al-maʿrūf wa al-nahy ʿan al-munkar* is obligatory even if it necessitates the taking up of arms.

(ii) The leadership (*imāmah*) of the Rashidun Caliphs was correct in the order it occurred.

(iii) ʿAlī (A) was superior to the Caliphs who preceded him (this is the view of some of the Muʿtazilites, not of all. The earlier Muʿtazilites – with the exception of Wāsil ibn ʿAtā' – considered Abū Bakr as the best, but the majority of the latter Muʿtazilites considered ʿAlī (A) to be superior).

(iv) Evaluation and criticism of the companions of the Prophet (S) and their deeds are permissible.

(v) A comparative study and analysis of the state policies of ʿUmar and ʿAlī (A).

These represent a sample of the issues touched on by the Muʿtazilites, which are far more numerous than those to which we have referred. In some of these problems, they were contradicted by the Ashʿarites, in some by the philosophers, in some by the Khawārij and in some by the Murjiʿah.

The Mu'tazilites never submitted to Greek thought and did not accept Greek philosophy indiscriminately, which entered the Islamic world at the same time as the emergence and rise of the Mu'tazilites. On the other hand, with great courage, they wrote books against philosophy and philosophers, boldly expressing their own opinions. The controversy between *mutakallimīn* and philosophers benefited both *kalām* and philosophy. Both of them made progress, and in the course of time came so close to each other that there remained no disagreement except on a few issues.

Transitions in the History of the Mu'tazilites

Obviously, all the above-mentioned problems were not posed at one time or by any single individual. Rather, they were raised gradually by several individuals, expanding the scope of *'ilm al-kalām*.

Among these mentioned, apparently the oldest problem was that of free will and determinism, in which the Mu'tazilites, of course, adhered to the notion of free will. This is a problem that is posed in the Qur'ān. That is, the Qur'ān refers to this issue in such a way as to stimulate thought on the subject. Some verses clearly indicate that man is free, not coerced in any of his acts. On the other hand, there are verses that, with equal clarity, indicate that all things depend on the Divine Will.

Here it may be thought that these two types of verses contradict each other. Accordingly, some explained away the verses upholding free will and supported determinism and predestination, while others explained away the verses that refer to the role of Divine Will and Intention and came down on the side of human freedom and free will. There is in fact a third group who see no contradiction between those two sets of verses.[11]

Moreover, the controversy between freedom and fate is frequently taken up in the utterances of 'Alī (A). Therefore, it is almost contemporaneous with Islam itself. However, the division of Muslims into two opposite camps, one siding with free will and the other with fate, took place in the second half of the first/seventh century.

It is said that the idea of free will was first put into circulation by Ghaylan al-Dimashqi and Ma'bad al-Juhani. The Banu Umayyah were inclined to propagate the belief in fate and predestination among the people, because it served their political interests. Under the cover of this belief that 'everything is by the Will of God' (*āmannā bi al-qadar khayrihi wa sharrihi* – 'We believe in fate, whether it bring good or evil'), they justified their oppressive and illegitimate rule. As a result, they repressed any notions of free will or human freedom, and Ghaylan al-Dimashqi and Ma'bad al-Juhani were both killed.

During that period the supporters of the belief in free will were called 'Qadariyyah'.

However, the problem of the infidelity or otherwise of the evildoer (*kufr al-fāsiq*) had become a subject of controversy even before the issue of freedom and fate, because it was raised by the Khawārij during the first half of the first century about the time of the caliphate of 'Alī (A). But the Khawārij did not defend this view in the fashion of the *mutakallimīn*. Only when the problem was raised among the Mu'tazilites, with the emergence of their doctrine of *manzilah bayna al-manzilatayn*, did it take on the colour of a problem of *kalām*.

The problem of fate and freedom (*jabr wa ikhtiyār*) automatically brought in its wake such other problems as these: the problem of Divine Justice; the rational and essential goodness or badness (*ḥusn wa qubḥ dhāti wa 'aqli*) of things and acts; dependence of Divine Acts on purposes; the impossibility of burdening a person with a duty exceeding his capacities; and the like.

During the first half of the second/eighth century one Jahm ibn Safwān (d. 128/745) voiced certain beliefs regarding the Divine Attributes. The writers of intellectual and religious history of Islam (*milal wa niḥal*), claim that the problem of *al-tawḥīd al-ṣifāti* (that the Divine Attributes are not separate from the Divine Essence – which the Mu'tazilites call their 'doctrine of *tawḥīd*') and the problem of *nafy al-tashbīh*, also called *aṣl al-tanzīh*, (which means that nothing can be likened to God) was expressed for the first time by Jahm ibn Safwān, whose followers came to be called the 'Jahmiyyah'. The Mu'tazilites followed the Jahmiyyah in their doctrines of tawḥīd and *tanzīh*, in the same way as they followed the Qadariyyah on the issue of free will. Jahm ibn Safwān himself was a Jabrite (i.e. a supporter of fate or predestination). The Mu'tazilites rejected his view of fate but accepted his view of *tawḥīd*.

The foremost among the Mu'tazilites, who established Mu'tazilism (*al-i'tizal*) as a school of thought was Wāsil ibn 'Ata', who, as mentioned earlier, was a pupil of al-Ḥaṣan al-Baṣri and who parted company with his teacher and established his own school. We mentioned above two different explanations of the source of the name Mu'tazilites. Another version is that the term '*mu'tazilite*' originally referred to a group of individuals who remained neutral during the events of the Battle of al-Jamal and the Battle of Siffin, such as Sa'd ibn Abi Waqqāṣ, Zayd ibn Thābit and 'Abd Allāh ibn 'Umar.

Later, when the issue of the faith or infidelity of the *fāsiq* was raised by the Khawārij, Muslims divided into two camps. One group took the third path, dissociating itself from the rest and maintaining a position of indifference to their debates. They adopted a neutrality with regard to a theoretical problem just as did such people as Sa'd ibn Abi Waqqāṣ in the midst of the heated social political climate of their time. Consequently they were called '*mu'tazilah*', 'the indifferent', and the name became stuck permanently.

Wāsil was born in the year 80/699 and died in 141/758–59. His views were limited to those on the negation of the Attributes (as distinct from the Essence of God), free will, *manzilah bayna al-manzilatayn*, *al-wa'd wa al-wa'id* and opinions on some differences among the companions.

After Wāsil came 'Amr ibn 'Ubayd, who extended and gave final shape to the views of Wāsil. After him came 'Amr ibn Abi al-Hudhayl al-'Allaf and Ibrahim ibn Sayyar al-Nazzām. Abū al-Hudhayl and al-Nazzām are both considered eminent Mu'tazilites. *kalām* attained its philosophical tinge at their hands. Abū al-Hudhayl studied philosophical works and wrote books in refutation of them. Al-Nazzām presented certain views in the sphere of physics, and it was he who offered the view that bodies are constituted of atoms. Abū al-Hudhayl died, most probably, in the year 255/869, and al-Nazzām in 231/845–46.

Al-Jāhiẓ (159/775 to 254/868), the famous author of the *al-Bayān wa al-tabyīn*, was another eminent Mu'tazilite of the third/ninth century.

During the rule of the Banū Umayyah, the Mu'tazilites did not have good relations with the ruling authorities. In the early days of the Banū al-'Abbās, they took on a neutral stand.[12] But under al-Ma'mūn, who was himself learned in literature, sciences and philosophy, they attracted the ruler's patronage. Al-Ma'mūn and after him al-Mu'taṣim and al-Wāthiq were staunch patrons of the Mu'tazilites and all three of these caliphs called themselves Mu'tazilites.

It was during this period that a heated controversy began that ultimately extended to all corners of the vast Islamic dominions of the period. The issue under debate was whether Speech is an attribute of the Divine Act or an attribute of the Essence. Whether it is created and temporal (*ḥadīth*) or uncreated and eternal (*qadīm*) like Divine Knowledge, Power and Life. The Mu'tazilites believed that the Qur'ān is created (in time) and is therefore a creation of God (*mākhluq*) and so temporal. They also maintained that belief in the pre-eternity of the Qur'ān amounted to infidelity (*kufr*).

Opponents of the Mu'tazilites, by contrast, believed in the pre-eternity and uncreatedness of the Qur'ān. Al-Ma'mūn (r. 198/813 to 218/833) sent out a circular saying that any believer in the pre-eternity of the Qur'ān would be liable to punishment. Many persons were thrown into prison and subjected to torture.

Al-Mu'taṣim (r. 218/833 to 227/842) and al-Wāthiq (r. 227/842 to 232/847) also followed al-Ma'mūn's practice. One of those who went to prison during that time was Aḥmad ibn Ḥanbal. This policy remained in force until al-Mutawakkil assumed power (r. 232/847 to 247/861). Al-Mutawakkil was not inclined to favour the Muʿtazilites and most of the ordinary people were also opposed to them. As a result the Muʿtazilites and their admirers suffered a reverse and indeed persecutions and reprisals. In the purges that followed, much blood was shed and homes were ruined. The period is remembered by Muslims as *miḥnah* – times of adversity and trial.

The Muʿtazilites never recuperated after this and the field was left open forever for their opponents, the Ahl al-Sunnah and the Ahl al-Ḥadīth. Nevertheless, there appeared some prominent personalities even during the following periods of their decline, such as ʿAbd Allāh ibn Aḥmad Abū al-Qāsim al-Balkhi, well known as al-Kaʿbi (d. 319/ 931); Abū ʿAlī al-Jubbaʿi (d. 303/915–16); Abū al-Hāshim al-Jubbaʿi (d. 321/933) the son of Abū ʿAlī al-Jubbaʿi; Qāḍī ʿAbd al-Jabbar (d. 415/1024); Abū al-Ḥaṣan al-Khayyāṭ; al-Sāhib ibn ʿAbbād, al-Zamakhsharī (d. 538/1144); and Abū Jaʿfar al-ʿIskāfi.

Ashʿarites

As we have seen, the ideas and notions that led to the emergence of the Muʿtazilite school were born during the latter half of the first century of Hijrah. The Muʿtazilites characteristically used a kind of logical and rational method for understanding the basic doctrines of the Islamic faith. Obviously, the first condition for such an approach is belief in the freedom, independence and validity of reason. It is also true that people at large are not used to ratiocination and intellectual analysis and always tend to equate 'religiosity' with 'credulity' and intellectual submission to the apparent meanings of the Qur'ānic verses and in particular of the *aḥādīth*. They tend to look on every attempt at independent and original interpretation as a kind of rebellion against religion, especially if the political climate supports this attitude, and more so if some religious scholars propagate such an outlook, particularly when they really believe in their literalist outlook and are inflexible and fanatical in practice. The attacks of the Akhbaris on the Uṣūliyyūn and the *mujtahidūn*, and the attacks of some *fuqaha'* and *muḥaddithūn* against philosophers in the Islamic world had their roots in such thinking.[13]

The Muʿtazilites had a deep-rooted interest in understanding Islam and its propagation and defence against atheists, Jews, Christians, Magians, Sabaeans, Manichaeans and others. They even trained missionaries and dispatched them to various regions. Nevertheless, their existence was threatened by the literalists, who called themselves 'Ahl al-Ḥadīth' or 'Ahl al-Sunnah'. They were ultimately stabbed in the back and weakened and gradually became extinct.

Despite it all, until about the beginning of the fourth/tenth century, there existed no rival school of *kalām* that could challenge the Mu'tazilites. All opposition was based on the claim that the views of the Mu'tazilites were contrary to the externals of the *ḥadīth* and the Sunnah. The leaders of the Ahl al-Ḥadīth, such as Mālik ibn Anas and Aḥmad ibn Ḥanbal, basically considered any debate, inquiry or argument about matters of faith to be unlawful (*ḥarām*). Not only did the Ahl al-Sunnah lack any system of *kalām* challenging the Mu'tazilites, but they were also opposed to *kalām* itself.

About the late third/ninth century and the early fourth/tenth, a new phenomenon came into being, thanks to the appearance of a distinguished thinker who had received instruction in Mu'tazilite teachings under Qāḍī 'Abd al-Jabbar and had mastered them. He rejected Mu'tazilite tenets and inclined towards the doctrines of the Ahl al-Sunnah. Being a man of some genius and equipped with the tools used by the Mu'tazilites, he established all the doctrines of the Ahl al-Sunnah on a rational basis and gave them the form of a relatively closely-knit intellectual system. That distinguished person was Abū al-Ḥaṣan al-Ash'ari (d. circa 330/941–42). Al-'Ash'ari – unlike his predecessors among Ahl al-Ḥadīth, such as Aḥmad ibn Ḥanbal – considered debate and argument and use of the tools of logic in the matter of the doctrines of the faith as permissible, citing evidence from the Qur'ān and the Sunnah to support his claim. He wrote a treatise entitled *'Risālah fi istiḥsan al-khawḍ fi 'ilm al-kalām'* ('A Treatise on the Appropriateness of Inquiry into *'Ilm al-Kalām'*).[14]

It was at this point that the Ahl al-Ḥadīth split into two groups: the Ash'arites or followers of Abū al-Ḥaṣan al-Ash'ari, who considered *kalām* permissible; and the Ḥanbalis or followers of Aḥmad ibn Ḥanbal, who considered it unlawful. As already mentioned, Ibn Taymiyyah, a Ḥanbali, wrote a book on the unlawfulness of logic and *kalām*.[15] There was another reason why people began to detest the Mu'tazilites. It was the period of calamity, or *miḥnah*, and the Mu'tazilites, under the patronage of the caliph al-Ma'mūn, wanted to coerce the people into accepting their belief in the createdness of the Qur'ān. Their attempt at regimentation brought bloodshed, imprisonment, torture and exile, which shook Muslim society. The people held the Mu'tazilites responsible for that havoc and accordingly regarded them with much disfavour.

These two causes contributed to the public welcome given to the emergence of the school of Ash'arism. After Abū al-Ḥaṣan al-Ash'ari, other distinguished personalities appeared in this school and strengthened its foundations. Among them were: Qāḍī Abū Bakr al-Bāqillāni (a contemporary of al-Shaykh al-Mufīd), who died in the year 403/1012–13; Abū Ishāq al-'Asfarā'ini (who is considered to belong to the generation after al-Bāqillāni and al-Sayyid al-Murtaḍā 'Alam al-Hudā); Imām al-Ḥaramayn al-Juwayni, the teacher of al-Ghazzālī; Imām Muḥammad al-Ghazzālī, the author of *Ihya' 'Ulūm al-Dīn* himself (d. 505/1111–12); and Imām Fakhr al-Dīn al-Rāzi.

Of course, the Ash'arite school underwent gradual changes and, particularly in the hands of al-Ghazzāli, *kalām* somewhat lost its characteristic colour and took on the hue of *'irfān* (Sufism). Imām al-Razi brought it close to philosophy. After Khwājah Nāṣir al-Dīn al-Ṭūsī wrote his book *Tajrīd al-i'tiqad* more than ninety per cent of *kalām* took on a philosophical tone. After the publication of the *Tajrid*, all *mutakallimīn* – including the Mu'tazilites and the Ash'arites – followed the same path that had been trodden by that great philosopher and Shī'ī *mutakallīm*.

For instance, the later works of *kalām* such as *al-Mawāqif* and *Maqāṣid* and the commentaries written upon them were all in the same mould as the Tajrīd. In fact, it may be said that, the more time has elapsed since Abū al-Ḥaṣan al-Ash'ari, the more the leading Ash'arites have moved away from him, bringing his doctrines closer to the views of the Mu'tazilites or of the philosophers.

The following are the main doctrines of al-Ash'ari, which are aimed at defending the basic principles of the Ahl al-Sunnah or attempting a rational justification of their beliefs.

(i) The Divine Attributes, contrary to the belief of the Mu'tazilites and the philosophers, are not identical with the Divine Essence.

(ii) The Divine Will is all-embracing. Divine Providence and predestination encompass all events (this belief, too, is contrary to the view held by the Mu'tazilites, though in agreement with those of the philosophers).

(iii) All evil, like good, is from God (of course, this view is a logical corollary, in al-Ash'ari's view of the above belief).

(iv) Man is not free in his acts, which are created by God (this belief, too, in al-Ash'ari's view, necessarily follows from the doctrine of the all-embracing nature of the Divine Will).

(v) Acts are not intrinsically good or evil, i.e. *ḥusn* or *qubḥ* of deeds is not intrinsic, but determined by the Sharī'ah. The same is true of justice. What is 'just' is determined by the Sharī'ah, not by reason (contrary to the belief of the Mu'tazilites).

(vi) Grace (*luṭf*) and selection of the best for creation (*al-aṣlah*) are not incumbent upon God (contrary to the belief of the Mu'tazilites).

(vii) Man's power over his actions does not precede them (there is no *istita'ah qabl al-fi'l*), but is commensurate and concurrent with the acts themselves (contrary to the belief of the Muslim philosophers and the Muʿtazilites).

(viii) Absolute deanthropomorphism *(tanzīh muṭlaq)*, in other words, absolute absence of similarity between God and others does not hold (contrary to the Muʿtazilite view).

(ix) Doctrine of acquisition. Man does not 'create' his own acts; rather he 'acquires' or 'earns' them (this is in justification of the Ahl al-Sunnah's belief in the creation of human acts by God).

(x) Possibility of the beatific vision. God shall be visible to human eyes on the Day of the Resurrection (contrary to the view of the Muʿtazilites and the philosophers).

(xi) The *fāsiq* is a believer, or *mu'min* (contrary to the view of the Khawārij, who consider him *kāfir*, and contrary to the Muʿtazilite doctrine of *manzilah bayna al-manzilatayn*).

(xii) There is nothing wrong in God's pardoning someone without repentance. Similarly, nothing is wrong in God's subjecting a believer to chastisement (contrary to the Muʿtazilite position).

(xiii) Intercession (*shafāʿah*) is justifiable (contrary to the Muʿtazilite position).

(xiv) To tell a lie or break a promise is not possible for God.

(xv) The world is created in time (*ḥddīth*) (contrary to the view of the philosophers).

(xvi) The Qur'ān is pre-eternal (*qadīm*); however, this is true of *al-kalām al-nafsi* (meaning of the Qur'ān), not *al-kalām al-lafẓi* – the spoken word (this is in justification of the Ahl al-Sunnah's belief in the pre-eternity of the Qur'ān).

(xvii) The Divine Acts do not follow any purpose or aim (contrary to the view of the philosophers and the Muʿtazilites)

(xviii) It is possible that God may burden a person with a duty beyond his power (contrary to the belief of the philosophers and the Muʿtazilites).

Abū al-Ḥaṣan al-Ashʿari was a prolific writer and reportedly compiled more than two hundred books. As many as a hundred are mentioned in biographies, although most of those works have apparently perished. The most famous of his works is *Maqālāt al-Islāmiyyīn*, which has been published. It is a very disorderly and confused work. Another one printed is *al-Lumaʿ*, and other of his works may perhaps also have appeared in print.

Abū al-Ḥaṣan al-Ashʿari is one of those individuals whose ideas, regrettably, exercised a great influence on the Islamic world. Nevertheless, later, his works were subjected to severe criticism by philosophers and the Muʿtazilites. Ibn Sīnā, in *al-Shifā*, has refuted many of his ideas without mentioning his name. Even some of his followers, such as Qāḍī Abū Bakr al-Bāqillāni and Imām al-Ḥaramayn al-Juwayni, revised and modified his views about predestination and the createdness of (human) acts.

Imām Muḥammad al-Ghazzālī, although an Ashʿarite who to a great extent established and strengthened the Ashʿarite doctrines, put them on a different foundation. Thanks to al-Ghazzālī, *kalām* was brought closer to *ʿirfān* and Sufism. Mawlānā Muḥammad al-Rūmi, the author of the Mathnawī, is, in his own way, an Ashʿarite; but his deep *ṣūfī* inclinations give a different colour to all the issues of *kalām*. Imām Fakhr al-Dīn al-Rāzī, who was familiar with philosophic thought, transformed al-Ashʿari's *kalām*, further strengthening it.

The triumph of the Ashʿarite school cost the Muslim world dearly. Its triumph was the victory of the forces of stagnation over freedom of thought. Despite the fact that the battle between Ashʿarism and Muʿtazilism is related to the Sunni world, even the Shīʿī world could not remain unaffected by some of the stultifying effects of Ashʿarism. This triumph has particular historical and social reasons behind it, and certain political events effectively contributed to it.

As mentioned earlier, during the third/ninth century, the caliph al-Ma'mūn, himself an intellectual and a man of learning, rose to the support of the Muʿtazilites. After him al-Muʿtasim and al-Wāthiq also followed him – until al-Mutawakkil assumed the caliphate. Al-Mutawakkil played a basic role in the victory of the Ahl al-Sunnah's doctrines, which acquired dialectic foundations after one hundred years at the hands of al-Ashʿari. Had al-Mutawakkil's way of thinking been similar to that of his predecessors, Muʿtazilism would assuredly have had a different fate.

The rise of the Seljuq Turks to power in Iran was another effective factor in the triumph and propagation of the Ashʿarite ideas. The Seljuqs did not believe in the freedom of thought. They were the antithesis of the Buyids, some of whom were men of scholarship and literary merit. Shīʿism and Muʿtazilism flourished in the Buyid court. Ibn al-ʿAmid and al-Ṣāhib ibn ʿAbbād, the two learned ministers of the Buyids, were both anti-Ashʿarites.

It is not the intention here to support Muʿtazilite doctrines, and later we shall expose the feebleness of many of their beliefs. However, what deserves appreciation in the Muʿtazilites is their rational approach – something that died out with them. As we know, a religion as rich and resourceful as Islam needs a *kalām* that has an unshakeable faith in the freedom of reason.

The Shī'ite Kalām

Now we turn our attention, if only briefly, to the Shī'ite *kalām*. *kalām*, in the sense of logical and rational argument about the principal doctrines of Islam, has a special and distinguished place in the Shī'ī tradition. The Shī'ī *kalām* emerges from the core of Shī'ite *ḥadīth* but is also mixed with Shī'ī philosophy. We have seen how, in the early centuries, the Ahl al-Sunnah considered *kalām* to be inimical to the Sunnah and the *ḥadīth*. In fact, the opposite is true: the Shī'ite *kalām* is firmly rooted in the Sunnah and the *ḥadīth*. The reason is that the Shī'ite *ḥadīth*, unlike the Sunni corpus on *ḥadīth*, consists of numerous traditions in which profound metaphysical or social problems have been dealt with logically and analysed rationally. In the Sunni corpus such analytic treatment of these subjects is missing. For instance, wherever there is mention of such matters as Divine Providence and Preordination, the all-embracing Will of the Almighty, the Divine Names and Attributes, the soul, life after death, the final reckoning, the *Ṣirāt*, the balance or such issues as *imāmah*, *khilāfah* and the like, argument and rational explanation are absent. But in the Shī'ī corpus on *ḥadīth*, all such issues are dealt with in a rational and discursive manner. A comparison between the list of the chapters of the six *Sihah* and that of al-Kulayni's *al-Kāfi* will make this quite clear.

Accordingly, *kalām*, in the sense of rational and analytical treatment of problems, is found in the Shī'ī *ḥadīth*. This is the reason why the Shī'ites were not divided; whereas the Sunnis were divided into the 'Ahl al-Ḥadīth' and the 'Ahl al-kalām'.

We stated above, on the basis of the Sunni textual sources, that the first doctrinal issue to become a subject of controversy was the issue of the *kufr* of a *fāsiq*, brought up by the Khawārij during the first half of the first century. Then there emerged the problem of freedom and fate, which was raised and argued by two individuals named Ma'bad al-Juhani and Ghaylan al-Dimashqi. The belief they professed in this matter was contrary to the one held and propagated by the Umayyad rulers. Then, during the first half of the second century, the notion of the unity of Divine Attributes and Essence was posed by Jahm ibn Ṣafwān. There followed Wāsil ibn 'Atā' and 'Amr ibn 'Ubayd, the founders of the Mu'tazilite school, who adopted the belief in free will from Ma'bad and Ghaylan and the doctrine of the Unity of Divine Essence and Attributes from Jahm ibn Safwan, and themselves invented the doctrine of *manzilah bayna al-manzilatayn* in the issue of the faith or infidelity of *fāsiq*. In so doing, they initiated debates in some other issues and thus were responsible for founding the first school in Islamic *kalām*.

This is how Orientalists and scholars of Islam in the West and the East explain and interpret the origins of rational speculation and debate in the Islamic world. This group, whether by accident or design, ignores the profound rational and demonstrative arguments advanced for the first time by Amir al-Muminin 'Alī (A). The truth is that it was 'Alī (A), in his sermons and discussions, who introduced the rational approach to Islamic teachings and initiated profound discussion on the subjects of Divine Essence and Attributes, temporality (*ḥudūth*) and pre-eternity (*qidām*), simplicity (*basāṭah*) and compositeness (*tarkīb*), unity (*waḥdah*) and plurality (*kathrah*), etc. These are recorded in the *Nahj al-balāghah* and other authentic texts of Shī'ī *ḥadīth*. The discussions have a colour, flavour and spirit that are totally distinct from the approaches of the Mu'tazilites and the Ash'arites to the controversies of *kalām*, or even from that of the Shī'ites scholars, who were influenced by their contemporary *kalām*.

I have discussed this matter in *Sayr dar Nahj al-balāghah* ('A Journey through the "Nahj al-balāghah"') and in the preface to Vol. V of *Uṣūl-e falsafah wa rawishe riyalism*.

Sunni historians confess that from the earliest days the Shī'ite thinking was philosophical in approach. The Shī'ite intellectual and theoretical approach is opposed not only to Ḥanbali thinking – which fundamentally rejects the idea of using discursive reasoning in religious belief – and the Ash'arite approach – which denies the independence of reason and subordinates it to literalist appearance – but also to Mu'tazilite thinking with all its predilection for reason. Because, although Mu'tazilite thought is rational, it is dialectical or polemical (*jadali*), not discursive or demonstrative (*burhāni*).

In our discussion of the basics of Islamic philosophy, where we looked at the difference between peripatetic (*ḥikmat al-mashshā'*) and illuminationist (*ḥikmat al-'ishrāq*) philosophies, we also explained the difference between dialectical (Mu'tazilite and Ash'arite) *kalām* and mystical or intuitive approaches to philosophical issues.[16] The reason why most Islamic philosophers have been Shī'ites is that only the Shī'ites have preserved and kept Islamic philosophy alive, since they acquired this spirit from their Imāms (A), particularly from the first Imām, Amir al-Mu'minin 'Alī (A).

The Shī'ī philosophers, without having to mould philosophy into *kalām* and without transforming rational philosophy into dialectical philosophization, consolidated the doctrinal basis of Islam under the inspiration of the Qur'ānic Revelation and the guiding principles of their spiritual leaders. If we wish to enumerate the Shī'ī *mutakallimīn*, that is, those who have applied rational thought to the doctrines of the Faith, we shall have to include a group of *muḥaddithūn* as well as a group of Shī'ī philosophers among them. This is because, as was said earlier, both Shīʿite *ḥadīth* and Shīʿite philosophy have accomplished the function of *ʿilm al-kalām* to a greater extent than *kalām* itself.

But if by *mutakallimīn* we mean only those who, under Muʿtazilite or Ashʿarite influence, resorted to the tools of dialectical reasoning, we are forced to select only a particular group of them. However, there is no reason to concentrate our attention on this particular group only.

If we discount the utterances of the infallible Imāms (A) about doctrines, delivered in the form of sermons, narratives or prayers, the first Shīʿī writer to compile a book on doctrines of faith was ʿAlī ibn Ismaʿil ibn Mitham al-Tammar. Mitham al-Tammar himself was an orator and expert debater, and was one of the closest companions of Amir al-Mu'minin ʿAlī (A). ʿAlī ibn Ismaʿil was his grandson. He was a contemporary of ʿAmr ibn ʿUbayd and Abū al-Hudhayl al-ʿAllaf, the famous figures of *kalām* during the first half of the second century, who were from the first generation of the founders of Muʿtazilite *kalām*.

Among the companions of al-Imām al-Ṣādiq (A), there is a group of individuals, referred to as *mutakallīm* by the Imām (A) himself, who included Hishām ibn al-Hakam, Hishām ibn Sālim, Humran ibn Aʿyan, Abū Jaʿfar al-Aḥwal (known as Mu'min al-Taq), Qays ibn Masar and others.

Al-Kāfi relates the story of a debate between this group and an opponent in the presence of al-Imām al-Ṣādiq (A), which pleased him. This group lived during the first half of the second century, and was trained in the school of al-Imām al-Ṣādiq (A). This shows that the Imāms of the Ahl al-Bayt (A) not only themselves engaged in discussion and analysis of the problems of *kalām* but also trained some of their pupils for the express purpose of conducting such debates and arguments. Of these Hishām ibn al-Hakam distinguished himself only in *ʿilm al-kalām*, not in *tafsīr*, *fiqh* or *ḥadīth*. Al-Imām al-Ṣādiq (A) used to treat him with more respect than the others, even when he was a raw youth, and used to offer him a preferred seat, all because of his expertise in *kalām*.

By showing preference for Hishām the *mutakallīm* over other pupils who were experts in *ḥadīth* and *fiqh*, al-Imām al-Ṣādiq (A), in fact, hoped to raise the status of *kalām* as against *ḥadīth* and *fiqh*. Obviously, this played a decisive role in the promotion of *ʿilm al-kalām* and consequently gave Shīʿī thought a dialectical and philosophical character.

Al-Imām al-Riḍā (A) personally participated in debates in which al-Ma'mūn invited *mutakallimīn* of various schools to take part. The records of such meetings are preserved in the Shīʿī texts.

It is indeed amazing that Orientalists should be completely silent about all such events pertaining to the efforts of Amir al-Mu'minīn ʿAlī (A) and ignore the role of the Infallible Imāms (A) in the revival of rational inquiry in matters of religious doctrine.

Faḍl ibn Shadhan al-Nishāburi, a companion of al-Imām al-Riḍā (A), al-Imām al-Jawad (A) and al-Imām al-Hadi (A), whose tomb is in Nishabur, apart from being a *faqīh* and a *muḥaddith*, was also a *mutakallīm*. He is reported to have written a large number of books.

The Nawbakht family produced many illustrious personalities, most of whom were *mutakallimīn*. Faḍl ibn Abi Sahl ibn al-Nawbakht, a contemporary of Harūn, was attached to the famous Bayt al-Hikmah library and well known as a translator from Persian into Arabic; Ishaq ibn Abi Sahl ibn al-Nawbakht; his son, Isma'il ibn Ishaq ibn Sahl ibn al-Nawbakht; another of his sons, 'Alī ibn Ishaq; his grandson, Abū Sahl Isma'il ibn 'Alī ibn Ishaq ibn Abi Sahl ibn al-Nawbakht (called '*shaykh al-mutakallimīn*' of the Shī'ites); Ḥaṣan ibn Musa al-Nawbakht, a nephew of Isma'il ibn 'Alī; and several others of this family were all Shī'ī *mutakallimīn*.

Ibn Qubbah al-Rāzi in the third/ninth century and Abū 'Alī ibn Miskawayh, the famous doctor of medicine and author of *Tahdhīb al-'akhlāq wa tathir al-a'raq*, who lived during the early fifth/eleventh century, are also Shī'ī *mutakallimīn*.

The Shī'ī *mutakallimīn* were many in number. Khwājah Nāṣir al-Dīn al-Ṭūsī, the famous philosopher and mathematician and author of the *Tajrīd al-I'tiqād*, and al-'Allāmah al-Ḥilli, the well-known *faqīh* and commentator of the *Tajrīd al-I'tiqād*, were well-known *mutakallimīn* of the seventh/thirteenth century.

Khwājah Nāṣir al-Dīn al-Ṭūsī, himself a learned philosopher, created the most solid work of *kalām* in the *Tajrīd al-I'tiqad*, which has always attracted the attention of all *mutakallimīn*, whether Shī'ī or Sunni. Al-Ṭūsī has, to a great extent, brought *kalām* out of the dialectical labyrinth and made it closer to discursive (rational) philosophy. In later times, *kalām* almost completely lost its dialectical form and thinkers abandoned dialectical philosophy in favour of discursive (rational) philosophy.

The Shī'ite philosophers after al-Ṭūsī brought the essential problems of *kalām* into philosophy and applied philosophical methods of inquiry to the study and analysis of these problems, with greater success than had been attained by the *mutakallimīn* who employed older methods. For example, Mullā Ṣadrā and Mullā Hādi Sabzawari, though not usually counted among *mutakallimīn*, have been far more influential in Islamic thought than any of the true *mutakallimīn* themselves.

If we compare their approach to that of the basic Islamic texts, such as the Qur'ān, the *Nahj al-balāghah* and the prayers and traditions transmitted from the Ahl al-Bayt (A), we find this approach and style of reasoning to be closer to that of the original teachers of the faith.

The Shī'ī Standpoint

Here we shall briefly explain Shī'ite views on the issues current among Muslim *mutakallimīn*. Earlier, when we looked at the Mu'tazilite viewpoint, we noted that the Mu'tazilites considered their five doctrines, viz. *tawḥīd, 'adl, al-wa'd wa al-wa'īd, manzilah bayna al-manzilatayn* and *al-'amr bi al-ma'rūf wa al-nahy 'an al-munkar*, to be fundamental to their school of thought. We said also that the reason for giving prominence to these doctrines above all other Mu'tazilite beliefs is that they characterize their school and distinguish it from the schools of their opponents. We should not construe from this that the five principles constitute the basic doctrines of the faith (*uṣūl al-Dīn*) of the Mu'tazilites and that all the remaining beliefs are regarded as subsidiary.

The Shī'ite scholars – not the Shī'ite Imāms (A) – from the earliest days also introduced five doctrines, which they held to be characteristic of Shī'ism. They were: *tawḥīd, 'adl, nubuwwah, imāmah* and *ma'ād* (Resurrection). It is generally said that these five are the basic tenets of the faith (*uṣūl al-Dīn*) and the rest have a subordinate significance, or are *furu' al-Dīn*. If by *uṣūl al-Dīn* we mean the doctrines in which it is essential to believe in order to be a Muslim, their number falls to two, namely, *tawḥīd* and *nubuwwah*. These are the only two beliefs contained in the Shahadatayn (*'ashhadu 'an lā ilāhā illallāhu wa 'ashhadu 'annā Muḥammadan rasūlūllāh*). Moreover, the second testimony is related in particular to the prophethood of Muḥammad (S), not to prophethood in general, and the prophethood of other prophets is not covered by it. However, belief in the prophethood of all the other prophets (A) is a part of the *uṣūl al-Dīn* and faith in it is compulsory for all believers.

If by *uṣūl al-Dīn* we mean the doctrines in which it is essential to have faith, as they form part of the totality of Islamic faith, then the number increases to include other matters such as belief in the existence of angels – which is explicitly stated in the Qur'ān.[17] Furthermore, what is special about the Attribute of *'adl* (justice) that only this Divine Attribute should be included in the essential doctrine, to the exclusion of all other attributes, such as Knowledge, Life, Power, Hearing or Vision? If belief in the Divine Attributes is necessary, it should be necessary to believe in all of them; if not, none of them ought to be made the basis of the faith.

Actually, the fivefold principles were selected in such a manner as, to determine certain tenets essential to the Islamic faith, on the one hand, and to specify the particular identity of the school, on the other. The doctrines of *tawḥīd*, *nubuwwah* and *ma'ād* are the three in which it is essential for every Muslim to believe. These three are, in other words, part of the objectives of Islam, the doctrine of *'adl* being the specific mark of the Shī'ite school.

The doctrine of *'adl*, although it is not part of the main objectives of the Islamic faith – in the sense that it does not differ from the other articles of faith pertaining to Knowledge, Life, Power, etc. – is one of those doctrines that represent the specific Shī'ī outlook with regard to Islam.

The article on *imāmah*, from the Shī'ite viewpoint, covers both these aspects, i.e. it is a part of the essential doctrines and it also characterizes the Shī'ite school.

If faith in the existence of angels is also, on the authority of the Qur'ān, essential and obligatory, then why was it not stated as a sixth article of the faith? The answer is that the above-mentioned articles are part of the objectives of Islam. That is, the Holy Prophet (S) called the people to believe in them. This means that the mission of the Prophet (S) prepared the ground for the establishment of these beliefs. But the belief in angels or in obligatory duties such as prayer and fasting is not a part of the objectives of the prophethood; it rather forms an essential accessory to it. In other words, such beliefs are essential accessories of faith in prophethood, but are not the objectives of prophethood.

The issue of *imāmah*, if viewed in socio-political terms or from the point of view of government and leadership, is similar to that of *'adl*, in that it is not an essential part of the faith. However, if viewed from a spiritual viewpoint – that is, recognizing that the Imām, to use the terminology of *ḥadīth*, is the *ḥujjah* (proof) of God and His *khalīfah* (vicegerent), who at all times serves as a spiritual link between every individual Muslim and the perfect human being – then it is to be considered as one of the articles of faith.

Now let us look separately at each of the particular doctrines of Shī'ite *kalām*, including the above-mentioned five doctrines.

(i) Tawḥīd

Tawḥīd is one of the five doctrines of the Mu'tazilites, as also of the Ash'arites, with the difference that in the case of the Mu'tazilites it specifically means *al-tawḥīd al-ṣifāti*, which is denied by the Ash'arites. On the other hand, the specific sense of this term as affirmed by the Ash'arites is *al-tawḥīd al-af'āli*, which is rejected by the Mu'tazilites.

As mentioned above, *al-tawḥīd al-dhāti* and *al-tawḥīd al-'ibādi*, since they are admitted by all, are outside the scope of our discussion. The concept of *tawḥīd* upheld by the Shī'ites, in addition to *al-tawḥīd al-dhāti* and *al-tawḥīd al-'ibādi*, also includes *al-tawḥīd al-ṣifāti* and *al-tawḥīd al-af'āli*. That is, in the controversy regarding the Attributes, the Shīʿites are on the side of *al-tawḥīd al-ṣifāti*, and in the debate on human acts, they are on the side of *al-tawḥīd al-afʿāli*. Nevertheless, the Shīʿī concept of *al-tawḥīd al-ṣifāti* is different from that of the Muʿtazilites. Also, their notion of *al-tawḥīd al-afʿāli* differs from that of the Ashʿarites.

The Muʿtazilites concept of *al-tawḥīd al-ṣifāti* is synonymous with the idea of the absence of all Attributes from the Divine Essence or, to put it another way, with the concept that the Divine Essence is devoid of all qualities. But the Shīʿī notion of *al-tawḥīd al-ṣifāti* means identity of the Attributes with the Divine Essence.[18] For further elaboration of this issue one must have recourse to works on Shīʿite *kalām* and philosophy.

The Shīʿī conception of *al-tawḥīd al-afʿāli* differs from the one held by the Ashʿarites. The Ashʿarite notion of *al-tawḥīd al-afʿāli* means that no creature is of any consequence in the scheme of things and everything is directly ordained by God. Accordingly, He is also the direct creator of the deeds of human beings and they are not creators of their own acts. Such a belief is similar to the idea of absolute predestination and has been refuted through many an argument. However, the notion of *al-tawḥīd al-afʿāli* upheld by the Shīʿites means that the system of causes and effects is real, and every effect, while being dependent on its proximate cause, is also dependent on God. These two modes of dependence do not operate in parallel but in series. For further clarification of this subject see my book *Insān wa sarnewisht* ('Man and Destiny').

(ii) ʿAdl

The doctrine of *ʿadl* is common to both the Shīʿites and the Muʿtazilites. *ʿAdl* means that God bestows His mercy and blessings and so also His trials and chastisement according to the prior and intrinsic deservedness of beings, and that Divine mercy and trial, reward and punishment are determined in accordance with a particular order or law (which is also of Divine origin).

The Ashʿarites deny this notion of *ʿadl* and such an order. In their view, belief in *ʿadl* in the sense of a just order necessitates God's subjection and subordination to something else and thus contradicts His Absolute Power. *ʿAdl* in itself implies several corollaries, to which we shall refer while explaining other doctrines.

(iii) Free Will and Freedom

The Shīʿī doctrine of free will is to some extent similar to that of the Muʿtazilites. But the two differ with regard to its meaning. Human freedom or free will for the Muʿtazilites is equivalent to Divine Resignation (*tafwid*), i.e.

leaving man to his own devices and suspending the Divine Will from any effective role. Of course, this is impossible, as has been shown.

Freedom and free will, in the understanding of the Shīʿites, mean that men are created as free beings. But they, like any other creature, are entirely dependent on the Divine Essence for their existence and all its multifarious modes, including the mode of action, all of which are derived from and dependent on God's merciful care, and they seek help from His Will.

Accordingly, free will and freedom in Shīʿism occupy an intermediate position between the Ashʿarite (absolute) predestination (*jabr*) and the Muʿtazilite doctrine of freedom (*tafwīḍ*). This is the meaning of the famous dictum of the Infallible Imāms (A), *'la jabra wa la tafwīḍa bal amrun bayna 'amrayn'* (Neither *jabr* nor *tafwīḍ*, but something intermediate between the two [extreme] alternatives).

The doctrine of free will is a corollary to the doctrine of Divine Justice.

*(iv) Inherent Morality or Immorality of Deeds (*Ḥusn wa Qubḥ Dhāti*)*

The Muʿtazilites believe that all deeds are inherently and intrinsically either good or evil. For example, justice is intrinsically good and oppression is inherently evil. The wise man selects the good works and abstains from bad deeds. And since God the Almighty is Wise His Wisdom necessitates that He should do good and abstain from evil. Thus the inherent goodness or badness of acts, on the one hand, and the Wisdom of God, on the other, inevitably make some acts 'obligatory' for God and some 'undesirable'.

The Ashʿarites are strongly opposed to this belief. They deny both the inherent goodness or badness of acts and the applicability of such judgements as 'obligatory' or 'undesirable' to God.

Some Shīʿī thinkers, under the influence of the Muʿtazilite *kalām*, accepted the Muʿtazilite view in its above-mentioned form, but others, with greater insight, while accepting the doctrine of inherent morality or immorality of acts, rejected the view that the judgements of permissibility or undesirability are applicable to the Divine realm.[19]

(v) Grace (Lutf*) and Choice of the Best (*Intikhāb al-Aṣlah*)*

There is a controversy between the Ashʿarites and the Muʿtazilites as to whether or not Grace or 'choice of the best' for the good of human beings is a principle that governs the universe. The Muʿtazilites considered Grace as a duty and obligation incumbent upon God. The Ashʿarites denied Grace and 'choice of the best.'

However, the principle of Grace is a corollary to the doctrine of justice and the doctrine of the innate goodness or badness of deeds. Some Shīʿite *mutakallimīn* have accepted the doctrine of Grace in its Muʿtazilite form, but others who consider it absolutely wrong to apply the notion of 'duty' and 'obligation' to God, advance another version of the doctrine of the 'choice of the best'. Space does not allow us to elaborate this here.

(vi) Independence and Validity of Reason

Shīʿism affirms a greater independence, authority and validity for reason than the Muʿtazilites.

According to certain indisputable traditions of the Maʿsumun (A), reason is the internalized prophetic voice in the same way as a prophet is reason externalized. In the Shīʿite *fiqh*, reason (*'aql*) is considered one of the four valid primary sources of the Law.

(vii) 'Aim' and 'Purpose' of Divine Acts

The Ashʿarites reject the notion that the Divine Acts may be for one or several purposes or aims. They state that possession of a purpose or goal is solely applicable to man and other similar creatures. But God is above such matters, since having a purpose and aim implies subjection of a doer to that purpose or aim. God is free from and above every kind of limit, restriction and subordination, even though it be the limit imposed by a purpose.

The Shīʿites affirm the Muʿtazilite belief with regard to purposiveness of Divine Acts. They believe that there is a difference between the purpose of the act and the purpose of the doer. What is impossible is that God may seek to satisfy some purpose of His own through His Acts; however, a purpose or aim that is directed to the benefit of a creature is not at all incompatible with Divine perfection and the supremacy of His self-sufficing Essence.

(viii) The Possibility of Badaʿ *(Divine Abrogation of Predestiny)*

Badaʿ is possible in Divine Acts, in the same way as it occurs in the abrogation of the Divinely decreed laws. An elaborate and satisfactory study of the issue of *badaʿ* may be found in such profound philosophical books as *al-Asfār*.

(ix) Vision (Ru'yah*) of God*

The Muʿtazilites vehemently deny the possibility of seeing God with the eyes. They believe that one may only have faith in the existence of God, a firm conviction in the depth of one's soul and mind, but that this is the highest faith that one may attain. The Qur'ān lends credence to this belief:

The sights do not perceive Him, and He perceives the sights, and He is All-subtle [incapable of being perceived] and All-knowing [i.e. He perceives the eyes and the rest of things]. (6:103).

The Ashʿarites, with equal vehemence, assert that God can be seen with the eyes, but only on the Day of Resurrection. They also cite as evidence certain Qurʾānic verses and prophetic traditions, including the following:

[Some] faces on that Day shall be bright, looking towards their Lord. (75:22–23)

The Shīʿites believe that God can never be seen with the eyes, neither in this life nor in the hereafter. Nevertheless, the highest kind of faith is not an intellectual one. Intellectual faith is *ʿilm al-yaqīn*. A higher level of faith is *ʿayn al-yaqīn* – certitude of the heart. *ʿAyn al-yaqīn* (literally 'certitude by sight') means witnessing God with the heart, not with the eyes. Thus, God is 'visible' to the heart. ʿAlī (A) was once asked, 'Have you seen God?' He replied, 'I have not worshipped a god whom I have not seen. But He is visible to the hearts, not to the eyes.' The Imāms (A) were asked whether the Prophet (S) saw God during his Ascension (*miʿrāj*). Their reply was, 'With the eyes? No. With the heart? Yes.' In this matter only the *ṣūfis* share a similar position to that of the Shīʿites.

(x) The Faith or Infidelity of the Fāsiq

On this issue, which has been referred to earlier, the Shīʿī position coincides with that of the Ashʿarites, but differs from that of the Khawārij (who believe that a *fāsiq* is *kāfir*) and the Muʿtazilites (who believe in *manzilah bayna al-manzilatayn*).

*(xi) The Infallibility (*ʿIṣmah*) of the Prophets and the Imāms*

This belief is characteristic of the Shīʿites, who hold that the prophets (A) and the Imāms (A) are infallible and do not commit any major or minor sin whatsoever.

(xii) Forgiveness (Maghfirah*) and Intercession (*Shafāʿah*)*

On this issue also the Shīʿites differ from the cut-and-dried Muʿtazilite position that anybody who dies without repentance cannot possibly receive Divine forgiveness or (the Prophet's) intercession. Similarly, their position is also at variance with the indulgent and extravagant notion of *shafāʿah* held by the Ashʿarites.[20]

Notes

1. See Murtaḍā Muṭahharī, *Sayri dar Nahj al-balāghah*, pp. 69–76, where the author discusses the difference between the approach of the *Nahj al-balāghah* to the problems of theology and metaphysics and the approach of Muslim *mutakallimīn* and philosophers to such problems.
2. *Zanādiqah* (sing. *zindiq*), a term applied heterogeneously and relatively, is used to describe any heretical group whose belief deviates radically from Islamic doctrines. The author probably uses the term to refer to one or more of such sects as the Mu'attilah, who denied the Creation and the Creator, reducing the world to an unstable mixture of the four elements, the Manawiyyah (Manichaeans); and Mazdakiyyah, who were dualists, etc.
3. See Murtaḍā Muṭahharī, *Insān wa sarnewisht* ('Man and Destiny').
4. See Murtaḍā Muṭahharī, *'Adl-e ilāhi* ('Divine Justice'), Introduction, pp. 7–43.
5. Translator's note: There are at least seventy-five places where the various derivatives of the root *kalimah* occur in the Qur'ān. In three places the phrase *Kalām Allāh* is used in reference to the Qur'ān (2:75, 9:6, 48:15). The word *kalimah* ('word', 'statement') or the plural *kalimah* with reference to God occurs at least thirty times in the Qur'ān, twice with reference to Jesus (A) who is called a '*kalimah*' of God. The Gospel of John designates Jesus Christ (A) as the 'Eternal Word of God'. The Qur'ān also speaks of Jesus as a Word of God, while according to John's Gospel he is the Word, eternal and uncreated: 'Before the world was created, the Word already existed; he was with God, and he was the same as God.' We are further told: 'Through him God made all things, not one thing in all creation was made without him. The Word was the source of life . . . the Word became a human being and, full of grace and truth, lived among us. We saw his glory, the glory that he received as the Father's only Son.'

   Probably the Christian belief in Jesus as the uncreated *kalimah* Allāh (Word of God), some kind of a demiurge – a belief that probably emerged as a result of Manichaean influence on early Christianity – had prompted the early Muslims, engaged in polemics with Christians on the nature of Jesus Christ, to consider, in their turn, the Qur'ān, the *Kalām* Allāh, as uncreated and eternal.
6. Allamah Sayyid Muḥammad Husayn Tabataba'i, *Uṣūl-e falsafah wa rawishe riyalism* ('The Principles and Method of Realism'), vol. V, chapter XIV, Introduction by Murtaḍā Muṭahharī, who has written very elaborate footnotes to the text of 'Allamah Tabataba'i's book.
7. *'Abd al-Raḥmān al-Badawi, Madhāhib al-'Islāmiyyīn*, vol. I, p. 34. Apparently, the author does not number the Tahawiyyah, the Maturidiyyah and the Zahiriyyah among the major schools of *kalām* or important enough to be included in this brief survey.
8. Translator's note: Both theology and metaphysics are referred to by the common term *al-'ilāhiyyat* (literally 'theology'). Whenever theology proper only is meant, the phrase *bil-ma'na al-'akhass* (literally 'in its special sense') is added. Metaphysics, which deals with general problems, is termed *al-'umūr al-'āmmah* (literally 'the general issues').

9. Translator's note: Some of these reasons are as follows: (1) Every human being is aware that his daily acts, such as going to the market or having a walk, depend on his will; he is free to do them if he likes and to abstain if he so chooses. (2) If all our acts were imposed upon us, there would be no difference between a virtuous act and a wicked one; whereas it is obvious that even a child can distinguish between a kind and a cruel act and will enjoy the first and detest the second. If all our acts were determined by God, they would be all alike; that is, there would be no difference between good and evil, between virtue and vice. (3) If God creates all our acts, it is pointless for Him to command some things and forbid others and consequently to reward and punish accordingly. (4) If we are not free in our acts, it is unjust of God to create sins in creatures and then punish them on account of sinning.
10. Translator's note: The notion of motion in leaps (*tafrah*) was first suggested by al-Nazzām. It means that a body undergoes discrete leaps during motion. The modern parallel of this idea of motion is one employed by quantum mechanics. In 1900 Max Planck put forward the hypothesis that the charged particle – usually called the oscillator or vibrator – that is the source of monochromatic light absorbs and emits energy only in discrete quanta. It changes its energy not continuously, as was supposed in the classical theory of radiation, but by sudden jumps (*tafrah*). In 1913 Niels Bohr, applying quantum theory to subatomic phenomena, published the quantum theory of the atom. Since then quantum mechanics has become an important part of atomic physics.
11. Translator's note: The verses 57:22 and 4:78 seem to convey a meaning contradictory to that of 4:79 and 18:29. While the former imply total predestination, the latter explicitly support the idea of freedom. The Ash'arites attach basic importance to the former and the Mu'tazilites to the latter kind. The Shī'ites reconcile the two sets of verses and take an intermediary position. The following traditions from al-Shaykh al-Saduq's *al-Tawḥīd*, pp. 360–62 (Jāmī'at al-mudarrisin fi al-Hawzat al-'Ilmiyyah, Qum), explain the Shī'ī position:

> Al-Imām al-Baqir (A) and al-Imām al-Ṣādiq (A) said, 'Indeed God is of greater mercy than that He should coerce His creatures into sin and then punish them for that; and God is of greater might than that He should will something and it should fail to happen.' They were asked, 'Is there any third position between absolute predestination (*jabr*) and absolute freedom (*qadar*)?' They said, 'Yes, vaster than the space between the heaven and the earth.'
>
> . . . Muḥammad ibn 'Ajun says, 'I asked Abū 'Abd Allāh (A), "Has God left men free [to do what they may like]?" He replied, "God is nobler than that He should leave it up to them [to do whatever they may like]." I said, "Then God has imposed their deeds upon them?" He said, "God is more just than that He should coerce a creature into committing some act and then punish him on its account."'
>
> . . . Al-Ḥasan ibn 'Alī al-Washsha' says, 'I asked al-Imām al-Riḍā (A) whether God has given men total freedom in their acts. He said, "God is mightier than that." I said, "Then, has He coerced them into sins?" He replied, "God is more just and wiser than that He should do such a thing." Then he added, "God, the Almighty, has said, 'O son of Adam! I deserve more credit in your virtues than

yourself, and you deserve more discredit for your sins than I; you commit sins with the power I have given you."'

. . . Al-Mufaddal ibn 'Umar reports that al-Imām Abū 'Abd Allāh (al-Ṣādiq) (A) said, 'Neither total predetermination (*jabr*), nor total freedom (*tafwīḍ*), but a position intermediate between the two (*amr bayna amrayn*).' I said, 'What is *amr bayna amrayn*?' He replied, 'It is as if you see someone committing a sin. You stop him, but he does not desist. So you leave him alone. Then if he commits that sin, it does not mean that since he did not heed you and you left him alone, you asked him to commit it."'

See also Murtaḍā Muṭahharī, *Insān wa sarnewisht* ('Man and Destiny'), for an elaborate discussion of this point.

12. Translator's note: Some historians have advanced the theory of a connection between Mu'tazilite theology and the 'Abbasid movement. H. S. Nyberg, in his article on the Mu'tazilites in the *Shorter Encyclopedia of Islam*, after remarking that 'Wāsil adopted a somewhat ambiguous attitude regarding 'Uthman and his murderers and that he left undecided the question of knowing who had the superior claim to caliphate, Abū Bakr, 'Umar, or 'Alī,' says that, 'All these apparently dissimilar lines converge on a common centre: the 'Abbasid movement. It is precisely Wāsil's attitude which we must regard as characteristic of the partisans of the 'Abbasids . . . Everything leads us to believe that the theology of Wāsil and the early Mu'tazilites represents the official theology of the 'Abbasid movement. This gives us an unforced explanation of the fact that it was the official doctrine of the 'Abbasid court for at least a century. It seems even probable that Wāsil and his disciples took part in the 'Abbasid propaganda . . .' Although Nyberg's conjecture is not sufficient to establish this hypothesis, further research may bring to light some conclusive evidence in the matter.

13. Translator's note: Akhbarism is a movement that started within the Shī'ī world about four hundred years ago. Its originator was Mullā Muḥammad Amin ibn Muḥammad Sharif al-'Astarabadi (d. 1033/1623–24). He openly attacked the Shī'ites *mujtahidūn* in his work *al-Fawa'id al-madaniyyah*, vehemently contesting the Usuliyyun's claim that reason is one of the sources of *fiqh*. The Usuliyyun hold the Qur'ān, the Sunnah, reason and *ijma'* (consensus) to be valid sources for deduction of the rules of the Sharī'ah. The Akhbaris accepted the validity only of the Sunnah and rejected the rest. Understanding the Qur'ān, they claimed, is beyond the capacity of an ordinary person, being restricted exclusively to the Ahl al-Bayt (A).

Regarding *ijmā'*, they said that it was an innovation (*bid'ah*) of the Ahl al-Sunnah. Reason, they held, is valid only in empirical sciences. Its applicability cannot be extended to the realm of the Sharī'ah. Accordingly, they rejected *ijtihād*, considering the *taqlid* (following the authority, imitation in legal matters) of a non-*Ma'sum* as forbidden. However, they considered the reliability of all the *aḥadīth* of the four books, viz. *al-Kāfī*, *al-Tahdhīb*, *al-'Istibsār*, and *Man la yaḥḍuruhu al-faqīh* as being authentic and undisputable. They held that it was the duty of the people to refer directly to the *ḥadīth* texts in order to discover the commands of the Sharī'ah. There was no need of the *mujtahid* as an intermediary. The Usuliyyun, in particular such scholars as Aqa Muḥammad Baqir al-Bahbahani (1118/1706–1205/1788) and

Shaykh Murtaḍā al-Anṣārī (d. 1281/1865–66) refuted the Akhbari position and effectively repulsed the threat posed by them to the Shīʿī institution of *ijtihād*. Some prominent Akhbaris among Shīʿī scholars were Sayyid Niʿmat Allāh al-Jaza'iri (d.1050/1640), Muḥammad ibn Murtaḍā Mullā Muhsin Fayd al-Kashānī (d 1091/1680), Shaykh Yusuf ibn Aḥmad al Bahrani al Ha'iri (1107/1695–1186/1772), and Ṣadr al-Dīn Muḥammad ibn Muḥammad Baqir al-Ḥamadānī (d. after 1151/1738–39)

14. This treatise has been published as an appendix to his *al-Lum'ah*, and 'Abd al-Rahman al-Badawi has included it in the first volume of *Madhahib al-'Islāmiyyīn*, pp.15–26.
15. See Muḥammad Abū Zuhrah, *Ibn Taymiyyah*.
16. Murtaḍā Muṭahharī, *Ashna'i bi 'ulūm-e Islami* ('An Introduction to the Islamic Sciences'), see the section on philosophy, the fourth lecture entitled 'Rawishha-ye fikri-ye Islami'.
17. The Qur'ān, 2:285.
18. This is the stand on *sifat* that is usually attributed to the Muʿtazilites. Ḥajji Sabzawari (in *Manzumah*, his philosophical poem) says:

    al-Ash'ari bizdiyadin qa'iluhu
    wa qala binniyabati'l Mu'tazilitesu

    However some Muʿtazilites, such as al-Hudhayl, have held a position exactly similar to the Shīʿī position.
19. Murtaḍā Muṭahharī, *'Adle Ilāhi* ('Divine Justice').
20. Ibid., the discussion on *shafā'ah*.

Part Three

'Irfān: Islamic Mysticism

'Irfān is one of the disciplines that originated within the realm of Islamic culture and developed there to attain a high level of sophistication. But before we can begin to discuss *'irfān*, we must realize that it can be approached from two viewpoints: the social and the academic. Unlike the scholars of other Islamic disciplines – such as the Qur'ānic commentators (*mufassirūn*), the scholars of *ḥadīth* (*muhaddithūn*), the jurisprudents (*fuqahā'*), the theologians (*mutakallimīn*), the philosophers, the men of literature and the poets – the *'urafā'* are a group of scholars who have not only developed their own science, *'irfān*, producing great scholars and important books, but have also given rise within the Islamic world to a distinct social grouping. In this the *'urafā'* are unique; for the scholars of the other Islamic disciplines – the jurisprudents, for instance – form solely academic groupings and are not viewed as a social group distinct from the rest of society.

In view of this distinction the gnostics, when referred to as belonging to a certain academic discipline, are called *'urafā'* and when referred to as a social group are generally called *ṣūfis* (*mutaṣawwifah*).

The *'urafā'* and *ṣūfis* are not regarded as forming a separate sect in Islam, nor do they claim to be such. They are to be found within every Islamic school and sect, yet, at the same time, they coalesce to form a distinct social group. The factors that set them apart from the rest of Islamic society are a distinctive set of ideas and opinions, a special code governing their social intercourse, dress and even, sometimes, the way they wear their hair and beards and the fact that they live communally in hospices (Pers. *Khāniqah*, *Ar-ribāt*, *zāwiyah*; Turk. *tekkiye*).

Of course, there are and have always been *'urafā'* – particularly among the Shī'ites – who bear none of these external signs that distinguish them socially from others; yet, at the same time, they have been profoundly involved in the spiritual methodology of *'irfān* (*sayr wa sulūk*). It is these who are the real gnostics; not those who have invented hundreds of special mannerisms and customs for themselves and have brought innovations into being.

In the present work, in which we are taking a general look at Islamic sciences and disciplines, we shall not be dealing with the social and sectarian aspect of gnosis, that is to say, *taṣawwuf* (Sufism). We shall limit ourselves to an examination of *'irfān* as a discipline and a branch among the branches of Islam's scientific culture. To look thoroughly at the social aspects of Sufism would require us to examine its causes and origins, the effects – positive and negative, beneficial and detrimental – it has had and continues to have upon Islamic society, the nature of the relations between the *ṣūfis* and other Islamic groups, the hue it has given to the whole of Islamic teaching and the role it has played in the diffusion of Islam throughout the world. This is far beyond the range of the present work, and here we will consider the tradition of *'irfān* only as a science and as one of the academic disciplines of Islam.

'Irfān, as a scientific and academic discipline, itself has two branches: the practical and the theoretical. The practical aspect of *'irfān* describes and explains the relationship and responsibilities the human being bears towards himself, towards the world and towards God. Here, *'irfān* is similar to ethics (*akhlāq*), both of them being practical sciences. There do exist differences, however, and we shall explain them later.

The practical teaching of *'irfān* is also called the itinerary of the spiritual path (*sayr wa sulūk*; literally 'travelling and journeying'). Here, the wayfarer (*sālik*) who desires to reach the goal of the sublime peak of humanness – that is to say, *tawḥīd* – is told where to set off, the ordered stages and stations that he must traverse, the states and conditions he will undergo at these stations and the events that will befall him. Needless to say, all these stages and stations must be passed under the guidance and supervision of a mature and perfect example of humanity, who, having travelled this path, is aware of the manners and ways of each station. If not, and there is no perfect human being to guide him on his path, he is in danger of going astray.

The perfect man, the master, who must necessarily accompany the novice on the spiritual journey according to the *'urafā'*, is known as *Ṭā'ir al-quds* (the Holy Bird) and Khidr:

Accompany my zeal on the path, O Ta'ir al-Quds,
The path to the goal is long, and I new to the journey.
Leave not this stage without the company of Khidr,
There is darkness ahead; be afraid of losing the way.

Of course, there is a world of difference between the *tawḥīd* of the *'ārif* and the general view of *tawḥīd*. For the *'ārif*, *tawḥīd* is the sublime peak of humanness and the final goal of his spiritual journey, while for ordinary people, and even philosophers, *tawḥīd* means the essential Unity of the Necessary Being. For the *'ārif*, *tawḥīd* means that the ultimate reality is only God, and everything other than God is mere appearance, not reality: 'other than God there is nothing'. For the *'ārif*, *tawḥīd* means following a path and arriving at the stage when he sees nothing but God. However, this view of *tawḥīd* is not accepted by the opponents of the *'urafā'*, and some of them have declared such a view to be heretical. Yet the *'urafā'* are convinced that this is the only true *tawḥīd* and that the other stages of it cannot be said to be free of polytheism (*shirk*).

The *'urafā'* do not see the attainment of the ideal stage of *tawḥīd* to be the outcome of reason and reflection. Rather, they consider it to be the work of the heart, and attained through struggle, through the journeying and through purifying and disciplining the self.

This, however, is the practical aspect of *'irfān*, which is not unlike ethics in this respect, for both discuss a series of things that 'ought to be done'. However, there are differences, and the first of these is that *'irfān* discusses the human being's relationship with himself, with the world and with God, and its primal concern is man's relationship with God. Systems of ethics, on the other hand, do not all consider it necessary for the relationship between man and God to be discussed; it is only the religious ethical systems that give importance and attention to this matter.

The second difference is that the methodology of spiritual progression, *sayr wa sulūk*, as the words *sayr* (travelling) and *sulūk* (journeying) imply, is a dynamic one, while ethics is static. That is, *'irfān* speaks about a point of departure, a destination and the stages and stations that the wayfarer must pass, in their correct order, in order to arrive at the final destination. In the *'ārif's* view, there really is a path in front of every human being – a path that is actual and not remotely metaphorical – and this path must be followed stage by stage, station by station; to arrive at any station without having passed through the preceding one is, in the *'ārif's* view, impossible. Thus the *'ārif* views the human soul to be a living organism, like a seedling or like a child, whose perfection lies in growth and maturation in accordance with a particular system and order.

In ethics, however, the subjects are handled solely as a series of virtues, such as righteousness, honesty, sincerity, chastity, generosity, justice and preferring others over oneself (*ithār*), to name but a few, with which the soul must be adorned. In the view of ethics, the human soul is rather like a house to be furnished with a series of beautiful objects, pictures and decorations, and no importance is attached to a particular sequence. It is not important where one begins or where one ends. It is of no consequence whether one starts at the ceiling or at the walls, at the top of a wall or at the bottom and so on. On the contrary, in *'irfān* the ethical elements are discussed in a dynamic perspective.

The third difference between these two disciplines is that the spiritual elements of ethics are limited to concepts and ideas that are generally commonplace, while the spiritual elements of *'irfān* are much more profound and expansive. In the spiritual methodology of *'irfān*, much mention is made of the heart and the states and happenings it will experience, and these experiences are known only to the wayfarer of the path during the course of his struggles and his journey on the path, while other people have no idea of these states and happenings.

The other branch of *'irfān* is related to interpretation of being, that is, God, the universe and the human being. Here *'irfān* resembles philosophy, for both seek to understand existence, whereas practical *'irfān* seeks, like ethics, to change the human being. However, just as there are differences between practical *'irfān* and ethics, so also there are differences between theoretical *'irfān* and philosophy. In the following section we shall explain these differences.

Theoretical 'Irfān

Theoretical *'irfān*, as we said before, is concerned with ontology and discusses God, the world and the human being. This aspect of *'irfān* resembles theological philosophy (*falsafeh-ye ilāhi*), which also seeks to describe being. Like theological philosophy, *'irfān* defines its subject, essential principles and problems, but whereas philosophy relies solely on rational principles for its arguments, *'irfān* bases its deductions on principles discovered through mystic experience (*kashf*) and then reverts to the language of reason to explain them.

The rationalistic deductions of philosophy can be likened to studying a passage written originally in the same language; the arguments of *'irfān*, on the other hand, are like studying something that has been translated from some other language. To be more precise, the *'ārif* wishes to explain those things that he claims to have witnessed with his heart and his entire being by using the language of reason.

The ontology of *'irfān* is in several ways profoundly different from the ontology of philosophers. In the philosopher's view, both God and other things have reality, with the difference that while God is the Necessary Being (*wajib al-wujūd*) and Existing-By-Himself, things other than God are only possible existents (*mumkin al-wujūd*), existing-through-another, and are effects of the Necessary Being. However, the *'ārif's* ontology has no place for things other than God to exist alongside Him, even if they are effects of which He is the cause; rather, the Divine Being embraces and encompasses all things. That is to say, all things are names, qualities and manifestations of God, not existents alongside Him.

The aim of the philosopher also differs from that of the *ʿārif*. The philosopher wishes to understand the world; he wishes to form in his mind a correct and relatively complete picture of the realm of existence. The philosopher considers the highest mark of human perfection to lie in perceiving, by way of reason, the exact nature of existence, so that the macrocosm finds a reflection within his mind while he in turn becomes a rational microcosm. Thus philosophy may be defined as the (final) development of a rational knower (*ʿālim*) into an actual world (*ʿalam*).

This means that philosophy is a study in which a human being becomes a rational microcosm similar to the actual macrocosm. The *ʿārif*, on the other hand, will have nothing to do with reason and understanding; he wishes to reach the very kernel and reality of existence, God, to become connected to it and witness it.

In the *ʿārif's* view, human perfection does not mean having a picture of the realm of existence in one's mind; rather it is to return, by means of treading the spiritual path of progression, to one's origin, to overcome the separation of distance between oneself and the Divine Essence and, in the realm of nearness, to obliterate one's finite self to abide in Divine Infinitude.

The tools of the philosopher are reason, logic and deduction, while the tools of the *ʿārif* are the heart, spiritual struggle, purification and disciplining of the self and an inner dynamism.

Later, when we come to the world view of *ʿirfān*, we shall also discuss how it differs from the world view of philosophy.

ʿIrfān, both practical and theoretical, is closely connected with the holy religion of Islam. Like every other religion – in fact, more than any other religion – Islam has explained the relationships of man with God, with the world and with himself; and it has also given attention to describing and explaining existence.

The question inevitably arises here about the relation between the ideas of *ʿirfān* and the teachings of Islam. Of course, the *ʿurafāʾ* never claim that they have something to say that is above or beyond Islam, and they are earnest in their denials of any such imputations. In fact, they claim to have discovered more of the realities of Islam and that they are the true Muslims. Whether in the practical teaching of *ʿirfān* or the theoretical, the *ʿurafāʾ* always support their views by reference to the Qurʾān, the Sunnah of the Prophet and the Imāms, and the practice of the eminent among the Prophet's companions.

However, others have held different views about the *'urafā'*. They include the following.

(a) Some *muḥaddithūn* and jurisprudents have been of the view that the *'urafā'* are not practically bound to Islam, that *'irfān* basically has no connection with Islam and that the references by the *'urafā'* to the Qur'ān and the Sunnah are merely a ruse to deceive simple-minded people and to win the hearts of Muslims.

(b) Some modernists who do not have favourable relations with Islam and are prepared to welcome wholeheartedly anything that gives the appearance of freedom from the observances prescribed by the Sharī'ah (*ibāḥah*) and that can be interpreted as a movement or uprising in the past against Islam and its laws. Like the first group, they believe that in practice the *'urafā'* had no faith or belief in Islam, and that *'irfān* and *taṣawwuf* constituted a movement of non-Arab peoples against Islam and the Arabs, disguised under the robes of spirituality.

This group and the first are united in their view that the *'urafā'* are opposed to Islam. The difference between them is that the first group hold Islam to be sacred and, knowing that they can reckon with the Islamic sentiments of the Muslim masses, try to condemn the *'urafā'* and thus drive them off the stage of the Islamic sciences. The second group, however, draw attention to the great personalities of the *'urafā'* – some of whom are world renowned – and use them as a means of propaganda against Islam. They disparage Islam on the grounds that the subtle and sublime ideas of *'irfān* found in Islamic culture are in fact alien to Islam. They consider that these elements entered Islamic culture from outside, for, they say, Islam and its ideas thrive on a far lower level. This group also claim that the *'urafā* cited the Qur'ān and *ḥadīth* solely from dissimulation, fear of the masses and to save their own lives.

(c) A third group take a rather neutral view of *'irfān*, namely, that *'irfān* and Sufism contain many innovations and deviations that do not accord with the Qur'ān and the traditions; that this is more true of the practical teaching of *'irfān* than its theoretical ideas, especially where it takes on a sectarian aspect. Yet, they say, the *'urafā'*, like the Islamic scholars of other ranks and the majority of Islamic sects, have had the most sincere intentions towards Islam, never wishing to make any assertions contrary to its teachings. It is quite possible that they have made mistakes, just as other scholars – theologians, philosophers, Qur'ānic commentators and jurisprudents – have made mistakes, but this has never been due to an evil intention towards Islam.

In the view of this group, the *'urafā'*s supposed opposition to Islam was alleged by those who harboured a special prejudice either against *'irfān* or against Islam. If a person were disinterestedly to study the books of the *'urafā'*, provided that he were acquainted with their terminology and language, although he might come across many a mistake, he would be left in no doubt about the sincerity of their complete devotion to Islam.

Of the three views, I prefer the third. I do not believe that the *'urafā'* have had evil intentions towards Islam. At the same time I believe that it is necessary for those who have specialized knowledge of *'irfān* and of the profound teachings of Islam to undertake objective and disinterested research into the conformity of the issues of *'irfān* with Islamic teachings.

Sharī'ah, Tariqah and Haqīqah

One of the important points of contention between the *'urafā'* and the non-*'urafā'*, especially the jurisprudents, is the particular teaching of *'irfān* regarding the Sharī'ah, the Tariqah (the Way) and the Haqīqah (the Reality). Both agree in saying that the Sharī'ah, the body of Islamic laws, is based upon a series of realities and beneficial objectives. The jurisprudents generally interpret these goals to consist of certain things that lead the human being to felicity, that is, to the highest possible level of benefit from God's material and spiritual favours to man. The *'urafā'*, on the other hand, believe that all the paths end in God, and that all goals and realities are merely the means, causes and agencies that impel the human being towards God.

Jurisprudents say only that underlying the laws of the Sharī'ah is a series of benign objectives, that these objectives constitute the cause and spirit of the Sharī'ah, and that the only way of attaining these objectives is to act in accordance with the Sharī'ah. But the *'urafā'* believe that the realities and objectives underlying the laws of the Sharī'ah are of the nature of stations and stages on the human being's ascent towards God and access to the ultimate reality.

The *'urafā'* believe that the esoteric aspect of the Sharī'ah is the Way, the Tariqah, at whose end is the Reality (al-Haqīqah), that is *tawḥīd* (in the sense mentioned earlier), which is a stage acquired after the obliteration of the *'ārif's* self and his egoism. Thus the gnostic believes in the Sharī'ah, the Tariqah and the Haqīqah, and that the Sharī'ah is the means to, or the shell of, the Tariqah, and that the Tariqah in turn is the means to, or the shell of the kernel of, the Haqīqah.

We have explained above, in the discussion of *kalām*, how jurisprudents view Islam.[1] They believe that the Islamic teachings can be grouped into three branches. The first of these is *kalām*, which deals with the principal doctrines (*uṣūl al-'aqa'id*). In matters related to the doctrines it is necessary for the human being to acquire, through reason, unshakeable belief and faith.

The second branch is ethics (*akhlāq*). It sets forth the instructions about one's duty in regard to ethical virtues and vices.

The third branch, *fiqh*, deals with the laws (*aḥkām*) that relate to our external actions and behaviour.

These three branches of Islamic teachings are separate from each other. The branch of *kalām* is related to thought and reason; the branch of *akhlāq* is related to the self, its faculties and habits; and the branch of *fiqh* is related to the organs and limbs of the body.

However, on the subject of doctrines, the *'urafā'* do not consider merely mental and rational belief to be sufficient. They claim that whatever is to be believed in must be arrived at; one must strive to remove the veils between oneself and those realities.

Similarly, with respect to the second branch they do not consider ethics to be adequate on account of its being static and limited. In place of a philosophical ethics, they suggest a spiritual methodology (*sayr wa sulūk*) with its particular composition.

Finally, in the third branch, they have no criticisms; only in specific instances do they express opinions that could, possibly, be taken as being opposed to the laws of *fiqh*.

The *'urafā'* thus term these three branches Sharī'ah, Tariqah, and Haqīqah. Yet they believe that, precisely as the human being cannot be divided into three sections, that is, the body, the self and reason, which are not separate from each other and form an indivisible whole of which they constitute inward and outward aspects, so it is with the Sharī'ah, the Tariqah and the Haqīqah. One is outward shell, another is inward kernel and the third is the kernel of the kernel. There is a difference, however, in that the *'urafā'* consider the stages of human existence to be more than three; that is, they believe in a stage that transcends the domain of reason.

The Origins of Islamic 'Irfān

In order to understand any discipline or science, it is essential to study its history and the historical developments associated with it. One must also be acquainted with the personalities who have originated or inherited it and with its source books. In this section and the next, we shall examine these matters.

The first issue to arise is whether Islamic *'irfān* is a discipline that originated in the Islamic tradition, such as *fiqh*, *uṣūl al-fiqh*, *tafsīr*, and *'ilm al-ḥadīth*, deriving its inspiration, sources and raw material from Islam and then developing thanks to the discovery of rules and principles? Or is it one of those sciences that found their way into the Islamic world from outside, like medicine and mathematics, which were then developed further by the Muslims in the environment of Islamic civilization and culture? Or is there a third possibility?

The *'urafā'* themselves maintain the first of these alternatives and will admit no other. Some Orientalists, however, have insisted – and some still insist – on the second view, that *'irfān* and its subtle and sublime ideas have come into the Islamic world from outside. Sometimes they maintain a Christian origin for it, and claim that mysticism in Islam is the result of early contact between the Muslims and Christian monks. At other times they claim it to be a result of the Persians' reaction against Islam and the Arabs. Then again sometimes they make it entirely a product of Neo-Platonism, which itself was composed of the ideas of Plato, Aristotle and Pythagoras, influenced by Alexandrian gnosticism and the views and beliefs of Judaism and Christianity. Sometimes they claim that it was derived from Buddhism. Similarly, opponents of *'irfān* in the Islamic world also strive to cast the whole of *'irfān* and Sufism in a light that is alien to Islam, and to that end they too maintain that gnosis has non-Islamic origins.

A third view admits that *'irfān*, whether practical or theoretical, draws its primary inspiration and material from Islam itself; it has imposed a structure on this material by devising certain rules and principles and in process has been influenced by external currents, especially the ideas of scholasticism and philosophy, notably those of the Illuminationist school. A number of questions arise in this context. First, to what extent have the *'urafā'* been successful in developing correct rules and principles for structuring their material? Have the *'urafā'* been as successful in this exercise as the jurisprudents? To what extent have the *'urafā'* felt themselves bound not to deviate from the actual principles of Islam? And, similarly, to what extent has *'irfān* been influenced by the ideas of outside traditions? Has *'irfān* assimilated these external ideas by shaping them in its particular moulds, and used them in its development? Or, on the contrary, have the waves of foreign currents carried away *'irfān* in their flow?

Each of these questions requires separate study and careful research. But what is certain is that *'irfān* has derived its basic sources of inspiration from Islam itself and from nowhere else. Let us consider this point.

Those who accept the first view and to some extent also those who take the second view see Islam as a simple religion, popular and unsophisticated, free of all sorts of mysteries and difficult or unintelligible profundities. To them, the doctrinal system of Islam rests on *tawḥīd* (monotheism), which means that, just as a house has a builder other than itself, so the world has a transcendent Creator other than itself. Also, the basis of man's relationship with the enjoyments of this world is, in their view, *zuhd* (abstinence). In their definition of *zuhd*, it means refraining from the ephemeral pleasures of this world in order to attain the everlasting enjoyments of the hereafter. Besides these, there are a series of simple and practical rituals and laws that are handled by *fiqh*. Therefore, in this group's view, what the *'urafā'* call *tawḥīd* is an idea that goes beyond the simple monotheism of Islam; for the *'ārif's* view of *tawḥīd* is existentialist monism in the sense that he believes that nothing exists except God, His Names, Attributes and manifestations.

The *'ārif's* concept of the spiritual path (*sayr wa sulūk*) likewise, they say, goes beyond the *zuhd* enjoined by Islam, for the spiritual path of *'irfān* involves a number of ideas and concepts – such as love of God, annihilation in God, epiphany – that are not to be found in Islamic piety.

Similarly, the *'ārif's* concept of the Tariqah goes beyond the Sharī'ah of Islam; for the practice of the Tariqah involves matters unknown to *fiqh*. Furthermore, in the view of this group, the pious among the Holy Prophet's companions whom the *'urafā'* claim to be their precursors were no more than pious men. Their souls knew nothing of the spiritual path of *'irfān* and its *tawḥīd*. They were simple otherworldly people who abstained from worldly pleasures and directed their attention to the hereafter and whose souls were dominated by mixed feelings of fear and hope – fear of the punishment of Hell and hope of the rewards of Paradise. That is all.

In reality this view can in no way be endorsed. The primal sources of Islam are far more extensive and richer than this group – out of ignorance or knowingly – supposes. The Islamic concept of *tawḥīd* is neither as simple and empty as they suppose, nor does Islam reduce human spirituality to a dry piety. The pious companions of the Holy Prophet were not simple ascetics, nor is the Islamic code of conduct confined to the actions of bodily limbs and organs.

As we shall see here, Islam's fundamental teachings are capable of having inspired a chain of profound spiritual ideas, both in the theoretical and the practical realms of *'irfān*. However, the question of the extent to which the Islamic mystics have used and benefited from Islam's fundamental teachings and the extent to which they may have deviated is one that we cannot go into in this work.

On the subject of *tawḥīd*, the Holy Qur'ān never likens God and the creation to a builder and a house. The Qur'ān identifies God as the Creator of the world, stating at the same time that His Holy Essence is everywhere and with everything:

> Wheresoever you turn, there is the Face of God . . . (2:115)
> . . . And We are nearer to him than the jugular vein. (50:16)
> He is the First and the Last, the Outward and the Inward . . . (57:3)

Verses such as these represent a call to thinking minds to a concept of *tawḥīd* that goes beyond commonplace monotheism. A tradition of al-Kāfi states that God revealed the opening verses of the *Sūra al-Ḥadīd* and the *Sūra al-'Ikhlās* because He knew that in future generations people would emerge who would think profoundly about *tawḥīd*.

As to the spiritual path of *'irfān*, which conceives of a sequence of stages leading to ultimate nearness to God, the Islamic origin is sufficiently proven with Qur'ānic verses that mention such notions as *liqā 'Allāh* (meeting with God), *riḍwān Allāh* (God's good pleasure) or those that relate to *waḥy* (revelation), *ilhām* (inspiration), and the angels' speaking to others who are not prophets – Mary, for instance – and especially the verses relating to the Holy Prophet's Ascension (*mi'raj*; 17:1).

In the Qur'ān there is mention of the 'commanding self' (*al-nafs al-'ammārah*; 12:53), the 'self-accusative self' (*al-nafs al-lawwāmah*; 75:2), and the 'contented self' (*al-nafs al-muṭma'innah*; 89:27). There is mention of 'acquired knowledge' (*al-'ilm al-'ifadi*) and inspired knowledge (*al-'ilm al-ladunni*; 18:65), and of forms of guidance resulting from spiritual struggle:

> And those who struggle in Us, We will surely guide them to Our paths . . . (29:69)

Mention is made in the Qur'ān of the purification of the self, and it is counted as one of the things that lead to salvation and deliverance:

> [By the self] . . . verily he who purifies it has succeeded, while he who corrupts it has indeed failed. (91:7–10)

There is also repeated mention there of the love of God as a passion above all other human loves and attractions.

The Qur'ān also speaks about all the particles of creation glorifying and praising God (17:44), and this is phrased in such a way as to imply that if anyone were able to perfect his understanding, he would be able to perceive the praise and magnification of God. Moreover, the Qur'ān raises the issue of the Divine breath in relation to the nature and constitution of the human being (32:9).

This, and much more besides, is sufficient to have inspired a comprehensive and magnificent spirituality regarding God, the world and man, particularly regarding his relationship with God.

As previously mentioned, we are not considering how the Muslim *'urafā'* have made use of these resources, or whether their utilization has been correct or incorrect. We are considering whether great resources existed that could have provided effective inspiration for *'irfān* in the Islamic world. Even if we suppose that those usually classed as *'urafā'* could not make proper use of them, others who are not classed as such did make use of them.

In addition to the Qur'ān, the traditions, sermons, supplications (*du'ā'*), polemical dialogues (*ihtijājāt*) and biographies of the great figures of Islam all show that the spiritual life current in the early days of Islam was not merely a lifeless type of asceticism blended with a worship performed in the hope of the rewards of Paradise. Concepts and notions are found in the traditions, sermons, supplications and polemical dialogues that stand at a very high level of sublimity. Similarly, the biographies of the leading personalities of the early days of Islam display many instances of spiritual ecstasy, visions, miraculous occurrences, inner insights and burning spiritual love. Here let us consider an example of it.

Al-Kāfi relates that one morning after performing the dawn prayer, a young man (Harithah ibn Mālik ibn Nu'man al-'Anṣārī) caught the Prophet's eye. Lean and pale, his eyes sunken, he gave the impression of being unaware of his own condition and of being unable to keep his balance. 'How are you?' inquired the Prophet. 'I have attained certain faith,' the youth replied. 'What is the sign of your certainty?' the Prophet asked. The youth replied that his certainty had immersed him in grief. It had kept him awake at night (in worship) and thirsty by day (in fasting), and had separated him from the world and its matters so completely that it seemed to him as if he could see the Divine Throne already set up (on Judgement Day) to settle the people's accounts, and that he and all of mankind were raised from the dead. He said that it seemed to him that even at that moment he could see the people of Paradise enjoying its bounties, and the people of Hell suffering torments and he could hear the roar of its flames.

The Holy Prophet (S) turned to his companions and told them, 'This is a man whose heart has been illuminated with the light of faith by God.' Then he said to the youth, 'Preserve this condition you are in, and do not let it be taken away from you.' 'Pray for me,' the youth replied, 'that God may grant me martyrdom.'

Not long after this encounter, a battle took place, and the youth was granted his wish and was martyred on the battlefield.

The life, utterances and prayers of the Holy Prophet (S) are rich with spiritual enthusiasm and ecstasy and full of indications of gnosis; the *'urafā'* often rely on the Prophet's supplications as reference and evidence for their views.

Similarly, the words of Amir al-Mu'minin ʿAlī (A), to whom nearly all the *'urafā'* and *ṣūfis* trace the origin of their orders, are also spiritually inspiring. I wish to draw attention to two passages of the *Nahj al-balāghah*. In Khutbah No. 222, ʿAlī states:

> Certainly, God, the glorified, has made His remembrance the means of burnishing hearts, which makes them hear after deafness, see after blindness and makes them submissive after unruliness. In all the periods and times when there were no prophets, there have been individuals with whom God – precious are His bounties – spoke in whispers through their conscience and intellects.

In Khutbah No. 220, speaking about men of God, he says:

> He revives his intellect and mortifies himself, until his body becomes lean and his coarseness turns into refinement. Then an effulgence of extreme brightness shines forth to illuminate the path before him, opening all the doors and leading him straight to the gate of safety and the place wherein he may abide forever. His feet, carrying his body, become fixed on safe, comfortable ground on account of the goodness of his heart and on having won the good pleasure of his Lord.

The Islamic supplications, especially those of the Shīʿites, are also replete with spiritual teachings. The Duʿaʿ Kumayl, the Duʿaʿ Abi Hamzah, the supplications of al-Sahifat al-Kamilah and the group of supplications called *Sha'baniyyah* all contain the most sublime spiritual ideas.

With all these resources in Islam, is there a need for us to search for the origin of Islamic *'irfān* elsewhere?

One is reminded of the case of Abū Dharr al-Ghifari and his protest against the tyrants of his time and his vocal criticism of their practices. Abū Dharr was severely critical of the favouritism, partisan politics, injustice, corruption and tyranny of the post-Prophetic era in which he lived. As a result he suffered torture and exile and finally it was in exile, deserted and alone, that he died. A number of Orientalists have pondered on what it was that motivated Abū Dharr to act as he did. They have been seeking something foreign to the world of Islam to explain his behaviour. George Jurdaq, a Lebanese Christian, provides an answer to these Orientalists in his book *al-Imām 'Alī, ṣawt al-'adālah al-insāniyyah* ('Imām 'Alī, the Voice of Human Justice'). There he says that he is amazed at the people who seek to trace Abū Dharr's mentality to an extra-Islamic source. He says it is as if they see someone standing beside the sea or a river with a pitcher of water in his hands, and, completely ignoring the nearby sea or river, go off in search of a pool or pond to explain how he has a full pitcher of water in his hands.

What source other than Islam could have inspired Abū Dharr? What source could equal the power of Islam in inspiring a man like Abū Dharr to rise up against such tyrants as Mu'awiyah? We can see a similar pattern in regard to *'irfān*. Orientalists seek a non-Islamic source of inspiration for *'irfān*, yet they completely overlook the great ocean of Islam. Can we really be expected to overlook all these resources – the Holy Qur'ān, the traditions, the sermons, the polemical dialogues, the supplications and the biographies – simply in order to give credence to the view of a group of Orientalists and their Eastern followers?

Formerly, Orientalists took great pains to portray the origins of Islamic *'irfān* as lying outside the original teachings of Islam. Lately, however, such individuals as the Englishman R. A. Nicholson and the Frenchman Louis Massignon, having made extensive studies in Islamic *'irfān* and having some acquaintance with Islam in general, have expressly admitted that the principal sources of *'irfān* are the Qur'ān and the Prophet's Sunnah.

We conclude this section by quoting a passage by Nicholson from the book *The Legacy of Islam*:

> Though Muḥammad left no system of dogmatic or mystical theology, the Qur'ān contains the raw materials of both. Being more the outcome of feeling than reflection, the Prophet's statements about God are formally inconsistent, and while Muslim scholastics have embodied in their creed the aspect of transcendence, the *ṣūfis*, following his example, have combined the transcendent aspect with that of immanence, on which, though it is less prominent in the Qur'ān, they naturally lay greater emphasis.[2]

> Allāh is the Light of the heavens and the earth. (xxiv:35)
> He is the first and the last and the outward and the inward. (lvii:3)
> There is no god but He; everything perishes except His Face. (xxviii:88)
> Have breathed into him (man) of My spirit. (xv:29)
> Verily, We have created man and We know what his soul suggests to him, for We are nigher unto him than the neck artery. (l:15)
> . . . wheresoever ye turn, there is the Face of Allāh (ii:114)
> . . . he to whom Allāh giveth no light hath no light at all. (xxiv:40)

Surely the seeds of mysticism are here. And, for the early *ṣūfīs*, the Qur'ān is not only the Word of God: it is the primary means of drawing near to Him. By fervent prayer, by meditating profoundly on the text as a whole and in particular on the mysterious passages (xvii:1; liii:1–18) concerning the Night journey and Ascension, they endeavoured to reproduce the Prophet's mystical experience in themselves.[3]

> . . . The doctrine of a mystical union imparted by divine grace goes beyond anything in the Qur'ān, but is stated plainly in apocryphal traditions of the Prophet, e.g. God said, 'My servant draws nigh unto Me by works of supererogation, and I love him; and when I love him, I am his ear, so that he hears by Me, and his eye, so that he sees by Me, and his tongue, so that he speaks by Me, and his hand, so that he takes by Me.'[4]

As has been said above, our concern here is not whether the *'urafā'* have correctly used the inspiration provided by Islam but whether the main source of their inspiration lay within Islam or outside it.

A Brief History

The previous section asked whether the principal sources of Islamic *'irfān* lay within the teachings of Islam and the lives of the Holy Prophet and the Imāms The answer to this question was seen to be affirmative.

The genuine teachings of Islam and the lives of its spiritual leaders, so rich in spirituality and spiritual splendour, which have provided the inspiration for profound spirituality in the Islamic world, are not encompassed by what is termed *'irfān* or Sufism. However, it is beyond the scope of this work to discuss other Islamic teachings that are not included under this term. Instead, we shall focus on the currents and events that have occurred within *'irfān* or Sufism. For this purpose, it appears appropriate to begin by providing a simple history of *'irfān* or Sufism from the beginnings of Islam until at least the tenth/sixteenth century, before turning to some analysis of the issues of *'irfān*.

What seems certain is that in the early era of Islam, that is throughout the first/seventh century at least, there were no Muslims known as *'urafā'* or *ṣūfīs*. The name *ṣūfī* was first used in the second/eighth century.

The first person to be called a '*ṣūfī*' was Abū Hāshim al-Kufi. He lived in the second/eighth century and he it was who first built, at Ramallah in Palestine, a hospice for worship by a group of ascetically minded Muslims.[5] The date of Abū Hāshim's death is not known, but he was the teacher of Sufyan al-Thawri who died in 161/777.

Abū al-Qāsim Qushayri, himself an eminent *'ārif* and *ṣūfī*, states that the name *ṣūfī* had appeared before the year 200/815. Nicholson also states that the name appeared towards the end of the second century H. From a tradition contained in ***kitāb** al-ma'ishah* (vol. V) of al-Kāfi, it appears that a group –Sufyan al-Thawri and a number of others – existed in the time of al-'Imām al-Ṣādiq (A) (that is to say, during the first half of the 2nd century H.), who were already called by this name.

If Abū Hāshim al-Kufi was the first to be called *ṣūfī*, then, since he was the teacher of Sufyan al-Thawri who died in 161/777, the designation must have been used for the first time during the first half of the second century H., not at its end (as Nicholson and others have stated). There appears no doubt that the derivation of the term *ṣūfiyyah* was their wearing of wool (*ṣūfī*: wool). In keeping with their asceticism, the *ṣūfīs* abstained from wearing fine garments and instead habitually wore clothes made of coarse wool.

As for the date when this group first began to call themselves *'urafā'*, again there is no precise information. All that is certain, as confirmed by the remarks of Sari Saqati (d. 243/867)[6] is that the term was current in the third century H. However, in the book *al-Luma'* of Abū Nasr al-Sarraj al-Ṭūsī, a reliable text of *'irfān* and Sufism, a phrase is quoted of Sufyan al-Thawri, which seems to indicate that the term appeared some time in the second century.[7]

At all events, there was no group known as *ṣūfīs* during the first century H. It seems that the *ṣūfīs* emerged as a particular group in the second century, not in the third as some people believe.[8]

However, the absence of a distinct group or name in the first century does not imply that the eminent companions were merely pious and ascetic persons and that all of them led lives of simple faith devoid of spiritual depth. Perhaps it is true that some of them knew nothing beyond mere piety and worship, but it is obvious that others led a profound spiritual life. Nor did all of them think and live at the same level, as the cases of Salman and Abū Dharr show. Salman adhered to his faith to a degree that Abū Dharr found extreme. According to many chroniclers,

> If Abū Dharr knew what was in Salman's heart, he would (considering him a heretic) have killed him.[9]

We come now to the different generations of the *'urafā'* and *ṣūfis* from the second/eighth century to the tenth/sixteenth.

'Urafā' *of the Second/Eighth Century*

1. Al-Ḥaṣan al-Baṣri

The history of what is termed *'irfān* begins, like *kalām*, with al-Ḥaṣan al-Baṣri (d. 110/728). He was born in 22/642 and lived for eighty-eight years, having spent nine-tenths of his life in the first century H. Of course, al-Ḥaṣan al-Baṣri was never known by the term *ṣūfi*, but there are three reasons for counting him among the *ṣūfis*. The first is that he compiled a book called *Ri'āyah li huquq Allāh* ('Observance of the Duties to Allāh'),[10] which is arguably the first book on Sufism. A unique manuscript of this book exists at Oxford. Nicholson has this to say on the subject:

> The first Muslim to give an experimental analysis of the inner life was Harith al-Muhasibi of Basrah . . . 'The Path' (*tarīqah*), as described by later writers, consists of acquired virtues (*maqāmāt*) and mystical states (*aḥwāl*). The first stage is repentance or conversion; then comes a series of others, e.g. renunciation, poverty, patience, trust in God, each being a preparation for the next.[11]

Second, the *'urafā'* themselves trace their orders back to al-Ḥasan al-Baṣri; and from him to 'Alī (A), among them the chain of shaykhs of Abū Sa'id ibn Abi al-Khayr.[12] Similarly, Ibn al-Nadīm, in his famous *al-Fihrist*, traces the chain of Abū Muḥammad Ja'far al-Khuldi back to al-Ḥaṣan al-Baṣri, stating that al-Ḥaṣan al-Baṣri had met seventy of the companions who had fought at Badr.

Third, some of the stories related of al-Ḥaṣan al-Baṣri give the impression that he was in fact part of a group that in later times became known as *ṣūfis*. We shall relate some of these stories where appropriate later on.

2. *Mālik ibn Dinār*

He was one of those who took asceticism and abstinence from pleasure to the extreme. Many stories are told about him in this regard. He died in the year 130/747.

3. *Ibrahim ibn Adham*

The famous story of Ibrahim ibn Adham resembles that of Buddha. It is said that he was the ruler of Balkh when something happened that caused him to repent and enter the ranks of the *ṣūfis*. *'Urafā'* attach great importance to this man, and a very interesting tale is told about him in Rūmi's *Mathnawī*. He died around the year 161/777.

4. *Rabi'ah al-'Adawiyyah*

This woman was one of the wonders of her time (d. 135/752 or 185/801). She was named Rabi'ah because she was the fourth daughter of her family (*rabi'ah* is the feminine word for 'fourth'). She is not to be confused with Rabi'ah al-Shamiyyah, who was also a mystic and a contemporary of Jāmī and lived in the ninth/fifteenth century.

Lofty sayings and soaring mystical verses are recorded of Rabi'ah al-'Adawiyyah,' and she is noted for amazing spiritual states (*ḥālāt*).

5. *Abū Hāshim al-Ṣūfi of Kūfah*

The date of this man's death is unknown. All that we can say is that he was the teacher of Sufyan al-Thawri; who died in 161/777. He appears to be the first person to have been called *ṣūfī*. Sufyan says about him, 'If it were not for Abū Hāshim I would not have known the precise details of ostentation (*riya'*).'

6. *Shaqīq al-Balkhi*

He was the pupil of Ibrahim ibn Adham. According to the author of *Rayhanat al-'adab*, and others quoted in *Kashf al-ghummah* of 'Alī ibn 'Isa al-'Arbili and *Nur al-'absar* of al-Shablanji, he once met al-'Imām Musa ibn Ja'far (A) and has given an account of the Imām's great reputation and miracles. Shaqiq died in 194/810.

7. *Ma'rūf al-Karkhi*

He is one of the famous *'urafā'*. It is said that his parents were Christian and that he became a Muslim at the hands of al-'Imām al-Riḍā (A), learning much from him. The lines of many orders, according to the claims of the *'urafā'*, go back to Ma'rūf, and through him to al-'Imām al-Riḍā, and through al-'Imām al-Riḍā to the preceding Imāms and thus to the Prophet himself. This chain is therefore termed the 'golden chain' (*silsilat al-dhahab*). Those known as the Dhahabiyyun generally make this claim.

8. Al-Fuḍayl ibn Iyāḍ

Originally from Merv, he was an Iranian of Arab descent. It is said that at first he was a highwayman, and that as he was preparing to carry out a robbery one night he heard the voice of his potential victim, reciting the Qur'ān. This had such an effect on him that he experienced a change of heart and repented. The book *Misbah al-Sharī'ah* is attributed to him and it is said to consist of a series of lessons that he took from al-'Imām Ja'far al-Ṣādiq (A). This book is considered reliable by an erudite scholar of traditions of the last century, the late Ḥajj Mirzā Husayn Nuri, in the epilogue to his *Mustadrak al-Wasa'il*. Fudayl died in 187/803.

'Urafā' *of the Third/Ninth Century*

1. Abū Yazid al-Basṭāmī (Bayāzīd)

One of the great mystics, it is said Bayazid was the first to speak openly of 'annihilation of the self in God' (*fanā fi 'Allāh'*) and 'subsistence through God' (*baqā' bi 'Allāh*). He said, 'I came forth from Bayazid-ness as a snake from its skin.' His ecstatic utterances (*shathiyyat*) have led others to call him a heretic. However, the *'urafā'* themselves consider him one of those given to mystical 'intoxication' (*sūkr*), that is, he uttered these ejaculations when he was beside himself with ecstasy.

Abū Yazid died in 261/874 or 264/877. Some have claimed that he worked as a water carrier in the house of al-'Imām Ja'far al-Ṣādiq (A). However, history shows this to have been impossible as Abū Yazid was not a contemporary of the Imām.

2. Bishr ibn al-Ḥārith al-Hāfi

This famous *ṣūfi* was another who led a corrupt life and then repented. In his book *Minhaj al-karamah*, al-'Allamah al-Hillī tells how Bishr repented at the urging of al-'Imām Musa ibn Ja'far (A), and because at the moment of his repentance he was barefoot in the street, he became known as *'al-Hāfi'* (*hāfi*: barefooted). However, others have suggested different origins of his name. Bishr al-Hafi (born near Merv c. 150/767) died in 226/840 or 227/841 in Baghdad.

3. Sari al-Saqati

One of the friends and companions of Bishr al-Hafi, Sari al-Saqati was one of those who bore affection for the creatures of God and who preferred others above themselves. In his book *Wafayat al-a'yan*, Ibn Khallikan writes that Sari once said, 'It is thirty years that I have been seeking forgiveness for one phrase, "Praise be to Allāh", that I allowed to pass my lips'. When asked to explain, he replied, 'One night the bazaar caught fire, and I left my house to see if the fire had reached my shop. When I heard that my shop was safe, I said, "Praise be to Allāh". Instantly I was brought to my senses with the realization that, though my shop was unharmed, should I not have been thinking about others'?' Sa'di is referring to this same story (with slight variations) when he says: 'One night someone's chimney kindled a fire/And I heard that half of Baghdad had burnt down./One said, thank God that in the smoke and ashes,/ My shop has not been damaged./A man who had seen the world replied, O selfish man,/Was your grief for yourself and no other?/Would you be content to see a town burnt to the ground,/As long as your own dwelling were left unscathed?

Sari was the pupil and disciple (*murid*) of Ma'rūf al-Karkhi, and the teacher and maternal uncle of Junayd of Baghdad. Sari was the author of many sayings on mystical unity (*tawḥīd*), love of God and other matters. It was also he who said, 'Like the sun, the *'ārif* shines on all the world; like the earth, he bears the good and evil of all; like water, he is the source of life for every heart; and like fire he gives his warmth to all and sundry.' Sari died in 253/867 at the age of ninety-eight.

4. Hārith al-Muḥāsibī

He was one of the friends and companions of Junayd. He was called '*al-muḥāsibi*' owing to his great diligence in the matter of self-observation and self-reckoning (*muḥāsābah*). He was a contemporary of Aḥmad ibn Ḥanbal, who, being an opponent of *'ilm al-kalām*, rejected Ḥārith al-Muḥāsibi for entering into theological debates, and as a result people avoided him. Born in Basrah in 165/781, he died in 243/857.

5. Junayd of Baghdād

Originally from Nahaw, Junayd received from the *'urafā'* and *ṣūfis* the title Sayyid al-Ṭa'ifah, just as Shī'ī jurisprudents called al-Shaykh al-Ṭūsī Shaykh al-Ta'ifah. Junayd is deemed one of the moderate mystics. The kind of ecstatic ejaculations uttered by others were never heard from his lips. He did not even put on the usual clothes of the *ṣūfis*, but dressed as scholars and jurisprudents did. It was suggested to him that for the sake of his associates he should wear *ṣūfi* dress. He replied, 'If I thought clothes were of any importance I would make an outfit of molten iron, for the call of truth is that "There is no significance in the [*ṣūfi*] cloak; importance lies only in the [inward] glow".'

Junayd's mother was the sister of Sari Saqati and Junayd became his pupil and disciple. He was also the pupil of Ḥārith al-Muḥāsibi. It seems that he died in Baghdad in 298/910 at the age of ninety.

6. Dhu an-Nūn al-Misri

An Egyptian, he was studied jurisprudence under the famous practitioner Mālik ibn Anas. Jāmī has called him the leader of the *ṣūfis*. It was he who first began to use symbolic language and to explain mystical matters through the use of a symbolic terminology which only the elect could understand. Gradually this became the standard practice, and mystical concepts were expressed in the form of love poetry (*ghazal*) and symbolic expressions. Some believe that Dhu al-Nun also introduced many Neo-Platonic ideas into *'irfān* and Sufism.[13] He died in 246/860 in Cairo.

7. Sahl ibn 'Abd Allāh al-Tustari

He was one of the great *'urafā'* and *ṣūfis*. A sect of gnostics who consider that the main principle of spirituality is combating the self is named 'Sahliyyah' after him. He associated with Dhu al-Nun of Egypt at Mecca. He died in Basrah in 282/895.[14]

8. Ḥusayn ibn Mansūr al-Ḥallāj

Now famous simply as al-Ḥallāj, he is one of the most controversial mystics of the Islamic world. The *shathiyyat* uttered by him are many, and he was accused of apostasy and of claiming divinity. Jurisprudents pronounced him an apostate and he was crucified during the reign of the 'Abbasid caliph al-Muqtadir. The *'urafā'* themselves accuse him of disclosing spiritual secrets. Ḥāfiẓ has this to say about him:

> He said, that friend, who was raised high on the Cross,
> His crime was that he used to reveal secrets.

Some consider him a mere conjuror, but the *'urafā'* themselves absolve him and say that the statements of al-Hallaj and Bayazid that gave the impression of unbelief were made when they were beside themselves in a state of 'intoxication'.

Al-Hallaj is remembered by the *'urafā'* as a martyr. He was executed in 309/913.[15]

'Urafā' *of the Fourth/Tenth Century*

1. Abū Bakr al-Shibli

A pupil and disciple of Junayd of Baghdad and among those who had met al-Hallaj, al-Shibli was one of the most famous mystics. He was originally from Khurasan. In the book *Rawḍat al-jannat* and in other biographies, many mystical poems and sayings have been recorded of him. Khawajah 'Abd Allāh al-'Anṣārī has said, 'The first person to speak in symbols was Dhu al-Nun of Egypt. Then came Junayd and he systematized this science, extended it and wrote books on it. Al-Shibli, in his turn, took it to the pulpit.' Al-Shibli died in 334/846 at the age of eighty-seven.

2. Abū 'Alī al-Rudbari

He traced his descent to Nushirwan and the Sasanids and was a disciple of Junayd. He studied jurisprudence under Abū al-'Abbas ibn Shurayh, and literature under Tha'lab. Thanks to his versatile knowledge, he was called the 'collector of the Law, the Way, and the Reality' (*jami' al-Sharī'ah wa al-Ṭarīqah wa al-Ḥaqiqah*). He died in 322/934.

3. Abū Naṣr al-Sarrāj al-Ṭūsī

Abū Naṣr al-Sarrāj is the author of the book *al-Luma'*, one of the principal and most ancient and reliable texts of *'irfān* and Sufism. Many of the shaykhs of the *ṣūfi* orders were his direct or indirect pupils. He passed away in 378/988 in Tus.

4. Abū Faḍl ibn al-Ḥaṣan al-Sarakhsi

He was the pupil and disciple of Abū Naṣr al-Sarrāj and the teacher of Abū Sa'id ibn Abi al-Khayr. He was a mystic of great fame. He died in 400/1009.

5. Abū 'Abd Allāh al-Rūdbārī

He was the son of Abū 'Alī al-Rūdbārī's sister. He is considered one of the mystics of Damascus and Syria. He died in 369/979.

6. Abū Tālib al-Makki

The fame of Abū Talib al-Makki rests largely on the book he authored on *'irfān* and Sufism, *Qut al-qulub*. This book is one of the principal and earliest texts of *'irfān* and Sufism. He passed away in 385/995 or 386/996.

'Urafā' *of the Fifth/Eleventh Century*

1. Shaykh Abū al-Ḥasan al-Kharqanī

One of the most famous *'urafā'*, and the subject of many amazing stories. One story relates how he would go to the grave of Bayazid and converse with his spirit, taking his advice in solving his difficulties. Rūmi says:

Many years had passed since the death of Bayazid/Before Bu'l-Ḥasan appeared./Now and then he would go and sit/By the side of his grave in his presence,/Until the spirit of his shaykh came to him,/And as soon as he uttered his problem, it was solved.

Rūmi includes many remembrances of Shaykh Abū al-Ḥasan in his *Mathnawī*, which shows his devotion and attachment to him. He is reputed to have met Abū 'Alī Sīnā, the philosopher, and Abū Sa'id ibn Abi al-Khayr, the famous *'ārif*. He died in 425/1033–34.

2. Abū Sa'id ibn Abi al-Khayr

One of the most famous of all mystics, Abū Sa'id ibn Abi al-Khayr is also one of those most noted for their spiritual states (*ḥālāt*). When once asked the definition of *taṣawwuf*, he replied, '*Taṣawwuf* means that you give up whatever is on your mind, give away whatever is in your hand and give yourself over to whatever you are capable of.'

He met Abū 'Alī Sīnā. One day Abū 'Alī was present at a meeting at which Abū Sa'id was preaching. Abū Sa'id was speaking about the necessity of deeds, and about obedience and disobedience to God. Abū 'Alī recited these verses (*ruba'ī*):

We are those who have befriended your forgiveness,
And seek riddance from obedience and disobedience.
Wherever your favour and grace are to be found,
Let the not-done be like the done, the done like the not-done.

Abū Sa'id immediately replied:

O you who have done no good, and done much bad,
And then aspire to your own salvation,
Do not rely on forgiveness, for never
Was the not-done like the done, the done like the not-done.

The following *ruba'i* is also of Abū Sa'id:

Tomorrow when the six directions fade away,
Your worth will be the worth of your awareness.
Strive for virtue, for on the Day of Retribution,
You shall rise in the form of your qualities.

Abū Sa'id passed away in the year 440/1048.

3. Abū 'Alī al-Daqqāq al-Nishābūrī

He is placed among those who have combined expertise of the Sharī'ah and the Tariqah. He was a preacher and an exegete (*mufassir*) of the Qur'ān. He used to weep so much while reciting supplications (*munajat*) that he was given the title 'the lamenting shaykh' (*shaykh-e nawhahgar*). He passed away in 405/1014 or 412/1021.

4. Abū al-Ḥaṣan 'Alī ibn 'Uthmān al-Hujwīrī

He was the author of one of the most famous *ṣūfi* books, *Kashf al-Mahjub*, which has recently been published. He died in 470/1077.

5. Khwājah 'Abd Allāh al-Anṣārī

A descendant of the great companion of the Prophet, Abū Ayyub al-'Anṣārī, Khwājah 'Abd Allāh was himself one of the most famous and pious of all *'urafā'*. His fame rests largely on his elegant aphorisms, *munājāt* and *ruba'iyyat*.

Among his sayings is this:

When a child you are low, when a youth you are intoxicated, when old you are decrepit; so when will you worship God?

And another:

Returning evil for evil is the trait of a dog; returning good for good is the trait of a donkey; returning good for evil is the work of Khwājah 'Abd Allāh al-'Anṣārī.

The following *ruba'i* also comes from him:

It is a great fault for a man to remain aloof,
Setting oneself above all the creation.
Learn thy lesson from the pupil of the eye,
That sees everyone but not itself.

Khwājah 'Abd Allāh was born in Herat where he died and was buried in 481/1088. For this reason he is known as 'the Sage of Herat' (*Pir-e Herat*). Khwājah 'Abd Allāh authored many books, the best-known of which, *Manāzil al-s'irin*, is a didactic manual on *sayr wa sulūk*. It is one of the best-written works of *'irfān*, and many commentaries have been written on it.

6. Imām Abū Ḥāmid Muḥammad al-Ghazzālī

One of the best-known scholars of Islam, whose fame has penetrated both East and West, he combined in his person the knowledge of the rational and traditional sciences (*ma'qul wa manqul*). He became head of the Nizamiyyah Academy in Baghdad and held the highest position of his age accessible to any scholar. However, feeling that neither his knowledge nor his position could satisfy him, he withdrew from public life and engaged in disciplining and purifying his soul. He spent ten years in Palestine, far from all who knew him, and it was during this period that he became inclined towards *'irfān* and Sufism. He never again accepted any post or position. Following his period of solitary asceticism, he wrote his famous *Ihya' 'ulum al-Dīn* ('Reviving the Sciences of Religion'). He died in his home city of Tus in the year 505/1111.

'Urafā' *of the Sixth/Twelfth Century*

1. 'Ayn al-Quḍāt al-Ḥamadānī

One of the most enthusiastic of mystics, 'Ayn al-Quḍāt al-Ḥamadānī was a disciple of Aḥmad al-Ghazzāli, younger brother of Muḥammad, who was also a mystic. The author of many books, he also composed some brilliant poetry, which, however, was not altogether free of theopathetic exclamations (*shathiyyat*). Charges of heresy were brought against him; he was executed, and his body burnt and his ashes cast to the winds. This occurred around 525–533/1131–1139.

2. Sanāi Ghaznawī

A famous poet, whose verse is laden with profound mystic sentiments. Rūmi, in his *Mathnawī*, cited some of his sayings and expounded on them. He died around the middle of the sixth/twelfth century.

3. Aḥmad Jāmī

Known as 'Zhand-e Pil', Jāmī is one of the most celebrated of *'urafā'* and *ṣūfīs*. His tomb lies at Turbat-e Jam, near the border between Iran and Afghanistan, and is well known. The following lines are among the verses he composed on fear (*khawf*) and hope (*rajā'*):

Be not haughty, for the mount of many a mighty man
Has been hamstrung among rocks in the desert;
But neither despair, for even wine-drinking libertines
Have suddenly arrived at their destination thanks to a single song.

Similarly, on achieving a balance between generosity and thrift, he offers the following advice:

Be not like an adze, drawing all to yourself,
Nor like a plane, gaining nothing for your work;
In matters of livelihood, learn from the saw,
It draws some to itself and lets some scatter.

Aḥmad Jāmī died around the year 536/1141.

4. 'Abd al-Qādir al-Jilānī

He is one of the most controversial figures of the Islamic world and it is to him that the Qaḍiriyyah order of *ṣūfīs* is attributed. He is the author of many supplications and elevated sayings. He was a sayyid descended from al-'Imām al-Ḥaṣan (A). He died in 560/1164 or 561/1165 and his grave at Baghdād is well known.

5. Shaykh Ruzbihān Baqli Shīrāzī

He is known as Shaykh-e Shattah on account of his prolific theopathetic exclamations. In recent years some of his books have been published, mainly through the efforts of Orientalists. He died in 606/1209.

'Urafa' *of the Seventh/Thirteenth Century*

This century produced some mystics of the highest stature. We shall mention some of them in chronological order.

1. Shaykh Najm al-Dīn Kubrā

One of the greatest and most celebrated of mystics, he is the source of many chains orders. He was the pupil and disciple of Shaykh Ruzbihan, and was also his son-in-law. He had many pupils and disciples, among whom was Baha' al-Dīn Walad, the father of Jalāl al-Dīn Rūmi.

He lived in Khuwarizm (in present-day Turkestan and Uzbekistan) at the time of the Mongol invasions. Before his city was attacked, he was sent a message informing him that he could lead a party of his family and disciples out of the city to safety. Najm al-Dīn's reply was that, 'Throughout all the days of comfort I have lived alongside these people. Now that the day of difficulties has come I will not leave them.' He then manfully strapped on a sword and fought alongside the people of the city until he was martyred. This happened in the year 624/1227.

2. Shaykh Farid al-Dīn al-'Aṭṭār

One of the foremost of mystics, al-'Aṭṭār wrote works both in verse and in prose. His book *Tadhkirat al-awliya'*, on the lives and characters of the *ṣūfis* and mystics – which begins with al-'Imām Ja'far al-Ṣādiq (A) and ends with al-'Imām Muḥammad al-Baqir (A) – is considered a source book of documentary significance, and great importance is attached to it by the Orientalists. Similarly, his work *Manṭiq al-ṭayr* ('The Speech of the Birds') is a masterpiece of mystical literature.

Rūmi, comments on al-'Aṭṭār and Sanāi thus:

'Aṭṭār was the spirit and Sana'i his two eyes,
We are following in the steps of Sana'i and 'Aṭṭār.

Rūmi also says:

'Aṭṭār passed through seven cities of love,
While we are yet in the bend of a single lane.

What Rūmi means by the 'seven cities of love' are the seven valleys of which al-'Aṭṭār speaks in his *Mantiq al-tayr*. Muḥammad Shabistarī in his *Gulshan-e raz* says:

I am not ashamed of my poetry,
For the like of 'Aṭṭār a hundred centuries will not see.

Al-'Aṭṭār was the pupil and disciple of Shaykh Majd al-Dīn of Baghdad, who was among the pupils and disciples of Shaykh Najm al-Dīn Kubra. He also benefited from the company of Qutb al-Dīn Ḥaydar, another of the shaykhs of the age and one after whom the town in which he is buried, Turbat-e Ḥaydariyyah, was named.

Al-ʿAṭṭār lived during the time of the Mongol invasions, and died – some say at the hands of the Mongols – around 626–28/1228–1230.

3. Shaykh Shihab al-Dīn al-Suhrawardi

He is the author of the celebrated *ʿAwārif al-maʿārif*, an excellent text of *ʿirfān* and Sufism. He claimed descent from Abū Bakr. It is said that he went each year to visit Makkah and al-Madinah. He met and conversed with ʿAbd al-Qaḍir al-Jilānī. Among his disciples were the famous poets Shaykh Saidi and Kamal al-Dīn Ismaʿil al-ʿIsfahan. Saʿdi had this to say about him:

> *My wise shaykh the murshid, Shihab, gave me two pieces of advice:*
> *One, not to be egocentric,*
> *The other, not to regard others with pessimism.*

This Suhrawardi is not the same person as the famous philosopher known as Shaykh al-Ishraq, who was killed around 581–590/1185–1194 in Aleppo, Syria. Suhrawardi the gnostic died around the year 632/1234.

4. Ibn al-Fārid al-Misri

He is considered one of the mystics of the first rank. His mystical poetry, in Arabic, reaches the loftiest summits and is of the greatest elegance. His *diwān* (collection of poems) has been published several times and has been the subject of many distinguished commentaries. One of those who wrote a commentary on his work was ʿAbd al-Rahman Jāmī, a well-known mystic of the ninth century.

The poetry of Ibn al-Fārid in Arabic is comparable to that of Ḥāfiẓ in Persian. Muḥyi al-Dīn ibn al-ʿArabi once suggested to him that he should write a commentary on his poems. Ibn al-Fārid replied that the commentary of his poems was Ibn al-ʿArabi's own *al-Futuhat al-Makkiyyah*.

Ibn al-Fārid was of those who went through abnormal, often ecstatic 'states' (*ahwal*) and it was in such states that he composed many of his poems. He died in the year 632/1234.

5. Muḥyi al-Dīn ibn al-ʿArabi

A descendant of Hatim al-Ta'i, Muḥyi al-Dīn ibn al-ʿArabi was originally from Spain. Most of his life, however, seems to have been spent in Makkah and Syria. He was a pupil of the sixth-century mystic Shaykh Abū Madyan al-Maghribi al-

'Andalusi. Through one intermediary link, the chain of his order goes back to the Shaykh 'Abd al-Qaḍir al-Jilānī mentioned above.

Muḥyi al-Dīn, also known by the name Ibn al-'Arabi, is certainly the greatest mystic of Islam. No one else has been able to reach his level, either before or after him. Thus he is known by the sobriquet 'al-Shaykh al-Akbar' ('the Greatest Shaykh').

Islamic mysticism, from the time of its first appearance, has made progress century upon century. Each century, as indicated above, produced great mystics who have developed *'irfān*, always adding to its heritage. This advancement had always been gradual. But in the seventh/thirteenth century, with the appearance of Ibn al-'Arabi, *'irfān* made a sudden leap and reached the summit of its perfection. Ibn al-'Arabi took *'irfān* to a stage it had never reached before.

The foundations for the second branch of *'irfān*, namely, theoretical *'irfān* and its attendant philosophy, were laid by Ibn al-'Arabi. In general, the mystics who came after him ate the crumbs from his table.

Besides bringing *'irfān* into a new phase, Ibn al-'Arabi was one of the wonders of all time. He was an amazing person, and this has led to wildly divergent views about him. Some consider him *al-Walī al-Kamil* ('Perfect Saint') and the *Qutb al-Aqtāb* ('Pole of Poles'). Others so disparage him as to label him a heretic, calling him *Mumit al-Dīn* ('Killer of the Faith') or *Maḥi al-Dīn* ('Effacer of the Faith'). Ṣadr al-Muta'allihin (Mullā Ṣadrā), the great philosopher and Islamic genius, had the greatest respect for him, considering him far greater than Ibn Sīnā or al-Fārābī.

Ibn al-'Arabi authored over two hundred books. Many of his works, perhaps all of those whose manuscripts are extant (numbering about thirty), have been published. Of his most important books, one is his *al-Futaḥat al-Makkiyyah*, a colossal work that is a veritable encyclopedia of *'irfān*. Another is his *Fuṣūs al-ḥikam*, which, although brief, is the most precise and most profound text of *'irfān*. Numerous commentaries have been written on it, yet perhaps there have been no more than two or three persons in any era who have been able to understand it.

Ibn al-'Arabi passed away in 638/1240 in the city of Damascus, where his grave is still well known today.

6. Ṣadr al-Dīn Qunawī

He was the pupil, disciple and son of the wife of Ibn al-'Arabi. He was a contemporary of Khwājah Nāṣir al-Dīn al-Ṭūsī and of Mawlānā Jalāl al-Dīn Rūmi. He corresponded with Khwājah Nāṣir, who respected him greatly, and at Qunyah (in present-day Turkey), there was perfect friendship and cordiality between him and Rūmi. Qunawī used to lead the prayers and Rūmi would pray behind him, and Rūmi may have been his pupil.

There is a story that when one day Rūmi came to join Qunawī's circle, he raised himself from his special *masnad* and offered it to Rūmi. Declining, Rūmi said that he would have no excuse before God for taking Qunawī's seat. At that, Qunawī threw away the *masnad*, saying, if it did not suit Rūmi it would not suit him either.

Qunawī provided the best exposition on the thought and ideas of Ibn al-'Arabi. In fact, without Qunawī it is possible that Ibn al-'Arabi would never have been understood. It was also through Qunawī that Rūmi became acquainted with Ibn al-'Arabi and his school, and one reason for surmising that Rūmi was Qunawī's pupil is that Ibn al-'Arabi's ideas are reflected in Rūmi's *Mathnawī* and his *Diwān-e Shams*.

Students of philosophy and *'irfān* have used Qunawī's books as textbooks for the last six centuries. His three famous books are *Miftāh al-ghayb*, *al-Nuṣūs* and *al-Fokūk*. Qunawī passed away in 672/1273 (the year in which both Rūmi and Khwājah Nāṣir al-Dīn died) or in 673/1274.

7. Mawlānā Jalāl al-Dīn Muḥammad Balkhi Rūmi

Known in the East as Mawlawi and in the West as Rūmi, author of the world-famous *Mathnawī*, this man was one of the greatest geniuses the world and Islamic *'irfān* have ever seen. He was descended from Abū Bakr. His *Mathnawī* is an ocean of wisdom and full of precise spiritual, social and mystic insights. He ranks among the foremost Persian poets.

Originally from Balkh, he left with his father when still a child. Together they visited Makkah, and at Nishabur they met Shaykh Fārid al-Dīn al-'Aṭṭār. On leaving Makkah his father went to Qunyah, where they settled. At first Rūmi, being a scholar, occupied himself, like other scholars of his rank, in teaching and he lived a respectable life. Then he met the famous mystic Shams-e Tabrizi. Rūmi was magnetized by this man and at once gave everything up. His *diwān* of *ghazal* is named after Shams, and he has repeatedly made ardent mention of him in his *Mathnawī*. Rūmi passed away in 672/1273.

8. Fakhr al-Dīn al-'Irāqi al-Ḥamadānī

A well-known poet of *ghazal* and a mystic, he was a pupil of Ṣadr al-Dīn Qunawī and a *murid* and protégé of Shihab al-Dīn al-Suhrawardi. He died in 688/1289.

'Urafā' *of the Eighth/Fourteenth Century*

1. 'Alā' al-Dawlah Simnānī

He began as an official secretary, then gave up his post and all his wealth to enter the path of the *'urafā'* and follow the way of God. He wrote many books and held his own beliefs in the field of theoretical *'irfān*, which are discussed in several important texts of *'irfān*. He died in 736/1335. Among his disciples was the well-known poet Khwajawi Kirmani, who describes him thus:

Whoever flourishes upon the path of 'Alī,
Like Khidr, finds the springs of life.
Delivered from the whisperings of the Devil,
He becomes like 'Alā' al-Dawlah Simnānī.

2. 'Abd al-Razzāq Kashānī

He was a scholar who wrote commentaries on the *Fuṣūs* of Ibn al-'Arabi and the *Manāzil al-sā'irin* of Khwājah 'Abd Allāh. Both of these have been published and scholars use them for reference.

According to the author of *Rawdat al-Jannat*, in his account of Shaykh 'Abd al-Razzāq Lahijī, 'Abd al-Razzāq Kashānī was eulogized by al-Shahīd al-Thānī. He and 'Alā' al-Dawlah Simnānī had heated discussions on theoretical issues of *'irfān* that had been raised by Ibn al-'Arabi. He passed away in the year 735/1334.

3. Khwājah Ḥāfiẓ Shirāzī

Despite his worldwide fame, the details of Ḥāfiẓ's life are not altogether clear. What is known is that he was a scholar, an *'ārif*, a *ḥāfiẓ* of the Qur'ān and an exegete of the Book. He himself repeatedly said as much in his verses:

I haven't seen more beautiful lines than yours, Ḥāfiẓ,
By the Qur'ān that you have in your breast.
Your love shall cry out if you, like Ḥāfiẓ,
Recite the Qur'ān memoriter with all the fourteen readings.
Of the memorizers of the world none has been my equal in gathering
Subtleties of wisdom with Qur'ānic delicacy.

In his poetry Ḥāfiẓ speaks much of the *pir-e tariqat* (spiritual guide) and of the *murshid* (master), yet it is not clear who was the teacher and guide of Ḥāfiẓ himself.

Ḥāfiẓ's poetry attains lofty mystical heights, and there are few people who are able to perceive his mystic subtleties. All the *'urafā'* who came after him admit that he had indeed covered all the most exalted stages of *'irfān*. Several important scholars have written commentaries on his verses. For example, a treatise was written by the well-known philosopher of the ninth century, Muḥaqqiq Jalāl al-Dīn Dawwani, on the following verse:

My teacher said: the pen of creation was subject to no error,
Bravo the pure eyes that hide all defects.

Ḥāfiẓ passed away in 791/1389.[16]

4. Shaykh Maḥmūd Shabistarī

He is the creator of the sublime mystic poem *Gulshan-e raz* ('The Garden of Secrets'). This poem is counted as one of the loftiest works of *'irfān* and has immortalized the name of its author. Many commentaries have been written upon it, perhaps the best of which was written by Shaykh Muḥammad Lahijī, which has been published and is available. Shabistarī passed away about the year 720/1320.

5. Sayyid Ḥaydar Amulī

One of the erudite mystics, Sayyid Ḥaydar Amulī is the author of the book *Jāmī' al-asrar* ('Collector of the Secrets'), which is a precise work on the theoretical *'irfān* of Ibn al-'Arabi. This book has lately been published. Another book by him is *Naṣṣ al-nuṣūs*, which is a commentary on Ibn al-'Arabi's *Fuṣūs al-Ḥikam*. He was a contemporary of the famous jurisprudent Fakhr al-Muḥaqqiqin al-Ḥillī, but the date of his death is not known.

6. 'Abd al-Karīm Jilāni

He is the author of the well-known book *al-Insān al-kamil* ('The Perfect Man'). The concept of the perfect man was first raised in its theoretical form by Ibn al-'Arabi, and has ever since occupied an important place in Islamic *'irfān*. Ibn al-'Arabi's pupil and disciple, Ṣadr al-Dīn Qunawī, discussed it fully in his *Miftāḥ al-ghayb* and, as far as we know, at least two mystics have written whole books on the subject. One is 'Aziz al-Dīn Nasafi, a mystic of the latter half of the seventh/thirteenth century; the other is 'Abd al-Karīm Jilāni. Jilāni died in 805/1402 at the age of thirty-eight.

'Urafā' *of the Ninth/Fifteenth Century*

1. Shah Ni'mat Allāh Walī
He claimed descent from the house of 'Alī. He is among the most famous of *'urafā'* and *ṣūfīs*. The current Ni'mat-ullahi order is one of the most famous of *ṣūfī* orders. His grave near the city of Kirman is still a *ṣūfī* shrine. He reportedly lived to the age of ninety-five and died in the year 820/1417, 827/1424 or 834/1430. He took inspiration from *ṣūfīs* of the seventh century and from Ḥāfiẓ Shirāzī. Much of his mystical poetry has survived.

2. Sa'in al-Dīn 'Alī Tarakeh Iṣfahānī
He was one of the most erudite of the *'urafā'*. He had a deep familiarity with the theoretical *'irfān* of Ibn al-'Arabi, as is evident in his book *Tamhid al-qawa'id*, which has been published and is still available and has been used as a source by later scholars.

3. Muḥammad ibn Mamẓah al-Fanari al-Rūmi
One of the scholars of the 'Uthmani empire, he distinguished himself in several fields. Author of many books, he is famous in *'irfān* for his book *Miṣbah al-uns*, a commentary on Qunawi's *Miftāḥ al-ghayb*. It is not within the capabilities of everyone to write a commentary and exposition on the books of Ibn al-'Arabi and his disciple Ṣadr al-Dīn Qunawī, and authorities in *'irfān* have all confirmed the value of this work. A lithograph print of the book with the *hawashi* of Aqa Mirzā Hāshim Rashti, a mystic of the last century, has been published in Tehran. Unfortunately, however, owing to bad print parts of the *hawashi* are illegible.

4. Shams al-Dīn Muḥammad Lahijī Nurbakhshī
The author of a commentary on the *Gulshan-e raz* of Maḥmūd Shabistarī, and a contemporary of Mir Ṣadr al-Dīn Dashtaki and 'Allamah Dawwani, he lived in Shiraz. These two, who were both outstanding philosophers of their age, had the greatest respect for Lahijī, according to Qadi Nur Allāh Shushtari in his *Majālis al-mu'minin*. Lahijī was a disciple of Sayyid Muḥammad Nurbakhsh, himself a pupil of Ibn Fahd al-Ḥillī. In his commentary on the *Gulshan-e raz* he traced his chain back from Sayyid Muḥammad Nurbakhsh to Ma'rūf al-Karkhi, thence to al-'Imām al-Riḍā and the preceding Imāms and thus to the Holy Prophet himself (S). This he calls the 'Golden Chain' (*silsilat al-dhahab*).

His fame rests largely on his commentary, which is itself one of the loftiest of mystic texts. As he says in the Introduction to the work, he began writing in

877/1472. The year of his death is not precisely known but it was probably before 900/1494.

5. Nur al-Dīn 'Abd al-Rahman Jāmī

Jāmī claimed descent from the well-known jurisprudent of the second century, Muḥammad ibn al-Ḥaṣan al-Shaybani. A powerful poet, he is considered the last great mystic poet of the Persian language. At first he assumed the *takhallus* 'Dashti', but he changed it to Jāmī in recognition of his place of birth, Jam, in the vicinity of Mashhad, and of Aḥmad Jāmī (*Zhand-e Pil*), from whom he claimed spiritual descent. In his own words:

My birthplace is Jam and the drops of my pen
Are the draught of the cup of Shaykh al-Islam,[17]
Thus in the pages of my poetry
In two ways my pen-name is Jāmī.

Jāmī was an accomplished scholar in the various fields of Arabic grammar and syntax, law, jurisprudence, logic, philosophy and *'irfān*. His many books include a commentary on the *Fuṣūs al-ḥikam* of Ibn al-'Arabi, a commentary on the *Luma'at* of Fakhr al-Dīn 'Irāqi, a commentary on the *Ta'iyyah* of Ibn al-Fārid, a commentary on the *Qaṣīdat al-Burdah* in praise of the Holy Prophet (S), a commentary on the *Qaṣīdah Mimiyyah* of Farazdaq in praise of al-'Imām 'Alī ibn al-Husayn, a book entitled *al-Lawdyih*, his *Bahdristan*, written in the style of Sa'di's *Gulistans*, and *Nafahat al-'uns*, a collection of biographies of mystics.

Jāmī was a disciple of Baha' al-Dīn Naqshaband, the founder of the Naqshabandi order. However, as in the instance of Muḥammad Lahijī, who was a disciple of Sayyid Muḥammad Nurbakhsh, his academic standing is above that of his peer. Jāmī, though counted as one of the followers of Baha' al-Dīn Naqshaband, achieved an academic standing several degrees higher than that of Baha' al-Dīn.

Thus in this brief history in which we are concentrating on the academic side of *'irfān* and not on the development of the various orders, special mention has been made of Muḥammad Lahijī and 'Abd al-Rahman Jāmī, rather than of the founders of their orders. Jāmī died in 898/1492 at the age of eighty-one.

This ends our brief history of *'irfān*, covering the period from its beginnings until the close of the ninth/fifteenth century. We end at this point because from the tenth/sixteenth century onwards *'irfān* took on a different form. Up until this time the learned and academic figures of *'irfān* had all been members of regular *ṣūfi* orders and the poles (*aqtab*) or masters of the *ṣūfi* orders were great academic figures of *'irfān*, to whom we owe the great mystic works. Around the beginning of the tenth/sixteenth century, however, this began to change.

First, the masters of the *ṣūfi* orders no longer possessed the academic prominence of their forerunners and formal Sufism became diffused in customs and externals that were occasionally of an innovative nature (*bid'ah*).

Second, scholars who were not members of any formal *ṣūfi* order began to show profound learning in the theoretical *'irfān* of Ibn al-'Arabi, such that none from among the *ṣūfi* orders could match them. Examples of such scholars are Ṣadr al-Muta'allihin of Shiraz (d. 1050/1640), his pupil Fayd Kashānī (d. 1091/1680) and Fayd's own pupil Qaḍi Sa'id Qummī (d. 1103/1691). Each of these had greater knowledge of the theoretical *'irfān* of Ibn al-'Arabi than the poles or masters of any *ṣūfi* order of their times, and they themselves were not attached to any of the *ṣūfi* orders. This development has, moreover, continued down to the present day, as can be seen in the examples of the late Aqa-Muḥammad Riḍā Qumsheh'i and the late Aqa Mirzā Hāshim Rashti. These two scholars of the last hundred years were both experts in the field of theoretical *'irfān*, yet they too were not members of any *ṣūfi* order.

On the whole, it can be said that it was in the time of Muḥyi al-Dīn ibn al-'Arabi, who laid the foundations of theoretical *'irfān* and philosophized *'irfān*, that the seed of this new development was sown.

Muḥammad ibn Hamzah Fanari, mentioned above, perhaps represented this type. But the new development that produced experts in theoretical *'irfān*, who were either not interested in practical *'irfān* and its spiritual methodology or, if they were (as most were, to some extent), had nothing to do with any formal *ṣūfi* order, is perfectly discernible from the tenth/sixteenth century onwards.

Third, since that period there have been individuals and groups devoted to the spiritual methodology of practical *'irfān*, who attained extremely high spiritual stature and yet were not members of any of the formal *ṣūfi* orders. Either they either indifferent to the formal *ṣūfis* or they regarded them as being partly or totally heretical. Among the characteristics of this new group of theoretical and practical *'urafā'* – who were also learned in law and jurisprudence – was a perfect loyalty to the Sharī'ah and a harmony between the rites of the path of progression and the rites of jurisprudence.

*The Mystic's Stations (*Maqāmāt*)*

The *'urafā'* maintain that in order to arrive at the stage of true gnosis, there are stages and stations that must be covered. Unless covered, the *'urafā'* believe, it is impossible to arrive at the station of true gnosis.

First, *'Irfān* has a facet that it shares with theosophy (*ḥikmat ilāhi*), although many of the facets of these two disciplines differ, the common facet being that the aim is knowledge of God (*ma'rifat Allāh*). They differ in that theosophy does not aim solely at knowledge of God but rather aims at a knowledge of the order of being. The knowledge that is sought by the theosophist (*ḥakīm*) is of the system of existence of which, naturally, knowledge of God is an important pillar. The goal of *'irfān*, on the other hand, is exclusively knowledge of God. In the view of *'irfān*, knowledge of God is total knowledge. Everything must be known in the light of knowledge of God and from the point of view of *tawḥīd*; such knowledge is a derivative of knowledge of God.

Second, the knowledge sought by the *ḥakīm* is intellectual knowledge and can be likened to the knowledge acquired by a mathematician after thought and reflection on a particular mathematical problem. However, the knowledge sought by the *'ārif* is experienced and witnessed; it can be likened to the knowledge acquired by an experimental scientist in his laboratory. The *ḥakīm* seeks certain knowledge (*'ilm al-yaqīn*), while the *'ārif* seeks the certainty of direct vision (*'ayn al-yaqīn*).

Third, the means employed by the *ḥakīm* are his reason, deductions and proofs, whereas those employed by the *'ārif* are the heart and the purification, disciplining and perfecting of the self. The *ḥakīm* seeks, through the telescope of his mind, to study the order of existence, while the *'ārif* seeks to prepare the whole of his being so as to arrive at the core of reality. He seeks to reach reality like a drop of water in search of the sea. In the view of the *ḥakīm*, the perfection expected of a human being lies in understanding reality, while in the *'ārif*'s view it lies in reaching reality. In the *ḥakīm*'s view an imperfect human being is one who is ignorant, while in the *'ārif's* view the imperfect human is one who has remained distant and separated from his origin.

The *'ārif* therefore sees perfection in reaching rather than in understanding. And in order to reach the principal goal and the stage of true gnosis, he regards the traversing of several stages and stations as necessary and essential. This he calls *sayr wa sulūk*, the science of inward wayfaring.

These stages and stations have been discussed in great detail in the books of *'irfān*. Here it is not possible to explain, even briefly, every one of them. However, in order at least to give a general impression, I believe that we can do no better than to turn to the ninth section of Ibn Sīnā's *al-'Ishārāt*. Although

Ibn Sīnā is mainly a philosopher, not a mystic, he is not a 'dry' philosopher, and especially towards the end of his life he developed mystic inclinations. In his *al-'Ishārāt*, which appears to be his last work, he has devoted a whole section to the 'stations' of the gnostics. This section being extraordinarily sublime and beautiful, we shall present a summary of this section, rather than citing or translating suitable passages from the books of the *'urafā'*.

Zāhid, 'Ābid *and* 'Ārif

He who abstains from the enjoyments of the world, even its wholesome ones, is called a *zāhid* (ascetic); and he who is careful to perform worship, prayer and fasting and the like is called an *'ābid* (devotee); and he who keeps his thought turned perpetually towards the realm of light in order that the light of the Real shine in his breast is called an *'ārif*; and sometimes two or more of these epithets may apply to the same person.

Although Ibn Sīnā defines here the *zāhid*, the *'ābid* and the *'ārif*, yet at the same time he is defining *zuhd*, *'ibādah* and *'irfān*. This is because a definition of *zāhid*, *'ābid*, or *tārif* per se includes implicitly a definition of *zuhd*, *'ibādah* or *'irfān*. Thus the conclusion to be drawn from this passage is that *zuhd* is abstinence from worldly enjoyments; *'ibādah* is the performance of specific acts like prayer, fasting, reciting the Qur'ān and the like; and *'irfān* is turning the mind from everything but Allāh and paying complete attention to the Divine Essence so that the light of the Real may shine on one's heart.

The last clause indicates an important point. One or more of these characteristics may occur in combination. Thus it is possible for an individual to be an *'ābid* and a *zāhid*, a *zāhid* and an *'ārif*, an *'ābid* and an *'ārif*, or an *'ābid*, *zāhid* and *'ārif* at one and the same time. Ibn Sīnā has not elaborated this, but he implies that although it is possible for one to be a *zāhid* or an *'ābid* and not be an *'ārif*, it is not possible for one to be an *'ārif* and not be a *zāhid* and an *'ābid*. One may be both a *zāhid* and an *'ābid* without being an *'ārif*, but an *'ārif* by definition is also a *zāhid* and an *'ābid*.

In the next passage we shall see that the *zuhd* of an *'ārif* differs in its goal from that of a *non-'ārif*. In fact, the spirit and essence of the *'ārif's zuhd* and *'ibādah* are different from those of the non-*'ārif*: the *zuhd* for the non-*'ārif* is a transaction by which he gives up the pleasures of the world for the pleasures of the hereafter, whereas for the *'ārif* it is something through which he dissociates himself from everything that keeps him from turning his attention towards God and he looks down on everything except God. Whereas worship for the non-*'ārif* is a transaction by which he performs actions in the world for a reward (*ajr, thawāb*) to be received in the hereafter, for the *'ārif* it is a kind of exercise that is aimed at strengthening his self's intellectual and imaginative faculties and that, by repetition, draws away the self from the realm of illusion to the realm of the Real.

The 'Ārif's *Goal*

The *'ārif* desires the Real (God) not for the sake of something else, and he values nothing above his knowledge of the Real, and his worship of Him is because He is worthy of worship and it is a worthy way of relating himself to Him; it is not out of desire (for rewards) or fear (of chastisement).

The meaning of this is that in terms of his aims the *'ārif* is a *muwahhid*. He seeks only God, yet his desire of God is not on account of His gifts in this world or in the hereafter. Were such to be the case, the real object of his desire would be the gifts, God being only the preliminary means by which the desired gifts are sought. In such a case, in reality, the final object of worship and desire would be one's own self; for the purpose of seeking those gifts is the pleasure of the self.

However, the *'ārif* desires whatever he desires for the sake of God. When he desires the gifts of God he does so because they are from Him and are His favours. They represent His Grace and Magnanimity. So, while the non-*'ārif* seeks God for the sake of His gifts, the *'ārif* seeks the gifts of God for the sake of God.

Here the question may arise, if the *'ārif* does not seek God for the sake of anything, then why does he worship Him? Is it not true that every act of worship must have a purpose? Ibn Sīnā's passage contains the answer. He states that the goal and motivation of the *'ārif's* worship is one of two things. One is the inherent worthiness of the Worshipped to be worshipped, meaning that one worships God simply because He is worthy of worship. It is rather like someone who upon noticing some admirable qualities in a person or a thing praises that person or thing. If asked what motivated him to do so or of what benefit was it to him, he will reply that he sought no benefit from his praise, but simply saw that person or thing as being genuinely deserving of praise. This is true of the praise accorded to heroes or champions in whatever field.

The other motivation of the *'ārif's* worship is the worthiness of worship itself. It carries an intrinsic nobility and beauty of its own, for it is a connection, a tie, between oneself and God. Thus there is no reason why worship should necessarily entail desire or fear.

'Alī (A) has some famous words on this subject:

> My God, I do not worship You in fear of Your Fire, nor in desire for Your Paradise, but I find You worthy of worship, so I worship You.

The *'urafā'* place great importance on this issue, considering it a kind of *shirk* (polytheism) if one's goal in life and particularly in worship is something other than God Himself. *'Irfān* totally rejects this kind of *shirk*. Many have written elegantly and subtly on the subject, as in this allegory from Sa'di's *Bustan*:

> One with the Shah of Ghaznah found fault, saying,
> What charm has he, the Shah's friend Iyaz?
> A flower indeed with neither colour nor smell,
> How strange of the nightingale to set its heart upon such a thing.
> Someone conveyed this remark to Sultan Maḥmūd,
> Who, on hearing it, was besides himself with anguish.
> 'I love him for his disposition and character,
> Nor for his pleasing gait and stature.'
> Heard I once that in a narrow defile,
> The king's treasure-chest broke open after a camel fell.
> The king, after signalling his bequest,
> Spurred on his steed to make haste.
> The riders now fell upon the pearls and corals,
> Their thoughts turning from the king to the treasure.
> None of the proud lads remained that day
> To follow in the king's train except Iyaz.
> Looking out, the king beheld Iyaz and
> His face like a flower bloomed with delight.
> 'What booty have you brought along?, ' the king inquired.
> 'None,' said Iyaz. 'I hurried after you,
> Preferring your service to treasure and bounties.'

Sa'di then turns from this story to the point he wishes to make, which he expresses thus:

> If you look to your friend for his favours,
> You are tied to yourself, not to your friend,
> A breach of the Way it was if the saints
> Desired of God aught other than God.

The First Station

The first level of the *'ārif's* journey is what they call 'resolution' (*al-'irādah*). This is a fervent desire to catch hold of the Firm Tie (*al-'urwat al-wuthqā*) that is within reach of one who is perceptive of true proofs or who has settled himself through the covenant of faith, so that it impels his heart towards the Holy in order to attain the spirit of connection (with Him).

In order to explain the first stage of the spiritual path – which in one respect potentially embraces the whole of *'irfān* – some elaboration is necessary. The *'urafā'* primarily believe in a principle that they sum up in the phrase, 'The ends are the return to the beginnings'.

Clearly, for the end to be the beginning there are two possibilities. One is that the movement is in a straight line, and that once the object in motion reaches a certain point it changes its direction and retraces exactly the same route from which it came. In philosophy it has been proven that such a change of direction would entail an interval of motionlessness, even if imperceptible. Furthermore, these two movements would be opposite to each other. The second possibility is that the movement is along a curve, all of whose points are equidistant from a certain central point, in other words, a circle. If the movement takes the form of a circle, naturally the path will end at the point of commencement.

An object moving in a circle will move continuously away from the point of beginning until it reaches the point farthest from where it began, a point diametrically opposite to the point of commencement. It is from this point that, with no pause or interval, the return journey (*ma'ād*) to the point of departure (*mabda'*) commences. The *'urafā'* call the first part of the journey, i.e. from the point of departure to the point farthest from it, 'the arc of descent' (*qawṣ al-nozūl*), and the journey from there back to the point of departure 'the arc of ascent' (*qawṣ al-su'ūd*). There is a philosophical view associated with the movement of things from the point of departure to the farthest point, which philosophers call the 'principle of causality' (*asl al-'illiyyah*) and which *'urafā'* call the 'principle of emanation' (*asl al-tajalli*); in either case objects travelling along the arc of descent are as if driven from behind. Similarly, the movement of objects from the farthest point to the point of departure also has its own philosophical theory, which is that every being has a passionate desire to flee from all that is strange and remote and return to its origin and its homeland. This tendency, so the *'urafā'* believe, is inherent in each and every particle of existence, including the human being, though in man it can often be latent and hidden.

Man's preoccupations prevent the activity of this tendency, and a series of stimuli are required before this inner inclination will surface. It is the appearance of this inclination that the *'urafā'* term 'resolution' or 'will' (*irādah*). This resolution is in reality a type of awakening of a dormant consciousness. 'Abd al-Razzāq Kashānī, in his *Istilahat*, defines *irādah* as:

A spark in the heart from the fire of love that compels one to answer the summons of the Real (*Haqīqah*).

Khwājah 'Abd Allāh Anṣārī in his *Manazīl al-sa'irin* defines *irādah* as follows:

> It is the voluntary answer (in actions) to the summons of the Real (*Haqīqah*).

Here we should point out that the *irādah* is defined as the first stage in the sense that it is the first stage after a chain of other stages has been passed, stages that are called 'preparations' (*bidāyat*), 'doors' (*abwāb*), 'conduct' (*mu'āmilat*) and 'manners' (*akhlāq*). Thus *irādah* is the first stage, in the terminology of the *'urafā'*, in that it signifies a genuine gnostic awakening.

Rūmi describes the principle that 'the end is the return to the beginning' as follows:

> The parts face towards the Whole,
> Nightingales are in love with the rose's face;
> Whatever comes from the sea to the sea returns,
> And everything goes back to its source;
> Like the streams rushing down from mountain tops,
> My soul, burning with love, longs to leave the body.

Rūmi opens his *Mathnawī* by inviting the reader to listen to the plaintive cries of the reed, as it complains of its separation from the reed bed. Thus in those first lines Rūmi is actually bringing up the first stage of the *'ārif*, that is *irādah*, a desire to return to one's origins, which is accompanied by a feeling of separation and loneliness. Rūmi says:

> Listen to the reed as its story it relates
> And of its separation it complains.
> Since the time that from the reed bed was I taken,
> At my strains man and woman have lamented.
> O, a heart I seek that is torn with the pain of separation
> That it may hear the tale of my longing for return.

Whoever remains distant from his origins
Seeks again the life of reunion.

To sum up, *irādah* is a longing that makes its appearance in the human being and motivates him to seek reunion with the Real, a reunion that puts an end to his feelings of alienation, loneliness and helplessness.

Exercise and Self-Discipline

After the stage of *irādah* comes that of exercise (*riyāḍah*) and preparedness. The preparedness is termed *riyāḍah*. Nowadays this term is generally misunderstood and is taken to mean self-mortification. In some religions the principle of self-mortification is hallowed. Perhaps the best examples of this are to be seen in the Yogis of India. In the terminology of Ibn Sīnā, however, the word is not used in this sense. The original meaning of this Arabic word is 'to exercise', or 'to break in a colt'. Thereafter the word was applied to physical exercise, a sense it still bears today. The *'urafā'* borrowed this word and used it to mean exercising the soul and preparing it for the illumination of the light of knowledge (*ma'rifah*). It is in this sense that the word is used in the passage above.

Ibn Sīnā then declares this exercising and preparing of the soul to be directed towards three aims. The first relates to external matters and entails removing all distractions and causes of negligence (*ghaflah*) in order to clear the path of all but the Real. The second relates to the balance of inner forces and the removal of agitations from the soul, which he has described as the submission of the 'commanding self' (*al-nafs al-'ammārah*) to the 'contented self' (*al-nafs al-mutma'innah*). The third relates to qualitative changes in the soul, which he calls 'rendering the heart subtle'.

The first (of the three aims of *riyāḍah*) is aided by true *zuhd* (i.e. *zuhd* removes from the path the impediments and the preoccupations that hinder and cause neglect). The second is aided by several things: worship infused with (presence of heart, concentration and) reflection; melody that serves to strengthen the self and whose accompanying words have an effect on the heart (such as melodious reciting of the Qur'ān, supplications and litanies and the singing of mystic poetry); the instructive speech of a pure, eloquent person who speaks gently and effectively in the manner of a guide. The third goal is aided by subtle thoughts (contemplating subtle and delicate ideas and meanings that lead to spiritual refinement) and a chaste love (a love that is spiritual and not physical and sensual), which is directed by the virtues of the beloved and not ruled over by sensuality.

Then, when *irādah* and *riyāḍah* reach a certain degree, flashes (*khalāṣat*) of the dawning light of the Real will descend upon him. Delightful as they are, they are momentary like flashes of lightning appearing and instantly vanishing. These 'moments' (*awqāt*) increase in frequency with greater diligence in *riyāḍah*. As the believer advances deeper into this stage, the flashes descend upon him even when he is not exercising. Often now he will glance at something and his glance will be deflected from it towards the Holy, bringing to his attention some aspect of the Divine, and a state of trance (*kalseh*) will descend upon him, in which it is as if he sees God in everything.

It may be at this stage that his states of trance overwhelm him, disturbing his equanimity. Anyone near him will notice the change.

Then he reaches a point in his exercises when his 'moments' change into stable tranquillity, the brief snatches become familiar and the flashes become a prolonged blaze. He achieves an enduring gnostic state, which permanently accompanies him and from which he derives an ecstatic delight. And when it departs him he becomes sad and bewildered.

It may also be at this stage that his state will become apparent to others; but as he progresses deeper into this gnosis, its appearance will be less detectable in him and he will be absent when appearing to be present and travelling when appearing to be still.

This passage calls to mind a sentence spoken by 'Alī ibn Abi Talib (A) to his disciple Kumayl ibn Ziyad about the 'friends of God' (*awliya' al-Haqq*), who exist in every age:

> Knowledge has led them to the reality of insight, and they are in contact with the spirit of certainty. They find easy what is regarded as rough by those who live in comfort and luxury. They are intimate with what terrifies the ignorant. They are in the company of people with their bodies, yet their souls are lodged in the highest realm. (*Nahj al-balāghah*, Hikam, No. 147)

Until this stage, perhaps, this state of gnosis will occur to him only occasionally. Thereafter it will gradually become such that it is available to him whenever he wants.

He now advances further, until his state no longer depends on his own wish. Whenever he observes a thing he sees other than it (i.e. God), even if his observation is not for the sake of reflection. So, the opportunity presents itself to ascend from the plane of false appearances to the plane of Truth. He becomes stabilized upon it, while (in the world) he is surrounded by the heedless.

Up until this point we have been dealing with the stage of exercise, self-discipline, struggle and the spiritual itinerary. Now the *'ārif* has reached his goal.

When he crosses from the stage of *riyāḍah* to that of attainment, his inner self becomes like a clear mirror facing in the direction of the Real. Sublime delights shower down on him and he rejoices for what he sees in himself of the Real. Now (like one viewing an image in a mirror, who looks either at the image or at the mirror reflecting the image) he is perplexed by two views: the view of the Real and the view of his own self.

Then he becomes oblivious to himself and views only the Holy. And if he notices himself it is because he is the viewer, not because he is admiring his own beauty (as when one looks at an image in a mirror and sees the image only, and, although one does not pay attention specifically to the mirror, nevertheless one sees it as one looks at the image; the mirror is not viewed for its own beauty). It is at this point that the wayfarer attains union (and his journey from *khalq* to *Haqq* becomes complete).

This brings to an end our summary of the ninth section of Ibn Sīnā's Ishārāt and his account of the journey from creation (*khalq*) to God (*Haqq*). An additional point is that the *'urafā'* believe in four journeys: *sayr min al-khalq ila al-Haqq, sayr bi al-Haqq a al-Haqq, sayr min al-Haqq ila al-khalq bi al-Haqq, sayr fi al-khalq bi al-Haqq* (the journey from Creation to God; the journey with God in God; the journey with God from God to Creation; and finally, the journey in Creation with God).

The first journey is from creatures to the Creator. The second is in the Creator, in the course of which journey the *'ārif* becomes acquainted with His Qualities and Names and himself becomes adorned with the same. In the third journey, he returns towards Creation, without becoming separated from God, in order to guide the people. While he is still united with God, the *'ārif* makes the fourth journey with and among the people and seeks to guide their affairs so as to lead them towards God.

The summary from Ibn Sīnā's *al-'Ishārāt* given above is related to the first of these journeys. He also gives a brief account of the second journey, but it is not necessary for our purposes to include it. Khwājah Nāṣir al-Dīn al-Ṭūsī, in his commentary on *al-'Ishārāt*, says that Ibn Sīnā has explained the first journey of the *'ārif* in nine stages. Three stages are related to the beginning of the journey, three to the journey from its beginning to its end and three are related to the arrival or the union. Some reflection on Ibn Sīnā's account makes the point clear.

By '*riyāḍah*' which is translated as 'exercise', Ibn Sīnā means the exercises in self-discipline that the *'ārif* performs. There are many of these, and the *'ārif* must follow a chain of stations in these exercises too. On this matter Ibn Sīnā is extremely brief, yet the *'urafā'* have discussed this matter in depth and one can find details in their works.

Some Terms of 'Irfān

In this section we intend to cover some of the special terms used in *'irfān*. The *'urafā'* have coined a large number of terms, and without an acquaintance with them it is not possible to understand many of their ideas. In fact, one may draw a conclusion quite the opposite of the one intended. This is one of the characteristics of *'irfān*. However, of necessity, every branch of learning has its own set of terms. The commonly understood meanings of words used are often unable to meet the precise requirements of a science or discipline.

Thus there is no option but that in every discipline certain words be selected to convey certain specific meanings, thus coining for the practitioners of that discipline a special vocabulary. *'Irfān* is no exception to this general rule. Moreover, the *'urafā'* insist that none but those initiated to the Path should know their ideas, because – in their view, at least – none but the *'urafā'* are able to understand these concepts. Thus the *'urafā'*, unlike the masters of other sciences and crafts, deliberately try to keep their meanings concealed so that the vocabulary they devised has not only the usual aspects of a terminology but also an enigmatic aspect, leaving us to try to discover the enigma's secret.

A third aspect must occasionally be taken into account, which increases the difficulty. This arises from the practice of some *'urafā'* – at least, those called the Malamatiyyah – who adopted an inverted form of ostentation (*riya' ma'kūs*) in their discourses by cultivating ill fame instead of good name and fame among the people. This meant that, by contrast with those afflicted with the vice of ostentation (*riya'*), who wish to make themselves appear better than they actually are, the *'urafā'* practise self-reproach in a bid to be considered good by God and yet bad by the people. In this way they seek to cure themselves of all types of ostentation and egoism.

It is said that the majority of the *'urafā'* of Khurasan were Malamatiyyah. Some even believe that Ḥāfiẓ was one. Such words as *rindi* (libertinism), *lā ubāligarī* (carelessness); *qalandarī* (mendicancy), *qallāshī* (pauperism) and the like signify indifference to Creation, not to the Creator. Ḥāfiẓ has spoken a lot on the subject of giving the impression of doing things that earn one a bad name, while being inwardly good and righteous. A few examples:

An adherent to the path of love need not worry about a bad name.
The Shaykh-e San'an had his robe in pawn at a gambling house.
Even if I heed the reproaches of claimants,
My drunken libertinism would not leave me.
The asceticism of raw libertines is like a village path,
But what good would the thought of reform do to one of worldwide ill fame like me?
Through love of wine I brought my self-image to naught,
In order to destroy the imprint of self-devotion.
How happily passes the time of a mendicant, who, in his spiritual journey,
Keeps reciting the Name of the Lord, while playing with the beads of his pagan rosary.

However, Ḥāfiẓ elsewhere condemns the ostentatious cultivation of ill fame just as he condemns sanctimoniousness:

My heart, let me guide thee to the path of salvation:
Neither boast of your profligacy, nor publicize your piety.

Rūmi defends the Malamatiyyah in the following verses:

Behold, do not despise those of bad name,
Attention must be given to their secrets.
How often gold has been painted black,
For the fear of being stolen and lost.

This issue is one of those over which the *fuqaha'* have found fault with the *'urafā'*. Just as Islamic law condemns sanctimony (*riya'*) – considering it a form of *shirk* – so too it condemns this seeking of reproach. It says that a believer has no right to compromise his social standing and honour. Many *'urafā'* also condemn this practice.

In any case, the practice, which has been common among some *'urafā'*, led them to wrap their ideas in words that conveyed the very opposite of what they meant. Naturally this makes understanding their intentions a good deal harder.

Abū al-Qāsim Qushayri, one of the leading figures of *'irfān*, declares in his *Risalah* that the *'urafā'* intentionally speak in enigmas, for they do not want the uninitiated to become aware of their customs, states and their aims. This, he tells us, is because they are incapable of being understood by the uninitiated.[18]

The technical terms of *'irfān* are many. Some of them are related to theoretical *'irfān*, that is to say, to the mystic world view and its ontology.

These terms resemble the terms of philosophy and are relatively recent. The father of all or most of them was Ibn al-'Arabi. It is extremely difficult to understand them. They include *fayḍ al-'aqdas* (the holiest grace), *fayḍ al-muqaddas* (the holy grace), *al-wujūd al-munbasiṭ* (the extending existence), *haqq mākhluq bi ḥadarat al-khams*, *maqām al-'ahadiyyah* (the station of uniqueness), *maqām al-wahidiyyah* (the station of oneness) and so on.

The others are related to practical *'irfān*, i.e. the *sayr wa sulūk* of *'irfān*. These terms, being of necessity related to the human being, are similar to the concepts of psychology and ethics. In fact, they are part of a special type of psychology, a psychology that is indeed empirical and experimental. According to the *'urafā'*, philosophers – and, for that matter, psychologists, theologians and sociologists and other classes of scholars – who have not entered this valley to observe and study the self at close hand have no right to make judgements on this subject.

The terms of practical *'irfān*, as opposed to those of theoretical *'irfān*, are ancient, dating from as early as the third/ninth century, from the time of Dhu al-Nun, Ba Yazid and Junayd. Here we shall look at some of these terms, according to definitions ascribed to them by Qushayri and others.

1. Waqt *(Moment)*

In the previous section we came across this word in a passage from Ibn Sīnā. Now let us turn to the *'urafā'*'s definitions of it. What Qushayri has to say on this subject is, in brief, that the concept of *waqt* is relative. Each state or condition that befalls the *'ārif* requires of him a special behavioural response. The particular state that calls for a particular kind of behaviour is termed the 'moment' of a particular *'ārif*.

Of course, another *'ārif* in the same state may have a different moment, or the same *'ārif* in other circumstances may have a different moment that will require of him a different behaviour and a different responsibility. An *'ārif* must be familiar with these moments, that is, he must recognize each state that descends upon him from the unseen, as well as the responsibilities that accompany it. The *'ārif* must also count his moment as precious. Thus it is said that 'the *'ārif* is the son of the moment'. Rūmi says:

> The *ṣūfi* is to be the son of the moment, O friend;
> Saying 'tomorrow ' is not a convention of the Way.

The Arabic *waqt* has the same sense as *dam* (breath) and *'aysh-e naqd* (cash of life' or cash pleasure) of Persian poetry. Ḥāfiẓ especially makes much mention of 'the cash of life' and 'counting the moment as precious.' Some of those who are uninformed or who wish to exploit Ḥāfiẓ as an excuse for their own perverseness claim that Ḥāfiẓ's use of such words is an invitation to material pleasures and indifference to the cares of the future, to the hereafter and God – an attitude that is known in the West as Epicureanism.

The notions of 'counting the moment as precious' or 'ready pleasure' are recurring motifs in Ḥāfiẓ's poetry. He mentions it perhaps thirty times or more. It is obvious that since in his poetry Ḥāfiẓ observes the *'urafā*'s practice of speaking in enigmas and symbols, many of the ideas in his ambiguous verses may, on the surface, seem perverse. The following verses may serve to dispel any such illusions.

Whether I drink wine or not, what have I to do with anyone?
I am the guardian of my secrets and gnostic of my moment.
Get up, let's take the ṣūfi's cloak to the tavern,
And the theopathetic ravings to the bazaar of nonsense;
Let's be ashamed of these polluted woollens,
If the name of miracle be given to this virtue and skill,
If the heart fails to value the moment and does nothing,
Now the moments will bring much shame or us.
In a land, at morning time, a wayfarer
Said this to a companion on the way,
O ṣūfi, the wine becomes pure
When it remains in its bottle for forty days.
God is disdainful of that woollen cloak a hundred times
That has a hundred idols up its sleeve;
I see not the joy of 'aysh in anyone,
Nor the cure of a heart nor care for religion;
The interiors have become gloomy, perhaps perchance,
A lamp may be kindled by some recluse.
Neither is the memorizer alone [with God] during lessons,
Nor does the scholar enjoy any knowledge of certainty.

Ḥāfiẓ wrote many ambiguous verses on this subject. For example:

Grab the pleasure of the moment, for Adam did not tarry
More than a moment in the garden of Paradise.

Qushayri states that what is meant by 'the *ṣūfi* is the son of his moment' is that he performs whatever has utmost priority for him in his current 'state' (*ḥāl*);

and what is meant by 'the moment is a sharp sword' is that the requirement (*ḥukm*) of each moment is cutting and decisive; to fail to meet it is fatal.

2. & 3. Ḥāl *(State) and* Maqām *(Position)*

Well known among the terms of *'irfān* are *ḥāl* (state) and *maqām* (position). The state is what descends upon the *'ārif's* heart regardless of his will, while his position is what he earns and attains through his efforts. The state quickly passes but the position is lasting. The states are like flashes of lightning that quickly vanish. Ḥāfiẓ says:

A lightning flash from Layla's house at dawn,
Goodness knows what it did to the love-torn heart of Majnun.

And Sa'di says:

Someone asked of him who had lost his son,
O enlightened soul, O wise old man,
All the way from Egypt you smelt his shirt,
Why could you not see him in the well of Canaan?
Said he, my state is like a lightning flash,
A moment it's there, another moment gone;
Often it lifts me to the highest sky,
And often I see not what is at my feet.
Should a dervish in his state persist,
The two worlds will lie in his hands.

We have already quoted above the following sentence from the *Nahj al-balāghah*, which is relevant here too:

He revives his intellect and mortifies himself, until his body becomes lean and his coarseness turns into refinement. Then an effulgence of extreme brightness shines forth to illuminate the path before him ... (Khutab, No. 220, p. 337)

The *'urafā'* call these flashes *lawa'ih*, *lawami'* or *tawali'*, depending upon their degree of intensity and duration.

4. & 5. Qabd *(Contraction) and* Bast *(Expansion)*

These two words are also among those to which the *'urafā'* apply a special meaning, They refer to two contrasting spiritual states of the *'ārif's* soul; *qabd* (contraction) refers to a sense of desolation felt by it, while *bast* (expansion) is a state of expansion and joy. The *'urafā'* have discussed these two states and their respective causes extensively.

6. & 7. Jam' *(Gatheredness) and* Farq *(Separation)*
These two terms are much used by the *'urafā'*. According to Qushayri: 'What comes from the creature or is acquired by the creature and is worthy of the station of creaturehood is called *farq*; what comes from God – such as inspiration – is called *jam'*. He whom God makes halt at the station (*maqām*) of obedience and worship is at the station of *farq*; and he to whom God reveals His favours is at the station of *jam'*.

Ḥāfiẓ says:

Listen to me with the ear of awareness and strive for pleasure,
For these words came at dawn from the unseen caller;
Stop thinking of 'separation' so that you may become 'gathered',
For, as a rule, the angel enters as soon as the Devil leaves.

8. & 9. Ghaybah *(Absence) and* Ḥuḍūr *(Presence)*
Ghaybah is a state of unawareness of Creation that occasionally descends upon the *'ārif*, in which he forgets himself and his surroundings. The *'ārif* becomes unaware of himself owing to his presence (*ḥuḍūr*) before God. In the words of a poet:

I am not so occupied with you, O you of heavenly face,
For the memories of bygone selfhood still flash within my heart.

In this state of 'presence' with God and 'absence' from himself and his surroundings, it is possible that important occurrences take place around him without his becoming aware of them. In this connection the *'urafā'* have many famous stories. Qushayri writes that Abū Hafs al-Haddad of Nishabur left his trade as a blacksmith because of one incident. Once, as he was busy working in his shop, someone recited a verse of the Holy Qur'ān. This put al-Haddad in a state that rendered him totally heedless of his surroundings. Without realizing it he removed a piece of red-hot iron from the furnace with his bare hand. His apprentice cried out to him and he returned to his senses. Thereupon he gave up that trade.

Qushayri also writes that al Shibli once came to see Junayd while Junayd's wife was also sitting there. Junayd's wife made a movement as if to leave, but Junayd stopped her saying that al-Shibli was in a 'state' and heedless of her. She sat a while. Junayd conversed with al-Shibli for some time until al Shibli slowly began to cry. Junayd then turned to his wife, telling her to veil herself for al-Shibli was returning to his senses.

Ḥāfiẓ says:

As every report that I heard has led to perplexity,
From now on it is I, the cupbearer, and the state of heedlessness.
If it is presence you want do not be absent from Him, Ḥāfiẓ,
When you meet what you desire, abandon the world and forget it.

It is along these lines that the *'urafā'* explain the states of the *awliya'* during their prayers, in which they became totally heedless of themselves and of their surroundings. Later we shall see that there is a level higher than 'absence', and it was this that to which the *awliya'* were subject.

10.,11.,12. & 13. Dhawq, Shurb, Sukr *and* Riyy

The *'urafā'* believe that mere conceptual knowledge of anything has no attraction; the attractiveness of a thing and the ability to inspire passion follow 'tasting'. At the end of the eighth section of his *al-'Ishārāt* Ibn Sīnā mentions this; he gives the example of a man who is impotent. He says that, however much one may describe sexual pleasure to a person devoid of the sexual instinct or to one who has never tasted of this pleasure, he will never be sexually aroused. Thus *dhawq* is the tasting of pleasure. In the terminology of *'irfān* it means the actual perception of the pleasure derived from manifestations (*tajalliyat*) and revelations (*mukāshafāt*). *Dhawq* is the beginning of this; its continuance is called *shurb* (drinking), its enjoyment *sukr* (intoxication) and satiation *riyy* (thirst-quenching).

The *'urafā'* are of the view that whatever is derived from *dhawq* is 'an appearance of intoxication' (*tasakur*) and not 'intoxication' (*sukr*) itself. Intoxication, they say, is obtained from drinking (*shurb*). What is obtained by having one's 'thirst quenched' (*riyy*) is 'sobriety' (*saḥw*), or the return to the senses. It is in this sense that the *'urafā'* have often mentioned *sharab* and *mey*, which would ordinarily mean wine.

14., 15. & 16. Maḥw, Maḥq *and* Saḥw

In the *'urafā'*s discourses, the words *maḥw* (effacement) and *saḥw* (sobriety) are very common. What is meant by *maḥw* is that the *'ārif* reaches such a stage that his ego becomes effaced in the Divine Essence. He no longer perceives his own ego as others do. And if this effacement reaches such a point that the effects of his ego are also effaced, they call this *maḥq* (obliteration). *Maḥw* and *maḥq* are both higher than the stage of *ghaybah*, as indicated above. *Maḥw* and *maḥq* mean *fana'* (annihilation). Yet it is possible for an *'ārif* to return from the state of *fana'* to the state of *baqa'* (abiding in God). It does not, however, mean a retrogression from a higher state; rather it means that the *'ārif* finds subsistence in God. This state, loftier even than *maḥw* and *maḥq*, is called *saḥw*.

17. Khawāṭir *(Thoughts)*

The *'urafā'* call the thoughts and inspirations cast into their hearts *wāridāt* (arrivals). These *wāridāt* are sometimes in the form of states of 'contraction' or 'expansion', joy or sadness and sometimes in the form of words and speech. In the latter case they are called *khawāṭir* (sing. *khatirah*). It is as if someone inside him is speaking to the *'ārif*.

The *'urafā'* have much to say on the subject of *khawāṭir*. They say that they can be *rahmani* (i.e. from God), *shaytani* (inspired by the Devil) or *nafsani* (musings of the self). The *khawāṭir* constitute one of the dangers of the path, for it is possible that owing to some deviation or error the Devil may come to dominate the human being. In the words of the Qur'ān:

> *Verily the satans inspire their friends . . .* (6:121)

They say that the more adept should be able to discern whether the *khatirah* is from God or from the Devil. The fundamental criterion is to see what a particular *khatirah* commands or prohibits; if its command or prohibition is contrary to the dicta of the Sharī'ah, then it is definitely satanic. The Qur'ān says:

> *Shall I inform you upon whom the Satans descend? They descend upon every lying, sinful one.* (26:221–222)

18.,19. & 20. Qalb, Rūḥ *and* Sirr

The *'urafā'* have different words for the human soul; sometimes they call it *nafs* (self), sometimes *qalb* (heart), sometimes *rūḥ* (spirit) and sometimes *sirr* (mystery). When the human soul is dominated and ruled by desires and passions they call it *nafs*. When it reaches the stage of bearing Divine knowledge, it is called *qalb*. When the light of Divine love dawns within it, they call it *rūḥ*. And when it reaches the stage of *shuhūd*, they call it *sirr*. Of course, the *'urafā'* believe in levels beyond this, which they call *khafī* (the hidden) and *akhfā* (the most hidden).

ʿIrfān: *Islamic Mysticism*

Notes

1. Murtaḍā Muṭahharī, *An Introduction to Ilm al kalām*, transl. by ʿAlī Quli Qarāī, *Al-Tawḥīd*, Vol. II, No. 2
2. R. A. Nicholson, *Mysticism in the Legacy of Islam*, ed. by Sir Thomas Arnold and Alfred Guillaume (London, 1931), pp. 211–12
3. ibid.
4. ibid.
5. Dr Qāsim Ghani, *Tarikh e Taṣawwuf Dar Islam*, p. 19
6. Fārid al Dīn al Aṭṭār, *Tadhkirat al-awliya*
7. Abū Nasr al Sarraj, *al-Luma*, p. 427
8. Dr. Qāsim Ghani, op. cit.
9. Abbas al Qummī, *Safinat al Bihār*
10. Harith al Muhasibi, not Ḥaṣan al Baṣri
11. Nicholson, op. cit., p. 214
12. Dr Qāsim Ghani, op. cit., p. 462
13. op cit., p. 55
14. Abū Abd al Rahman al Sulami, *Tabqat al ṣūfiyyah*, p. 206
15. Author's work, *Ilal e girayeh be maddehgari*
16. Ḥāfiẓ is the most beloved figure of Persian poetry in Iran
17. Aḥmad Jāmī was known as Shaykh al Isma
18. al-Qushayri, *Risalah*, p. 33

PART FOUR

Islamic Law

Introduction

The study of jurisprudence is one of the most extensive studies in Islam. Its history is older than that of all the other Islamic studies. It has been studied on a very wide scale throughout the whole of its existence. So many jurisprudents have appeared in Islam that their numbers cannot be counted.

*The Word Jurisprudence (*fiqh*) in the Qur'ān and the Traditions*

The words *fiqh* and *tafaqquh*, both meaning 'profound understanding', have been often used in the Qur'ān and in the Traditions. In the Holy Qur'ān we read: 'Why should not a company from every group of them go forth to gain profound understanding [*tafaqquh*] in religion and to warn their people when they return to them, so that they may beware?'. (9:122)

In the Traditions, the Holy Prophet has told us: 'Whoever from my nation learns forty Traditions; God will raise him as a *faqīh* [jurisprudent], an *'ālim* [a man of *'ilm* or knowledge].'

We do not know for sure if the *ulamā'* and *fuzalā*, the learned and distinguished of the Prophet's companions, were called *fuqahā* (jurisprudents), but it is certain that this name was applied from the time of those who had not themselves witnessed the Prophet but had witnessed those who had (*tabi'in*).

Seven of the *tabi'in* were called 'the seven jurisprudents'. The year 94 AH, which was the year of the death of Imām 'Alī ibn Husein (d) and the year in which Sa'id ibn Masib and 'Urwat ibn Zubayr of the 'seven jurisprudents' and Sa'id ibn Jabir and others of the jurisprudents of Medina also passed away, was called the 'year of the jurisprudents'. Thereafter the word *fuqahā* gradually came to be applied to those with knowledge of Islam, especially of the laws of Islam.

The holy Imāms have repeatedly made use of these words. They have commanded some of their companions to profound understanding (*taffaqquh*) or have designated them masters of jurisprudence or *fuqahā* (the plural of *faqīh*, a jurisprudent). The prominent pupils of the Imāms during that same period were known as Shī'ite *fuqahā*.

The Word Jurisprudence (Fiqh) in the Terminology of the 'Ulamā'

In the terminology of the Qur'ān and the Sunnah, *fiqh* is the extensive, profound knowledge of Islamic instructions and realities and has no special relevance to any particular division. In the terminology of the ulamā', however, it gradually came to be applied especially to profound understanding of the Islamic laws. The ulamā' of Islam have divided the Islamic teachings into three parts:

First, the realities and beliefs, the aims of which are awareness, faith and certitude, and which are related to the heart and the mind, embracing issues such as those related to the unseen past and the unseen future, to prophethood, revelation, angels and the imamate.

Second, morality and self-perfection, the goals of which are the spiritual qualities of being, including issues such as cautiousness of God (*taqwā*), justice (*'adālat*), generosity, courage, fortitude and patience (*ṣabr*), the state of being satisfied and content with God (*riẓā*), firmness on the true path (*istiqāmat*) and so on.

Third, the laws and issues of actions, which are related to the special external actions that human beings must perform and how the actions they perform are to be and are not to be.

The jurisprudents of Islam have termed this last division *fiqh* (jurisprudence), perhaps on the basis that since the early days of Islam the laws were subject to the most attention and queries. Therefore, those whose speciality was in this subject came to be known as the *fuqaha* (jurisprudents).

Two Types of Law

Here we must mention some of the special terms used by jurisprudents. Among these are the names of the two divisions the jurisprudents have made of the Divine Laws: the laws of (human) duty (*ḥukm taklifī*) and the laws of (human) situations (*ḥukm waẓ'ī*). The laws of duty include those duties that relate to obligation, prohibition, desirability, undesirability and simple permissibility. These are termed 'the five laws' (*aḥkām khamsah*).

The jurisprudents say that in the view of Islam no single action is devoid of one of these five laws. It may be obligatory (*wājib*), meaning that it must be done and must not be left undone, such as the five daily ritual prayers, or it is forbidden (*ḥarām*), meaning that it is prohibited and must be avoided, such as lies, injustice, drinking alcohol and the like; or it may be desirable (*mustaḥāb*), meaning that it is good to do but leaving it undone is not a crime or sin, including such things as praying in a mosque; or it is undesirable (*makrūḥ*), meaning that it is bad to do but if done no sin is committed, for example talking about worldly affairs in a mosque, which is a place of worship; or it is permissible (*mubāḥ*), meaning that the doing of it and the not doing of it are exactly equal, and this includes most actions.

The laws regarding situation are not like the laws regarding duty. The laws regarding duty consist of 'do's' and 'don't's', commands and prohibitions, or the giving of permissions, while the laws of situation apply to situations such as marriage and ownership and the rights involved therein.

Types of Obligation

The obligations, that is, the actions that are obligatory are divided into many different classifications. First, they are divided into *ta'abbudi* and *tawassuli.*

Ta'abbudi means those things whose correct and valid performance depends on the intention (*niyyat*) of nearness of God. That is, if the obligatory action is performed solely with the intention of approaching the Divine without any worldly, material motive, it is correct and valid and, if not, it is invalid. Prayer and fasting are both *wājib ta'abbudi.*

Wajib tawassuli, however, is an action that, even if performed without the intention of nearness to God, still meets an obligation and fulfils a duty, for example, obedience to one's parents. Another example is the performance of responsibilities towards society, such as the performance of work that a person has undertaken to do for a certain payment. Absolute loyalty to all one's promises falls within the same definition.

Obligations may alternatively be divided into *'ainī* and *kifā'i.* An *'ainī* obligation is one that is obligatory on every individual, such as prayer and fasting, whereas a *kifā'i* obligation is one that is obligatory on the general Muslim population and that, when performed by one or a group of them, is no longer obligatory on any of them. This type of obligation includes the needs of the community, such as the need for doctors, soldiers, judges, farmers, traders and so on. In the same class are the burials of deceased Muslims, which the general Muslim population is commanded to perform: once some people have done this, the duty is no longer obligatory on any others.

Another way the obligations are divided is into *ta'yīni* and *takhyīri.* A *ta'yīni* obligation is the requirement that a specified act must be performed, such as the daily prayers, fasting, *ḥajj*, *khums*, *zakāt*, adhering to what is recognized as good (*amr bil ma'rūf*), struggle (*jihād*), etc.

A *takhyīri* obligation, on the other hand, is a duty to perform one thing of two or several things. For example, if a person has intentionally not fasted one day during the holy month of Ramaḍān, it is a *takhyīri* obligation for him to free a slave or to feed sixty poor people or to fast for two consecutive months.

Yet another way the obligations are divided is into *nafsi* and *muqaddami*. A *nafsi* obligation means that the duty itself is the concern of the Sharī'ah, and it is demanded for its own sake, while a *muqaddami* obligation is obligatory for the sake of something else.

For example, to save a respected person's life is obligatory but this obligation is not a preparation for some other obligation. However, the actions needed in preparation for saving him, such as acquiring a rope or a boat to rescue a non-swimmer who has fallen in a river, are also obligatory, not for their own sake but as a preparation for a different obligation, that of saving the person's life.

A further example is the *ḥajj*. The actions of the *ḥajj* are themselves obligatory, but the acquiring of a passport and ticket to travel there are obligatory in preparation. Prayer is a *nafsi* obligation, while to take *wuẓū* or *ghusl* or *tayammum* as a substitute for them in order to enter the state of cleanliness necessary for prayer are not obligatory until the time of prayer has begun, and then not for themselves, but as an obligatory preparation for the obligatory prayer. Thus the *ḥajj* and the ritual prayers are both *nafsi* obligations, while acquiring a passport or washing are *muqaddami* obligations.

Brief History of Jurisprudence and Jurisprudents

As was mentioned in the previous sections, one of the preparations for learning about any field of knowledge is to pay attention to the views and ideas of the leading personalities in that field, and to the important books on the subject.

Jurisprudence has a continuous history of eleven hundred years, during which books have been written and compiled that are still studied today and centres for the study of jurisprudence and related disciplines have existed. Masters have trained students and those students in their turn have trained other students, and this practice has continued down the ages until today, with never a break in the relationship between master and pupil.

Other fields, of course, such as philosophy, logic, arithmetic and medicine have been studied for far longer, and books exist on these subjects that are older than the books on jurisprudence. Perhaps in no other subject, however, has the relationship between master and pupil been so splendidly preserved. Even where such constant relationships existed in other subjects, still they are particular to Islamic studies. Only in the Islamic world does the system of teaching and studying have a continuous, uninterrupted history going back over a thousand years.

The Shī'ite Jurisprudents

We shall begin our review of the history of the Shī'ite jurisprudents from the period of the Imāms' 'minor occultation' (260–320 AH), and this for two reasons:

First, the period prior to the 'minor occultation' was the period of the presence of the holy Imāms, at which time, although there were jurisprudents and *mujtahid*s who were able to make their own decisions, who were indeed encouraged by the Imāms to do so, yet they were outshone by the brilliance of the Imāms. Moreover, people tried as far as possible to refer questions to the Imāms, as original sources, and to defer to their judgement. Even the jurisprudents, because of distances and other difficulties, used to place their own problems before the Imāms whenever they could. But thereafter, when access to the Imāms was not available, people had recourse instead to jurisprudents.

Second, in formal, classified jurisprudence, none of the books from the period of the 'minor occultation' or earlier have reached us, or, if any have, I have no information about them.

All the same, among the Shī'ites there were great jurisprudents during the days of the holy Imāms, whose value becomes apparent when one compares them with the jurisprudents of their period from other sects. The Sunni ibn Nadin writes in his book *Fihrist* about Husein ibn Sa'id Ahwazi and his brother, both notable Shī'ite jurisprudents, 'They were the best of those of their time in knowledge of jurisprudence, effects (i.e. writings and compilations) and talents'. In referring to 'Alī ibn Ibrahim Qummī he has the phrase 'among the ulamā' and jurisprudents', and of Muḥammad ibn Ḥasan ibn Aḥmad ibn Walid, he notes that 'he has among books the book *Jam'e fil-fiqh*'.

Apparently these books were compilations of traditions on the varying aspects of jurisprudence that the compilers considered to be reliable, and in accordance with which they acted, together with the comments of the compilers.

The scholar Ḥillī, in the introduction to his book *Mu'tabar* wrote, 'Bearing in mind that our jurisprudents (God be pleased with them) are many and their compilations numerous and to narrate the names of them all is not possible,

I will content myself with those who are the most famous in merit, research and good selection, and with the books of those paragons whose *ijtihād* is mentioned in other undoubtable books as reliable.

> Those I will mention include, from the 'earlier' period (i.e. the period of access to the Imāms), Hassan ibn Mahboub, Aḥmad ibn 'Alī Nasr Bazanti, Husayn ibn Sa'id, Faḍl ibn Shathan, Yunis ibn 'Abd ur-Rahman and, from the later period, Muḥammad ibn Babawayh Qummī (Shaykh Ṣadūq) and Muḥammad ibn Ya'qub Kulayni and from the authors of verdicts (*fatwas*) 'Alī ibn Bībawayh al-Qummī, ibn Jāmīd Iskafi, ibn 'Alī 'Agil, Shaykh Mufīd, Syed Morteza, 'Alam ul Huda and Shaykh Ṭūsī . . .

Notice that, although the first group are quoted as having their own views and good selection and *ijtihād*, they are not mentioned as being masters of verdicts. This is because their books, which were summaries of their *ijtihād*, took the form of collections of traditions and not the form of verdicts.

One of the earliest Shī'ite jurisprudents, from the period of the Imāms' occultation, was 'Alī ibn Babawayh Qummī, who died in 329 AH and was buried in Qum. He was the father of Shaykh Muḥammad ibn 'Alī ibn Babawayh, known as Shaykh Saduq, who is buried near Tehran. The son was learned in traditions, the father in jurisprudence and he compiled a book of his verdicts. Normally this father and son are called Saduqayn.

'Ayashi Samarqandi lived at the same time as 'Alī ibn Babawayh or a little before. The author of a famous commentary of the Qur'ān, he did indeed specialize in commentary, but he is still numbered among the jurisprudents and wrote many books on the subject. Ibn Nadīm writes that the books of this man were readily available in Khorasan, but I have not yet seen his views represented anywhere, and his books on jurisprudence no longer exist.

'Ayashi was originally a Sunni Muslim but later became a Shī'ite. He inherited vast wealth from his father and spent it on collecting and copying books and on teaching and training his students.

Ibn Jāmīd-Iskāfī was one of the teachers of Shaykh Mufīd. It seems he passed away in 381 AH, having purportedly produced fifty books and writings. His views on jurisprudence have always been respected and still are to this day.

Shaykh Mufīd, whose full name was Muḥammad ibn Muḥammad ibn No'mān, was both a *mutakallīm* (theologian) and a jurisprudent. Ibn Nadīm, in the section of his book *Fihrist* in which he discusses Shī'ite *mutakallimīn*, calls him 'ibn Mu'ālim' and praises him. Born in 336 AH, he passed away in 413. His famous book on jurisprudence, *Muqna'ah*, is still used today.

The son-in law of Shaykh Mufīd, Abū Y'ala Ja'fari, tells us that Shaykh Mufīd slept little at night and spent the rest of his time in worship, study and teaching or reciting the Qur'ān.

Seyyid Morteza, known as 'Alam ul Huda, was born in 355 AH and died in 436 AH Allamah Ḥillī called him the teacher of the Shī'ites of the Imāms. He was a master of ethics, theology and jurisprudence. His views on jurisprudence are still studied today. He and his brother, Seyyid Rāḍī, the compiler of the *Nahj ul-balāgha*, both studied under Shaykh Mufīd.

Shaykh Abū J 'afar Ṭūsī, one of the shining stars of the Islamic world, wrote many books on jurisprudence, traditions, commentaries, theology and the transmitters. Originally from Khorasan (in eastern Iran), he was born in 385 AH and after twenty-two years emigrated to Baghdad, which in those days was the great centre of Islamic studies and culture. He stayed in Iraq the rest of his life and after the demise of his teacher, Seyyid Morteza, the directorship of learning and the position of highest reference for verdicts (*fatwas*) was transferred to him.

Shaykh Ṭūsī remained for twelve more years in Baghdad but then, following a series of disturbances in which his house and library were ravaged, he left for Najaf where he formed the famous scholastic centre that still exists today. There, in 460 AH, he passed away.

One of the books on jurisprudence compiled by Shaykh Ṭūsī was called *An-Nihāya* and was used as a textbook for religious students. Another, *Mabsūt*, brought jurisprudence to a new stage and was the most famous Shī'ite book of jurisprudence of its time. In *Khilāf*, he wrote about the views of both Sunni and Shī'ite jurisprudents. He wrote other books about jurisprudence and, until about a century ago, whenever the name Shaykh was mentioned it was understood to mean Shaykh Ṭūsī. Shaykhayn meant Shaykh Ṭūsī and Shaykh Mufīd. According to some books, the daughters of Shaykh Ṭūsī were also distinguished *faqīh*.[1]

Ibn Idrīs Ḥillī, one of the distinguished Shī'ite ulamā', was an Arab, although Shaykh Ṭūsī is believed to have been his maternal grandfather. He is known for the freedom of his thought; he broke away from the awe and reverence in which his grandfather, Shaykh Ṭūsī, was held and his criticisms of the jurisprudents bordered on impertinence. He died in 598 AH at the age of fifty-five.

Shaykh Abūl-Qāsim J'afar ibn Ḥaṣan ibn Yahya ibn Sa'id Ḥillī, known as Muḥaqqiq Ḥillī, wrote many books about jurisprudence, among them *Sharay'e*, *Ma'arej* and *al-Mukhtasar an-naf'i*. He was the student of ibn Idrīs Ḥillī and the teacher of Allamah Ḥillī to whom we shall refer shortly. In jurisprudence he has no superior. Whenever the word *Muḥaqqiq* is used in this context it refers to him. Great philosophers and mathematicians used to consult him and attend his lessons on jurisprudence. The books of Muḥaqqiq, especially the book *Sharāi'*, have been and still are textbooks for students and have been the subject of commentaries by many other jurisprudents.

Ibn Ḥaṣan ibn Yusef ibn 'Alī ibn Muṭahhar Ḥillī, famous as 'Allamah Ḥillī, was one of the prodigies of the age. He wrote books about jurisprudence, principles, theology, logic, philosophy, transmitters and many other things. Around a hundred of his books have been recognized, some of which, such as *Tadhkirat ul-fuqahā*, are alone enough to indicate his genius. Allamah wrote many books on jurisprudence, which have mostly, like the books of Muḥaqqiq, been commented on by the jurisprudents who succeeded him. His famous books on jurisprudence include *Irshād*, *Tabṣiral al-Muta'alimin*, *Qawa'id*, *Taḥrir*, *Tadhkirat ul-fuqahā*, *Mukhtalif ash-shia'* and *Mutaha*. He studied under various teachers: jurisprudence under his paternal uncle, Muḥaqqiq Ḥillī, philosophy under Khawajeh Nāṣir ud-Dīn Ṭūsī and Sunni jurisprudence under the ulamā' of the Sunnis. He was born in the year 648 AH and passed away in 726 AH.

Muḥammad ibn Makki, known as Shahīd Awwal ('the First Martyr'), one of the great Shī'ite jurisprudents, ranks with Muḥaqqiq Ḥillī and 'Allamah Ḥillī. He was from Jabal 'Āmel, an area in present-day southern Lebanon, which is one of the oldest centres of Shī'ites and is still today a Shī'ite area. Shahīd Awwal was born in 734 AH and in 786 AH, according to the *fatwa* of a jurisprudent from the Māliki sect, which was endorsed by a jurisprudent of the Shaf'i sect, he was martyred. He was a pupil of the students of 'Allamah Ḥillī, among them Allamah's son, Fakhr ul-Muḥaqqiqin. The most famous books of Shahīd Awwal on jurisprudence include *Al-lum'ah*, which he composed during the brief period he remained in prison awaiting his martyrdom. Amazingly, this noble book was subject to a commentary two centuries later by another great jurisprudent who suffered the same fate as the author, receiving the cognomen Shahīd al-Thānī ('The Second Martyr'). The famous book *Sharh ul-lum'ah*, which has been the foremost textbook of students of jurisprudence ever since is the commentary of Shahīd Thānī. Other books of Shahīd Awwal include *Dorar*, *Dhikrā*, *Bayan*, *Alfiyeh* and *Qawa'id*. All of the books of the First Martyr are among the priceless writings of jurisprudence.

Shahīd Awwal came from a very distinguished family, and the generations that succeeded him preserved this honour. He had three sons who were all ulamā' and jurisprudents, and his wife and daughter were likewise jurisprudents.

Shaykh 'Alī ibn Abūl ul-Alā Karaki, known as Muḥaqqiq Karaki or Muḥaqqiq Thānī, was one of the Jabal 'Āmel jurisprudents and one of the greatest of the Shī'ite jurisprudents. He perfected his studies in Syria and Iraq and then went to Iran and for the first time the position of Shaykh ul-Islam went to Iran when it was entrusted to him. The order that the ruling king of Iran (Shah Tahmaseb) wrote in Muḥaqqiq Karaki's name, in which the king gave him complete control, declaring himself to be only his agent, is famous. A well-known book that is often spoken of in jurisprudence is Muḥaqqiq Karaki's *Jam'i ul-Maqāsid*, which is a commentary on the *Qawa'id* of 'Allamah Ḥillī.

When Muhaqqeq Thānī arrived in Iran and established a religious university in Qazvin and then in Iṣfahānī, and also began training outstanding pupils in jurisprudence, Iran became, for the first time since the time of the Saduqayn, a centre of Shī'ite jurisprudence. He died between the years 937 AH and 941 AH. He had been the pupil of the pupil of Ibn Fahd Ḥillī, who had been the pupil of the pupils of Shahīd Awwal, such as Fāzel Miqdad.

Shaykh Zayn ud-Dīn, known as Shahīd Thānī, the 'Second Martyr', was another of the great Shī'ite jurisprudents. A master of several sciences, he was from Jabal 'Amal and a descendant of a man called Saleh who was a student of 'Allamah Ḥillī. Apparently Shahīd Thānī's family was from Tus, and sometimes he would sign his name 'At-Ṭūsī Ash-Shami'. He was born in 911 AH and martyred in 966 AH. He travelled widely, to Egypt, Syria, Hejaz, Jerusalem, Iraq and Istanbul, and studied with local teachers wherever he went. His Sunni teachers alone numbered twelve. Besides jurisprudence and principles he was accomplished in philosophy, gnosis, medicine and astronomy. He was very pious and pure and his students wrote that he used to bring wood home at nights for fuel for his household and, in the mornings, sit and teach. He compiled and wrote many books, the most famous of those on jurisprudence being *Sharh lum'a*, his commentary on the *Lum'a* of Shahīd Awwal. He was a pupil of Muḥaqqiq Karaki (before Muḥaqqiq migrated to Iran), but Iran was one place that he himself never visited. The author of *M'ālim*, which is about the Shī'ite ulamā', was Shahīd Thānī's son.

Muḥammad ibn Baqer ibn Muḥammad Akmal Bahbahani, known as Wahid Bahbahani lived in the period after the fall of the Safavi dynasty of Iran. At that time Isfahan was no longer the centre of religion, and some of the ulamā' and jurisprudents, among them Seyyid Ṣadr ud-Dīn Razawi Qummī, the teacher of Wahid Bahbahani, left Iran as the result of the Afghan turmoil and went to the *atabāt*, the holy centres of Iraq.

Wahid Bahbahani made Karbala the new centre and there he tutored numbers of outstanding pupils, many of them famous in their own right. Moreover, it was he who led the intellectual fight against the ideas of the *akhbāriyyīn*, which in those days were extremely popular. As a result of his defeat of the *akhbāriyyīn* and his raising of so many distinguished *mujtahid*s, he was referred to as *Ustaḍ ul-kul* ('the general teacher'). His virtue and piety were perfect and his students held him in profound respect.

Shaykh Morteza Anṣārī, a descendant of Jaber ibn Abdullah Anṣārī, was one of the great companions of the Holy Prophet himself. On a visit with his father to the *atabāt* of Iraq at the age of twenty, the ulamā', appreciating his genius, asked his father to let him stay. He remained four years in Iraq and studied there under the leading teachers. Then, owing to a series of unpleasant events, he returned to his home. After two years he went once more to Iraq, stayed for two years, and again returned to Iran, this time deciding to benefit from the ulamā' in Iran. He set off to visit Mashhad and on the way visited Ḥajj Mullā Aḥmad Naraqī, the author of the famous *Jāmi' Sa'ādat* in Kashan. This visit became a three-year stay as he became a pupil of Mullā Aḥmad in Kashan. He then went to Mashhad and stayed there for five months. He also journeyed to Isfahan and to Burujerd in Iran, the aim of all these trips being to learn from men of knowledge. Around 1202/3 AH he went for the last time to the *atabāt* and began giving lessons. After the decease of Shaykh Muḥammad Ḥaṣan, he became recognized as the sole authority for referral for verdicts.

Shaykh Anṣārī is called the *Khātim ul fuqahā wa al-mujtahidin* ('the seal of the jurisprudents and the *mujtahids*'). In the preciseness and depth of his views, he had very few equals. Two of his books, *Risā'il* and *Mukāssib*, are today's textbooks for (higher) religious students, and many commentaries have been written on his books by later ulamā'. After Muḥaqqiq Ḥillī, 'Allamah Ḥillī and Shahīd Awwal, Shaykh Anṣārī is the first person whose books have been so regularly subject to commentaries. He passed away in 1281 AH in Najaf, where he is buried.

Ḥajj Mirzā Muḥammad Ḥaṣan Shirāzī, known as Mirzā Shirāzī, undertook his preliminary studies in Isfahan and then went to Najaf to take part in the lessons of Shaykh Anṣārī. He became one of the Shaykh's most prominent and outstanding students. After Shaykh Anṣārī's demise, he became the leading authority of the Shī'ite world, and he remained thus until his demise about 23 years later. It was because of this great man's prohibition of tobacco that colonialism's famous monopoly agreement in Iran was broken.

Ḥajj Mirzā Ḥusayn Nainī, one of the great jurisprudents and master of principles of the fourteenth-century *hejrat*, was a pupil of Mirzā Shirāzī and became a highly respected teacher. His fame rests mostly on his work on principles, into which he introduced new views. Many of today's jurisprudents were his pupils. He died in 1355 AH in Najaf. One of the books he wrote was in Persian and was called *Tanaziyeh al-āmeh* or *Hukūmat dar Islam*, which he wrote in defence of constitutional government and its roots in Islam.

Summary and Review

In total we have introduced sixteen of the recognized jurisprudents from the time of the minor occultation until the end of the thirteenth century *hejrat*. We have mentioned only the jurisprudents from the world of jurisprudence and principles who are very famous and who have been and still are continually mentioned in lessons and books. Many other such names could have been mentioned but, from those we have reviewed, certain points became clear:

First, ever since the third century AH, jurisprudence has had a continuous existence, with no break in operation among the schools and no severance of the teacher-student relationship. If we start with my own teacher, the late great Ayatollah Burujerdi, we can trace the line of his teachers back over a thousand years to the period of the Imāms. Such a constant chain is unusual among other cultures and civilizations.

Of course, as was stated above, the present survey begins in the third century because in the earlier period people had access to the holy Imāms, wand the Shīʿite jurisprudents were overshadowed and moreover had no independence. The beginnings of *ijtihād* and jurisprudence among the Shīʿites and the writing of books about jurisprudence actually occurred among the companions. The first treatise on jurisprudence was written by ʿAlī ibn ʿAlī Rafi, who was the brother of ʿAbdullah ibn Abī Rafi, the scribe and accountant of Amir al-Mu'minīn, ʿAlī (*ʿa*) during the period of the Imām's caliphate.

Second, contrary to the perception of some, the Shīʿite sciences, among them jurisprudence, have not been developed and systematized solely by the ulamāʾ and jurisprudents of Iran. The ulamāʾ of Iran and the ulamāʾ of other lands have both shared in this great work, and, until the commencement of the tenth century and the emergence of the Safavi dynasty, non-Iranians were predominant. It is only since the middle of the Safavi period that Iranians have gained predominance.

Third, the centre of jurisprudence and of jurisprudents has likewise not always been Iran. At first Baghdad was the centre of Shīʿite jurisprudence and then, thanks to Shaykh Ṭūsī, the centre was transferred to Najaf. It was not long before Jabal ʿAmal in today's southern Lebanon became the centre, followed by Ḥillah, a small town in Iraq, and then for a while Ḥalab, one of the districts of Syria. During the time of the Safavids it was transferred to Isfahan, while at the same time Najaf was revived by Muqaddas Ardabīlī and other greats and still functions today. Of the towns of Iran, it is only Qum that in the first centuries of Islam, thanks to men like ʿAlī ibn Babawayh, was a minor centre of jurisprudence and related studies, while Baghdad was the main centre. During the time of the Qajar dynasty, Qum was revived owing to the efforts of

Abūl Qāsim Qummī and it was revived a second time in 1340 AH (i.e. 61 years before this translation) by the late Shaykh Abdul Karīm Ha'iri Yazdi; today it is one of the two great centres of Shī'ite jurisprudence.[2]

Fourth, the jurisprudents of Jabal 'Āmel played an important role in the development of Safavi Iran. The Safavi dynasty, as we know, were inclined to Sufism. Their path was originally based on the methods and customs peculiar to Sufism. If they had not been corrected by the profound and unchallengeable understanding of the jurisprudents of Jabal 'Āmil, and if an important centre of Islamic studies not been established by those jurisprudents, things would have led in Iran to the same situation that now pertains in Turkey and Syria. Their action had many effects. For one thing, the population and government of Iran remained immune from that deviation and, second, Shī'ite Sufism likewise followed a more reasonable path. Thus, we owe a great debt to the jurisprudents of Jabal 'Āmel-Muḥaqqiq Karaki and others for their founding of the religious university in Isfahan.

Fifth, as has been pointed out by others, Shī'ism in Jabal 'Āmel existed for a long time before it did in Iran, which is one of the reasons for rejecting the common claim that Shī'ism was formed in Iran. Some believe that the Shī'ite penetration into Lebanon was due to the great companion of the Prophet, the *mujahid* Abūzar Ghaffari. During his stay in ancient Syria, which included all or part of modern Lebanon, at the same time as offering stiff opposition to the misappropriation of public wealth by Mu'awiyyah and the rest of Bani Umayyid, Abūzar also used to propagate the holy platform of Shī'ism.

The Sections and Chapters of the Issues of Jurisprudence

To develop some familiarity with jurisprudence, one must recognize its different sections. We said earlier that the range of jurisprudence is extremely wide, for it contains all the subjects related to all the actions about which Islam contains instructions.

The foremost classification of today is the same classification first introduced by Muḥaqqiq Ḥillī in his *Sharāi'* and which Shahīd Awwal has briefly commented on and explained in his *Qawa'id*. Amazingly, the most proficient writers of commentaries on the book *Sharāi'*, among them Shahīd Thānī in his *Masālik*, have not made the slightest comment or explanation about the classification of Muḥaqqiq, and the First Shahīd in *Lum'a* has not even followed Muḥaqqiq's system.

In Muḥaqqiq's classification all the issues of jurisprudence are divided into four parts: worship, two-party contracts, one-party contracts and (other) commands.

This division is based on the fact that the actions that must be performed in accordance to the Sharīʿah are either such that a condition of their validity is the intention of nearness to God, meaning that they must be done solely for God, or if there is any other motivation for their performance the obligation is not fulfilled and they must be done again, or they are not subject to this condition.

If they are of the first type, such as prayer, fasting, *khums*, *zakāt*, *ḥajj* and so on, they are termed 'worship' (*ʿibādat*).

If, however, they are of the second type and the intention of nearness to God is not a condition of their validity, but they are performed with a different intention and are still correct and valid, then they are of two types: either their actualization does not depend upon the execution of a special contract or it does.

Acts that do not depend upon the execution of a special contract, such as inheritance, punishments, retribution and so on, are grouped together in jurisprudence under the heading 'commands' (*aḥkām*). If they do depend upon the execution of a contract, then again they are of two types: either the contract must be recited by two parties or there is no need for two parties and the contract is unilateral.

If they are of the first type, such as selling, hire and marriage, they are called a 'contract' (*ʿaqd*), in which one party states the contract and the other agrees. If, however, one person can carry it out alone with no need of another party, such as changing one's mind regarding one's due, divorce and so on, it is called 'unilateral instigation'.

In this classification all the sections of jurisprudence have been divided into fifty-two chapters: ten chapters of worship, nineteen of contracts, eleven of unilateral instigations and twelve chapters of commands.

A further point must be mentioned. In the first and second centuries of Islam, the books of jurisprudence that were written were related to one or a few of the subjects of jurisprudence, not to all the subjects. For example, it is recorded that such-and-such a person wrote a book about prayer and such-and-such a person a book about marriage. For this reason, in later eras, when books about all the issues of jurisprudence were written, the different chapters of jurisprudence were all under the heading 'the Book'. The custom is that instead of writing 'the Chapter of the Ritual Prayer', or 'the Chapter of the *Ḥajj*', we write 'the Book of Ritual Prayer' or 'the Book of *Ḥajj*'.

Now, in the order first used by Muḥaqqiq Ḥillī, we shall look at the different sections and chapters of the issues of jurisprudence.

Worship

There are ten books of worship.

The Book of Cleanliness (kitāb ut-tahārat)
Cleanliness is of two kinds: being clean of external, non-inherent material, filth and pollution; and being spiritually clean of inherent pollution. The first type of cleanliness means the body, clothes and other things being clean from the ten types of filth that include urine, faeces, blood, sperm, corpses and carcasses and so on and which are termed *najāsat*. The second type of cleanliness means entering the state of purity by performing a partial ablution, or total ablution or earth ablution, which is a condition of certain forms of worship such as prayer and circumambulation of the Ka'ba, and which is annulled by a series of natural things such as sleep, urination, sexual intercourse and simple sperm discharge. After such interruptions or annulment the state of cleanliness must be re-entered.

The Book of Prayer (kitāb uṣ-ṣalāt)
In this book the obligatory prayers are all discussed in detail, i.e. the five daily ritual prayers, the prayers of *'īd ul fitr* and *'id al-aḍḥā*, the prayer for the deceased, the prayer of special signs such as earthquakes and eclipses, etc. and the prayer of the circumambulation of the Ka'ba; the *nafilah* prayers, i.e. the desirable prayers such as the daily desirable prayers; the conditions, preparations, essentials, preventions, delayers and annullers of prayer; and the qualities of prayer, such as the prayer of a person at home and the prayer of a person deemed to be travelling, individual prayer and congregational prayer, the prayer offered at the right time (*ida*) and the prayer missed and made up for after its time (*qaẓa*).

The Book of Zakāt
Zakāt is a way of handing over wealth that is similar to a tax and that is due from nine things: gold, silver, wheat, barley, dates, grapes, animals of the cow family, animals of the sheep family and animals of the camel family. In jurisprudence the conditions under which *ẓakāt* is due from these nine things, the amount of *ẓakāt* due and the ways it is to be spent are all discussed and determined from the authentic sources and in the recognized ways. *Zakāt* is

mostly mentioned along with prayer in the Qur'ān, which requires that it be given and explains how it is to be spent; the rest is known from the Sunnah.

The Book of Khums

Khums, like *zakāt*, is a way of giving up one's wealth in a way that resembles tax. *Khums* means a fifth. In the view of the ulamā' of our Sunni brothers it is only a fifth of the spoils of war that is to be transferred to the Bait ul-mal, or public treasury of Islam, and it is to be spent for the public benefit. In the Shī'ite view, however, the spoils of war are just one of the sources of payment of *khums*. In addition, profits from mining, buried and underwater treasure, wealth that is mixed with illegitimate wealth when the amount and/or the owner cannot be discerned, land that a *dhimmi kāfir*[3] buys from a Muslim, and whatever exceeds one's expenses from one's annual earnings must all be divided into five and one of those fifths be given as *khums*. *Khums* in the Shī'ite path of religion is the great budget that can secure an important part of the budget of the state.

The Book of Fasting (kitāb uṣ-ṣawm)

When one fasts, one must abstain not only from eating and drinking but also from sexual intercourse, from immersing one's head in water, from breathing in dust (even as far as the throat) and from certain other things. For one month each lunar year, the blessed month of *Ramaḍān*, it is obligatory for every mature, sane person who is not ruled an exception (such as a traveller or a woman who is menstruating) to fast each day from daybreak until sundown. Other than in the month of *Ramaḍān* fasting is generally desirable. On the days of the two festivals, fasting is forbidden, and on certain other days, such as the day of 'Ashura, it is undesirable (*makrūh*).

The Book of Going into Seclusion (i'tikāf)

This literally means 'to reside in a specified place'. In the terminology of jurisprudence, however, it means a type of worship whereby a person resides in a mosque for three days or more, not setting foot out of the mosque and fasting each day. This has laws and conditions that are determined in jurisprudence. In its essence *i'tikāf* is desirable, not obligatory, but if it is begun and kept up for two days, the third day becomes obligatory. *I'tikāf* is to be performed in the Masjid ul-Haram in Mecca or the Masjid un-Nabi in Medina, or in the *masjid* of Kufa in Iraq, the *masjid* of Basreh in Iraq or at least in the major *masjid* of a city. *I'tikāf* in minor *masjids* is not permissible. The Holy Prophet used to perform *i'tikāf* during the final days of the month of *Ramaḍān*.

The Book of Ḥajj

Ḥajj is that famous act of worship performed in Mecca and the outskirts of Mecca that is normally linked to *'umrah*. The performance of the *ḥajj* consists of binding *iḥram*[4] upon oneself in Mecca, a stay in 'Arafat, a stay for a night in Mash'ar, the symbolic ceremony of throwing stones at the furthest (of three) boulders, the sacrifice, the shaving of the head for men and the cutting of a few curls for women, circumambulation (walking seven times around the Holy Ka'ba), the prayer of the circumambulation, the walking of seven times between the two hills of Safa and Marwah, the final circumambulation, the prayer of the final circumambulation, throwing stones at (all three of) the boulders and a stay overnight at Mina.

The Book of 'Umrah

'Umrah is a kind of lesser pilgrimage. Normally it is obligatory for those about to perform the *ḥajj* to perform the *ḥajj 'Umrah* first. The actions of *'umrah* are as follows: binding *iḥram* on oneself at one of the special places (*mī'qāt*), circumambulation, the prayer of circumambulation, walking seven times between Safa and Marwa and, finally, the cutting of a few hairs or a fingernail or toenail.

The Book of Jihād

This book deals with the issues concerning Islamic warfare. Islam is a religion of society and community and of the responsibilities of society, and for this reason it includes a law of *jihād*. There are two types of *jihād*: *ibtidā'i* (to be initiated by Muslims) and *difa'i* (defensive). In the view of Shī'ite jurisprudence, *ibtidā'i jihād* can take place only under the direction of the Holy Prophet or one of the twelve immaculate and perfect Imāms, otherwise it is forbidden. This type of *jihād* is obligatory only on men, whereas the *jihād* of defence is obligatory on both men and women whenever the conditions demand it.

Similarly, *jihād* can be either internal or external. If some of the people for whom obedience to the Imām is obligatory rise up against him, just as the Khawārij at Nahrawan and other places, Talha and Zubayr at the battle of Jamal and Mu'awiyyah and his companies at Siffin all rose up against Amir ul-Muminin, 'Alī, internal *jihād* is also obligatory against them.

In jurisprudence, the laws of *jihād* and of *dhimmeh*, the conditions for allowing non-Muslims to live in the Islamic state as citizens of the state and for peace between Islamic and non-Islamic states, are all discussed in detail.

The Book Commending What is Recognized as Good and Prohibiting What is Rejected as Bad (al-amr bi m 'arūf wa nahy'an al-munkar)
Because Islam is a religion of society and of the responsibilities of society and sees its orderly environment as the essential condition for enacting its heavenly programs and bestowing prosperity and fulfilment, it has created a shared general responsibility. We are all duty bound to be guardians of virtue and goodness and to combat evil and wrong. The guarding of virtue and goodness is called *amr bil ma'rūf* and the combating of evil and wrong is known as *nahy'an al-munkar.* The conditions attached to these duties and their stipulations and regulations are all stated in jurisprudence.

We now turn from the books of worship to the contracts.

Contracts ('uqūd)

The second section, according to our classification, consists of the contracts and includes nineteen books.

The Book of Buying and Selling (kitāb ul-bay'i)
This book deals with buying and selling, the conditions that buyer and seller must meet, the conditions of the commodities exchanged, the conditions of the contract and the type of transaction. Cash transactions fall into two groups: *nisiyah* transactions, in which a commodity is handed over immediately and payment is delayed for a time; and *salaf* transactions, in which payment is made immediately but the commodity is not put at the buyer's disposal until after a period. Transactions in which both the payment and the product are to be exchanged after a delay are null and void. Similarly, in the chapter of selling, advantageous transfers, disadvantageous transfers and advantageless transfers are also discussed. What is meant by an advantageous transfer (*marābiḥah*) is that a person makes a transaction and then, having made a profit, transfers it to someone else. A disadvantageous transfer (*muwādah*) is the opposite, meaning a transaction which, after the person has suffered some loss and damage, is transferred to someone else. An advantageless transfer (*tuwliyah*) is that a transaction is transferred to someone else after the person has neither made profit nor suffered a loss.

The Book of Rahn
Rahn means mortgage and the laws connected with mortgaging are discussed in this book.

The Book of the Bankrupt (muflis)

Muflis means 'the bankrupt', i.e. a person whose assets do not meet his liabilities. In order to investigate the liabilities of such a person, the Ḥakim Sharīʿah i.e. a *mujtahid*, can prohibit him from the right to his possessions until a thorough investigation has been carried out and as far as possible the liabilities have been paid.

The Book of Prohibition (ḥajr)

Hajr means prohibition, specifically the prohibition of making use of property. In many cases, the use of property by the original owner is prohibited. As we have seen, the bankrupt is one instance. Another is an immature child (i.e. a girl under nine or a boy under fifteen). Other instances include insane individuals and persons who, though in other respects sane and reasonable, spend their money foolishly, for example buying unnecessary clothes when they are desperately in need of food.

The Book of Liability (ḍimān)

What is referred to here is the acceptance by one person of liability for another's debts. A difference exists between Shīʿite jurisprudents and the jurisprudents of our Sunni brothers about the reality of liability. In the view of Shīʿite jurisprudents *ḍimān* is the transference of the obligation of a debt from the debtor to a party who accepts liability, and it is valid only with the consent of the creditor; once the liability has been transferred, the creditor no longer has the right to seek it from the person who has made himself liable. Of course, if the liability was urged on the liable person by the debtor, then, once he has cleared the debt, the liable person can recover the amount from the original debtor. In Sunni jurisprudence, however, *ḍimān* is the annexing of the obligation of the debt on to someone else, who also becomes obliged to repay the debt. Thus, after the contract of liability, the creditor has the right to seek the debt both from the original debtor and from the person who has made himself liable.

Sometimes two other chapters, *ḥawālih* (another kind of liability) and *kafālah* (a kind of bail system) are also included in this book.

The Book of Peace (ṣulḥ)

The *ṣulḥ* (peace) that is studied in this book is different from the *ṣulḥ* that is studied in the Book of *jihād*. *Ṣulḥ* in the Book of *jihād* means 'political agreements', whereas the Book of Peace deals with property affairs and common rights. For example, if a debt is owed but the amount of the debt is not precisely known, the two parties make a *ṣulḥ* agreement and settle on a specified sum. *Ṣulḥ* agreements are generally made to settle arguments and disagreements.

The Book of Partnerships (sharikat)

Sharikat means that a property or a right belongs to more than one person. For example, if brothers inherit their father's property, then, until such time as they divide it, they are partners in that property. Or two people may become partners in the purchase of an automobile or a house or a piece of land. Or a group of people may join together to take possession of a piece of land that belongs to no one and may reclaim it or restore what was desert or marshland. Furthermore, a partnership is sometimes accidentally forced on someone, for example, when the wheat of two farmers accidentally becomes mixed and it is impossible to separate the wheat of one from the wheat of the other.

There are two types of partnership existing in Islam, contractual and non-contractual. The examples above are non-contractual partnerships. A contractual partnership is made when two or more people, by an agreement, compact or contract, form what in English is called a company, such as a trading company, a farming company or an industrial company. Contractual partnerships or companies are subject to many laws, which are still studied in jurisprudence. In the Book of Partnerships the laws of profit-sharing are also discussed.

The Book of the Partnership of Capital and Labour (muḍārabah)

A *muḍārabah* is a kind of contractual partnership, but not a partnership of two or more investors. Rather it is a partnership of capital and labour, meaning that one or more partners provide the capital for a trading business and one or more partners provide the labour involved in the actual trading. The partners must first be in agreement as to the division of profits, and then the contract of *muḍārabah* is to be formally executed or at least put into practice.

The Book of Agricultural Partnerships (mazāra'at and musāqāt)

Mazara'at and *musaqat* are two more types of partnership. They are like *muḍārabah*, which we have just mentioned, in that they are both types of partnerships between capital and labour. The difference is that *muḍārabah* is relevant to trading whereas *mazāra'at* is for farming. The owner of land and water makes an agreement with someone else who does the actual farming and they agree as to the specified proportion of the profits each party shall receive. Likewise, *musāqāt* is for the affairs of orchards. The owner of fruit trees concludes an agreement with someone else who becomes responsible for all the work involved in looking after those trees, such as watering them and all the other things effective in fruit production, and both investor and worker take their specified share of the profits as per their agreement.

In partnerships between capital and labour, whether *muḍārabah* agreements or *mazāra'at* or *musāqāt*, any kind of harm or loss to the capital is borne by the owner of the capital, the investor. Likewise, there is no certainty of making a profit on the capital, which means that it is equally possible that a profit will or will not accrue. The profit that is returned to the owner of the capital is limited to the amount of profit made by the partnerships and to his specified proportion of the profit. This being so, the financier, just like the worker, may make no profit, he may even lose his capital or become bankrupt.

In today's world, however, even in most parts of the Muslim world, bankers achieve their aims by practising usury and as a result they receive a specified profit in all circumstances, whatever the types of concern they finance. Should one of the concerns that they have financed return a loss instead of a profit, the manager of that concern is absolutely obliged to return the banker's profit, even if he has to sell his house. Likewise, in the financial system that operates in most parts of the world today, the financier never goes bankrupt; the financier entrusts his capital to the manager, who has to repay it many times over, and whatever happens the banker demands that profit, even if the capital has dwindled or even been dispersed altogether.

In Islam, profiting from capital on the basis of usury, i.e. lending money and demanding repayment of the loan, with interest or profit, whatever the circumstances, is strictly and severely prohibited.

The Book of Trusts (wadī'ah)

Wadī'ah, or trust, means entrusting property to someone and making that person one's agent in keeping and safeguarding it. This in turn creates duties for the trustee but if the property suffers or is lost and the trustee has performed and observed those duties, he is not liable.

The Book of Lending ('āriyah)

'Āriyah is the circumstance in which a person receives the property of a second person in order to benefit from it. *'Āriyah* and *wadī'ah* are two types of trusts, but in *wadī'ah* the owner entrusts his property into the safekeeping of another and the trustee has no right, without the owner's permission, to make use of it in any way. Under the provisions of *'āriyah*, however, the owner from the very beginning gives it to the other person for him to use and then return.

The Book of Hire (ijārah)

In Islam there are two types of hire. Either a person gives the benefit of his property to another in return for an amount of money, which is called 'the money of hire' (*mal-ijārah*), such as the normal practices of hiring out one's house or car; or a person may rent out his services and become *ājir*, which means that in return for carrying out specific work, such as repairing a pair of shoes, cutting a person's hair or building a house, he will receive a wage or payment. Hire is similar to buying and selling in as far as both involve an exchange. The difference is that in buying and selling the exchange is of a thing or money, while in hire the exchange is of the benefit of a thing or money. Hire also has an aspect in common with *'āriyah* in that both the hirer and the *'āriyah* trustee make use of a benefit, the difference being that the hirer, having paid the price of the hire, is the owner of the benefit, while the *'āriyah* trustee is not the owner of the benefit but merely has the right to make use of it.

The Book of Representatives (wakālah)

Sometimes one may need to have a representative for works that demand a contract. Marriage and divorce are good examples, for the contracts of marriage and divorce must be verbally recited in correct and valid Arabic. The person who is represented is called the *muwakkīl* and the representative is called the *wakīl*, while the act of representation itself is called *takwīl.*

The Book of Endowments and Charity (waqf and sadaqat)

An endowment is what a person sets aside from his property for a special use. According to one definition, *waqf* entails safeguarding the original article of *waqf* but making it untransferable, while at the same time freeing its benefits. There is a difference of opinion about whether an intention of *qorbat*, of nearness to God, is a condition of *waqf* or not. The fact that it is included in this section indicates that Muḥaqqiq Ḥillī did not consider the intention of *qorbat* to be an essential condition. In any case, there are two types of *waqf*, general *waqf* and special *waqf*. Both these and the commands of charity are discussed in detail.

The Book of Temporary Endowments (sukna and ḥabs)

Sukna and *ḥabs* are similar to *waqf*, with the difference that in *waqf* the original property or wealth is guarded forever and there is no longer any possibility of its being someone's property, whereas *ḥabs* means that a person designates the benefits of his property for a specified period to be spent in a charitable way, and after that period it again becomes his personal property. *Sukna*, however, means that a person designates a dwelling for the use of a poor, deserving person for a period and at the end of that period it becomes exactly the same as the owner's other property.

The Book of Giving (hibat)

One of the effects of ownership is that one has the right to give one's property to others. Giving is of two types, 'in exchange' and 'not in exchange'. Giving 'in exchange' means that one receives something in return for one's gift. Something given in exchange is not retrievable, i.e. it cannot be taken back. When something is given 'not in exchange', however, if it is given between the *maḥram* members of a family or if the gift itself is lost or broken, it cannot be taken back. In other circumstances it can be taken back and the giver can nullify the transaction.

The Book of Wagers (sabq and rimāyah)

Sabq and *rimāyah* are two forms of betting agreement between the competitors of horse races, camel races or shooting competitions. *Sabq* and *rimāyah* are forms of gambling, yet, because the purpose of the races and competitions is practice of the martial arts necessary for *jihād*, Islam reckons them permissible as a means of encouraging the participants. Of course, this permission does not extend to anyone other than the participants.

The Book of Wills (wasiyat)

This book is related to the provisions of a will with regard to the deceased's wealth or any children of whom he was guardian. Each person has the right to appoint a person as his executor (*wasi*) to be the guardian of his under-age children after his death; to supervise their education and other affairs. In the same way, each person also has the right to have up to one third of his wealth spent as he stipulates in his will.

The Book of Marriage (nikāḥ)

This book first discusses the conditions of marriage, such as the *muḥarām*, the prohibitions that prevent certain people from entering into a marriage, such as father and daughter, mother and son, brother and sister and so on. There are two types of marriage, permanent and temporary. The book deals with matters such as disobedience by the wife towards the husband, ill-treatment of the wife by the husband and the obligation of the man of the house to provide for his wife and children, along with a few other issues.

Unilateral Instigations (iyqā'at)

This part, according to the present classification, consists of *iyqaʿat*, which, as has been explained, are the actions that require a contract, but not a two-sided contract; a unilateral contract is enough. There are fifteen of these.

The Book of Divorce (ṭalaq)

Divorce here means the cancelling of the marriage compact by the husband. Divorce is either *bāʾin* or *rajʿi*. *Bāʾin* is the kind of divorce in which the man has no right to return to the woman. A *rajʿi* divorce is one in which the man can return. What this means is that, until such time as the woman's special period of restraint (*ʿiddah*) has come to an end, the man can return to the woman and thus nullify the divorce. A divorce is a *bāʾin* divorce either because the wife has no *ʿiddah*, such as a divorced woman with whom the husband has not had sexual intercourse or a woman who has reached the age of menopause, or because, even though the woman must keep *ʿiddah*, the nature of the divorce disqualifies the man's right to return. An example would be the third consecutive divorce of that couple, in which case, until she marries someone else who has sexual intercourse with her and then himself dies or divorces her and she keeps another *ʿiddah*, the first husband cannot remarry her.

It is a condition of divorce, first, that, at the time of the divorce, the woman must not be menstruating. Second, there must be two just witnesses present when the contract of divorce is recited. Divorce is divinely detested. The Prophet of God tells us, 'The most-detested permissible [thing] before God is divorce'.

The Book of Divorce Wholly or Partly Instigated by the Wife (khulʿa and mabārāt)

Khulʿa and *mabārāt* are two types of *bāʾin* divorce. A *khulʿa* divorce is a divorce that occurs because the wife is dissatisfied with the marriage and gives the husband something or releases him from all or part of the *mehr*[5] so as to persuade him to divorce her. In this case, by the act of divorcing his wife, the man disqualified himself from returning to her, unless she wants to take back what she has given or ceded to him, in which case the man has the right to return to her.

Mabārāt is also a type of *bāʾin* divorce, but differs from *khulʿa* in that both parties are dissatisfied with the marriage, although the wife must still give the husband a sum to persuade him to divorce her. The other difference is that the given sum in *khulʿa* divorce has no specified limit, whereas in *mabārāt* the sum must not be more than the amount of the *mehr*.

The Book of Illegal Divorce (Ẓihar)

In the 'ignorance' of pre-Islamic Arabia, *ẓahar* was a kind of divorce in which the husband might say to his wife, '*anti 'alayya kaẓahar ummi*', i.e. 'You are like the rear of my mother to me'. This was quite enough for the wife to be recognized as divorced. Islam changed this. In the view of Islam, *ẓihar* is not divorce. A man is forbidden to make this statement to his wife, on pain of a fine (*kafārah*). Until he pays the fine it is forbidden for him to have sexual intercourse with the wife. The fine of *ẓihar* is the freeing of a slave or, if that is not possible, fasting each day for two consecutive months or again, if this is not possible, the feeding of sixty poor people.

The Book of Vows of Abstention (iylā')

Iylā' is a general word meaning oath, but in jurisprudence it has a special meaning, which is that in order to annoy his wife, a man recites a statement swearing that he will not have sexual intercourse with her ever again or for a fixed period (four months or more). If the wife protests to the Ḥakim Sharī'ah, he will oblige the man to do one of two things: break the vow or divorce his wife. If the man breaks his vow, he must, of course, pay the fine. To break a vow is always forbidden but in these circumstances the husband may be obliged to do so.

The Book of Cursing (la'n)

La'n is again related to the marital affairs of man and wife. It means their cursing of each other, and it applies to a situation in which the husband accuses his wife of immorality, namely, adultery or lesbianism.

If someone accuses a woman of the said immorality and cannot produce four just witnesses, the person must undergo punishment for falsely accusing her. If a man accuses his own wife and cannot produce four witnesses, then rather than punish him, something else can be done, namely, *la'n*. *La'n* takes the place of any other punishment, but his wife becomes forbidden to him forever.

La'n takes place in front of the Ḥakim Sharī'ah, when the two parties curse each other. The procedure is as follows. First the man stands up in front of the Ḥakim and says four times, 'God is my witness, I am truthful in my claim'. The fifth time he says, 'God curse me if I am lying in my claim'. The woman then stands up in the presence of the Ḥakim and says four times, 'I call God as a witness that in his claim he is a liar'. The fifth time she says, 'The anger of God be upon me if he is truthful in his claim'.

The Book of Freeing (iṭq)

This refers to the freeing of slaves. In Islam a series of legislative measures has been introduced about slaves. Other than making slaves of prisoners of war, Islam considers no other form of slavery legitimate. Furthermore, the aim of taking slaves in Islam is not to profit from them, rather it is for them to stay for a period in the homes of genuine Muslims and come to understand Islamic teachings. This alone would draw them to an appreciation and acceptance of Islam and its sublime teachings. In reality, this form of slavery is the passage between the slavery of disbelief (*kufr*) and the freedom of Islam. So the aim is not that slaves remain slaves forever, but for them fully to discover the Islamic teachings and their liberating effect and earn the real, spiritual freedom in the freedom of society. Therefore, the aim of Islam is freedom following slavery.

Islam has provided many systems of *iṭq*. Because the goal of Islam is freeing and not enslaving, the jurisprudents have entitled the book dealing with slavery the Book of Freeing and not the Book of Enslaving.

The Book of Acquiring Freedom through Will, by Purchase and through Relationship (tadbir, mukātabah and istilad)

Tadbir, *mukātabah* and *istilad* are three of the ways in which slaves are freed. *Tadbir* means that the owner stipulates in his will that after his death his slave shall be free. *Mukātabah* means that a slave reaches an agreement with his owner under which he will pay a sum (or agree to pay a sum in the future) to gain his freedom. In the Qur'ān it has been stipulated that if such an application is made by a slave in whom good is discerned, or, to be exact, one in whom faith is discerned (or who is deemed to be capable of managing to exist independently and not to become helpless), not only is the application to be accepted but the slave is also to receive capital from the owner's wealth.

Istilad concerns a slave woman who is made pregnant by her owner. Such a woman definitely becomes part of the inheritance when the owner dies, a part of which is inherited by her child, and since no one can be the slave of one's parents or grandparents or of one's children or grandchildren, she automatically becomes free.

Similarly, there are many other ways for slaves to become free. A slave who has been afflicted by blindness may be freed. Making amends for a sin by paying a fine (*kafārah*) make take the form of freeing a slave. Or a slave may be freed by someone simply to please God. Such cases are generally discussed in the Book of Freeing.

The Book of Confessing (iqrar)
Iqrar is related to the Islamic laws of arbitration. One of the means by which a case is proven against a person is the person's own confession. If, for example, a person claims that he is owed something by a second person, he must produce evidence or testimony and if he does not his claim is rejected. If, however, the second person himself confesses to the debt, this confession renders evidence and testimony unnecessary. Confession is accepted only from sane adults.

The Book of Reward (jaʿalah)
Reward in its essence is similar to the hiring of people. In hire, however, a specific person is hired to do a specific job in return for a specific sum, whereas in reward no specific person is hired. Instead, the hirer simply announces that whoever does a certain job for him (such as finding his missing child, for example) will be paid a certain sum as a reward.

The Book of Vows (aymān)
If a person swears to do a certain thing, it becomes obligatory for him to do it. One condition is that the vow is in the Name of God. A vow made in the name of the Prophet or of an Imām or the Qur'ān is not binding on him according to the Divine Law. Another condition is that what he vows to do is ruled permissible in the Sharīʿah, so a vow to do something that is ruled forbidden (*ḥarām*) or repulsive (*makrūḥ*) is meaningless and not binding at all. Examples of legitimate vows would be swearing to study an educational book from beginning to end or swearing to brush one's teeth at least once a day. The breaking of such a vow necessitates a fine (*kafārah*).

The Book of Taking an Oath (nadhr)
Nadhr is a type of undertaking to do something that involves an oath but no special contract. For example, to make an oath to recite all the daily *nafilah* prayers, i.e. the desirable but voluntary prayers that accompany the obligatory prayers of the day, all that is required is a declaration to that effect. As we have just seen, the object of an *aymān* vow must be not forbidden (*ḥarām*) or repulsive (*makrūḥ*) but it may be simply permissible. A condition of *nadhr*, however, is that the object of the vow be useful in some way. So any *nadhr* to do something that is not beneficial is void. As in the *aymān* vows, the breaking of a *nadhr* warrants a fine.

The inner meaning of *aymān* and *nadhr* and of the necessity of acting in accordance with them lie in the fact that both are types of compact with God, and, in the same way as one must respect one's compacts with the creatures of

God ('O you who believe, be loyal to your compacts.' 15:1), so too one must respect one's compacts with God Himself. An *aymān* or a *nadhr* is normally made when one has little confidence in one's willpower. The *aymān* or *nadhr* makes a thing obligatory for the doer until he is able to form the desired habit.[6]

Laws

The ninth section of the four sections of jurisprudence consists of the issues grouped under the heading of 'laws' (*aḥkām*). This word has no special definition. The fact is that those issues of jurisprudence that do not fall into one of the other three groupings have been grouped together to form this one. This section contains twelve books.

The Book of Hunting and Slaughtering (ṣayd and dhibḥ)

First, it is necessary to state that the meat of permitted meat animals becomes permitted either when the animal is slaughtered in a special way (*dhibḥ* or *naḥr*) or, if the animal is a wild animal the meat of which is permitted, when it is properly hunted by specially trained dogs or my means of an iron missile (such as a sharp arrowhead or a sharp bullet).

It is not permissible to eat the meat of tame, permitted animals if they have been hunted, and they must be slaughtered in exact accordance with the Sharīʿah. The way of slaughtering most tame animals, such as hens, sheep and cows, is called *dhibḥ* and the way of slaughtering camels is called *naḥr*. There is a slight difference between the actual acts of *naḥr* and *dhibḥ*, but the conditions, such as that the slaughterer be a Muslim and that the animal be killed in the Name of God are the same.

Hunting is related to permitted-meat animals that are wild, like deer and mountain goats. If the animal is hunted using a dog, the dog must be so trained that it will do whatever it is commanded, and thus reflect its master's will, and the meat of permitted-meat animals that are hunted and killed by dogs that are not trained in this way must not be eaten. Similarly, hunting with animals other than dogs, such as hawks, is also not permissible.

In hunting without the use of animals, it is a condition that the weapon be iron, or at least metal, and it must be so sharp that it kills the animal by its sharpness. So hunting with stones and blunt metal missiles is not permissible. In both forms of hunting, just as in both forms of slaughtering, the conditions that the man responsible for the animal's death, i.e. the hunter, be a Muslim and that he begin in the Name of God must be met for the meat of that animal to be permissible. There are other detailed conditions, which cannot be discussed here.

The Book of Eating and Drinking

Islam has a series of instructions concerning the gifts of nature. The laws of slaughtering and hunting are among them, as are the laws of eating and drinking. In the view of Islam, all good things, i.e. things that are beneficial and useful, are permitted, while all foul things, i.e. things that are not beneficial and are abominable for man, are forbidden. Islam has not contented itself with explaining these generalities but has specified a whole group of things that are foul and must be shunned, and a group of other things that are good and may be used without hindrance.

Eating refers either to the eating of meat or to the eating of other things. Meat may come from the creatures of the sea, the land or the air. Of the creatures of the sea only fish are permissible, and then again only fish that have scales.[7] The creatures of the land are of two types, tame and wild. The tame animals are cows, sheep, camels, hens, horses, donkeys and mules. Their meat may be eaten, although the eating of meat of horses, donkeys and mules is undesirable (*makrūḥ*). The meat of dogs, cats and pigs is forbidden. Of the wild animals, the meat of carnivorous animals and insects is forbidden. However, it is permissible to eat the meat of deer, wild cows and goats and other wild animals whose tame counterparts may be eaten. The meat of hares and rabbits, though they are not carnivorous, in accordance with the famous verdict of the ulamā', is forbidden.

Of birds, the meat of the different types of pigeon, partridge, ducks, domestic hens and so on is permissible but the meat of hunting birds is forbidden. In cases where the Sharī'ah has not made clear the status of the meat of certain birds, there are two signs of its being forbidden. One is that when the bird flies it does not flap its wings all the time but mostly glides. The other is that it has no crop or no gizzard or no sign of a bump on the back of its leg.

Other than animals, it is forbidden to eat or drink anything that is intrinsically filthy (*najāsat*), such as urine, faeces, blood, sperm, alcohol, etc., or any intrinsically clean thing that has been dirtied by intrinsic filth (*mutanajas*). Similarly, one may not eat or drink anything that is significantly harmful to the body, such as poison, for example. If medicine discovers that a certain thing, tobacco for example, is definitely harmful to the body and shortens one's life expectation or produces cancer, then its use will be forbidden. If it is not consequential, however, like, for instance, breathing the air of most cities, it is not forbidden.

It is also forbidden for a pregnant woman to consume something that leads to the abortion of her child or for a person to consume something that leads to disorder of the senses or for a man to consume something that leads to his sterilization or for a woman to consume something that leads to her permanent sterility.

To eat earth is absolutely forbidden, whether it is harmful or not. The drinking of intoxicating liquors is also absolutely forbidden. Furthermore, to consume something that belongs to another without the consent of the owner is strictly forbidden, but this is an incidental prohibition, not an intrinsic one.

Some parts of permitted-meat animals are forbidden, including the spleen, the testicles and generative parts. Likewise, the milk of forbidden-meat animals is also forbidden.

The Book of Misappropriation (ghaṣb)

Misappropriation (*ghaṣb*) means the taking or using of the property of another by force, i.e. without the other's permission. In the first place, this is forbidden. In the second place, it renders the misappropriator (*ghaṣib*) liable, so that if the property is damaged or destroyed while in the control of the misappropriator he is liable for it whether the loss or damage was his fault or not. Any use of misappropriated property, whatever it may be, is forbidden. *Wuẓu* taken with misappropriated water and prayer in misappropriated clothes or in a misappropriated place is void.

Just as misappropriation results in liability, so destruction causes liability. If, for example, a person smashes someone else's window, he is liable for it. Causing such destruction to happen also produces liability. This means that if the person does no direct damage, such as smashing a window, but does something that causes damage, he is liable. If, for example, a man drops a banana skin on a public footpath and a pedestrian slips on it and as a consequence suffers injury, that man is responsible for the injury.

The Book of Right of Preference (shof'ih)

Shaf'ih means the right of precedence of one partner to buy the share of the other. If two people are legitimate partners according to the Sharīʿah and one of them wants to sell his share, the other partner has the right of precedence over others who wish to purchase it on the same terms and at the same price.

The Book of Reviving Dead Land (iḥyā al-mamāt)

This book concerns waste land, i.e. land that is dead or barren owing to the absence of buildings, farming or other use. The Holy Prophet told us, 'Whoever revives dead land owns it'. This issue has many facets, which are discussed at length in jurisprudence.

The Book of Finds

This book discusses the laws of finding things whose owners are not known. The find is either an animal or something other than an animal. If it is an animal that will not be harmed if left alone, the finder has no right to take it into his control. If the animal may be harmed if left alone, however, like a sheep in the middle of the desert, the finder can take it into his control, but he must search for its owner. If the owner is found, the animal must be returned to him, and if the owner is not found, with the permission of the Ḥakim Sharīʿah, the animal must be given to the poor.

If the find is not an animal and its value is less than that of 2.32 grams[8] of minted silver, the finder can keep it for himself, but if it is more he must search for the owner for one year (unless, like fruit, it cannot be kept for a year). If the owner is not found and if the find was not made in the sacred area of Mecca, the finder has the option of doing any one of three things. He can use it himself with the intention that, if the owner is discovered, he will repay the find itself or its value to the owner; or he may it to charity with the same intention; or he can keep it in the hope that the owner will be found.

If the find has no distinctive characteristics the search for the owner is not necessary and the finder has the same three options from the time of the find.

The Book of Inheritance

We know that in Islam there are laws of inheritance. Inheritance in Islam is not a matter of choice. In Islam, a person has no right to specify a certain sum for a certain heir or, for example, to leave all his wealth to a certain heir. After a person's death, his wealth (apart from 'his' third, which he dispose of as he likes in his will) is divided and shared among the heirs in accordance with the relevant laws.

The heirs in the view of Islam form different ranks. If members of the first rank exist the inheritance does not reach the second, and the third rank inherits only if there is no one from the first and second ranks to inherit.

The first rank consists of the deceased's parents and sons and daughters and, if the sons and daughters have died, the grandchildren.

The second rank includes the deceased's four grandparents and his brothers and sisters and, if the brothers and sisters have themselves passed away, their children.

The third rank is the deceased's uncles and aunts and their children.

Hitherto we have spoken about inheritance of kin. There is also the inheritance of husband and wife, who inherit their share from each other before the other three ranks receive their inheritance. The details of the shares each receives are too complex to go into here.

The Book of Arbitration (qāḍa)

The issues of arbitration, i.e. the settling in court of differences and disputes, are so many that they cannot even be summarized here. Islam has its own special system of arbitration and devotes extraordinary attention to the justice of the arbitrator (*qāḍi*). The knowledgeable personality of the arbitrator is emphasized to the extent that he must be a *mujtahid* and an expert on Islamic rights. His moral and ethical competence is precisely defined. He must be free from all types of sin, even those that do not directly affect his work. In no way does he have any right to accept payment from either of the two parties, even after arbitration. His expenses are to be liberally reimbursed from the public treasury. The position of the judge is to be so respected that the parties of the case to be arbitrated, whoever they may be (even a caliph, as the history of Amir ul-Muminin, ʿAlī, so clearly shows), must both present themselves before the judge with perfect respect for his position and in no way expect or demand partiality. Confession, testimonial and, in some cases, oaths play an important role in the Islamic arbitration system.

The Book of Testimony

This book is connected to the Book of Arbitration in the same way as the Book of Confession. If a person claims something, the other party either admits it or denies it. If he admits it, this is sufficient for the claim of the claimant to be proven and for the arbitrator to reach his verdict. If he denies it, the claimant is bound to produce testimony, and if he produces the testimony and it meets the conditions stipulated in the Sharīʿah, his claim is proven. The defendant is not bound to produce testimony .

In certain circumstances, the defendant must swear an oath, and if he swears an oath his prosecution is to go no further. In jurisprudence, it is said, 'Testimony upon the claimant, and an oath upon whoever denies it'. The issues of arbitration are so many that voluminous books have been written solely on this subject.

The Book of Punishments (ḥudūd and taʿzirāt)

This book is about Islamic punishments. Some of the systems of punishment have been precisely defined and determined in Islam, and these are to be performed in the same way regardless of the conditions or any other factors. These types of punishments are called *ḥudūd*. There are a few punishments, however, that the Sharīʿah considers to depend on the view of the Ḥakim,[9] who, by taking into consideration the causes and conditions of the crime and any motivating factors or factors that make the crime more serious, enforces a fitting punishment. These punishments are called *taʿzirāt*.

The crimes for which *ḥudūd* have been stipulated are adultery, homosexuality (including lesbianism), falsely accusing a person of committing one of these crimes, drinking alcohol, stealing and armed civil disturbance, which are all considered crimes against God. Although these have all been greatly misunderstood both inside and outside the Islamic world, they are detailed and here is not the place to discuss them further. It must be mentioned, however, that if a certain punishment has not been introduced in the Sharīʿah among the *ḥudūd*, the Islamic government must introduce punishments as it considers in the best interests of all concerned. These punishments are among the *taʿzīrāt*.

The Book of Retaliation (qiṣās)

Qisas is also a type of punishment, but for offences wherein one person criminally ends the life or harms the body of another person. In reality, *qiṣās* is the right Islam gives to the victim or to his heirs if the offence leads to the victim's death.

Such offences are either murder or loss or impediment of a part of the body, and are either intentional (*ʿamd*), quasi-intentional (*shabih ʿamd*) or purely a mistake (*khata mehd*).

An intentional offence is one that was committed with the intention to commit it, such as a person who intends to kill another person and does so, whether with a specific weapon of attack, such as a sword or a gun, or by some other means, such as with a stone.

An offence that is 'quasi-intentional' is one in which the intention is to commit the act but not to inflict the harm that the act causes. An example would be a situation in which a person, with the intention of hurting another, hits him with a club, which results in the victim's death. Another example would be a case in which someone hits a child, by way of teaching the child a lesson, and the child dies. Also in this same category would be the case of a doctor who treats his patient for a certain disease and the treatment causes the patient to die.

A mistake, however, implies no intention to kill or harm at all, such as when a person who kills someone when the rifle he is cleaning accidentally discharges or the driver who makes an error and runs someone over in the street.

In the cases of intentional killing or quasi-intentional killing the heirs of the deceased have the right of *qiṣās*, meaning that under the supervision of the Islamic government and at the discretion of the nearest of kin, the killer can either be executed or forced to pay recompense. In the case of a mistake the killer should not be executed but is obliged only to pay the heirs the *diyah*, the financial recompense.

The Book of Financial Recompense (diyah)

Diyah is like *qiṣās* in that it is a right of the offended person or the heirs of the offended person against the offender, with the difference that *qiṣās* is a payment in kind while *diyah* is a financial penalty. The laws of *diyah*, like the laws of *qiṣās*, are very detailed.

In the books of *qiṣās* and *diyah*, jurisprudents have gone into the question of the liability of doctors and of teachers.

If a doctor is not competent and makes a mistake in his treatment of the patient, which leads to the patient's death, he is liable. And if he is competent and he treats the patient without the permission of the patient or the patient's next of kin, and the treatment leads to the patient's death, he is again liable. However, if the doctor is competent and he treats the patient with the permission of the patient or the patient's next of kin, he must make it clear that he will do his utmost to cure the patient but that, should his efforts happen to lead to the patient's death, he will not be responsible. If the patient in such a case dies or is harmed by the treatment, the doctor is not liable and not subject to *qiṣās*. If, however, the doctor fails to set out this condition before beginning the treatment, some jurisprudents say that he is liable.

Likewise, if a teacher strikes a child unnecessarily and the blow leads to the death or injury of the child, the teacher is liable. If, however, the teacher is punishing the child, believing it to be in the child's best interests, and if this should happen to lead to the death or injury of the child, the teacher will be liable, unless he has received prior permission to administer punishment from the child's guardians.

Translator's Epilogue

From this brief introduction to the issues of jurisprudence, it can be seen how jurisprudence, like the Sharīʿah itself, enters into all the aspects, indeed, is the very essence of Islamic life.

There has never been general agreement as to how the different issues of jurisprudence (in other words, the laws of Islam) should be classified, as it is very difficult to order and classify the different aspects of life itself. After the success of the Islamic revolution in Iran, however, a new development has taken place in this regard, which, although such classifications are of little significance and although it is yet to be seen how this new classification can be adapted to the existing classifications, promises to revolutionize the face of jurisprudence.

The new classification is wonderful in its simplicity. It divides all the Islamic laws and legislations into four groups, under the headings of 'Worship and Self-Perfection', including the issues of cleanliness, ritual prayer, fasting and the *ḥajj*; 'Economic Affairs', which includes *khums*, *zakāt*, endowment, partnership, etc.; 'Family Affairs', including marriage, divorce, wills and inheritance; and 'Political Affairs', which includes arbitration, Islamic punishments, the *jihād* of defence and so on.

As has been said, Islamic teachings are basically divided into three: knowledge of the unseen reality, knowledge of the perfection of one's inner self and knowledge of the perfection of one's external actions. Perhaps the reason why, of the three, it is the least important external actions that have been given such importance within the schools is that they are less intrinsic than belief and virtue and are, therefore, more demanding of the intellectual capacities, as well as being dependent upon the other two. A person who has some knowledge of God, prophethood, imamate and the hereafter may become engaged solely in the struggle to purify himself, paying attention to his external actions only insofar as to ensure that they accord with his moral values. A person who has a mastery of the external laws of actions, however, must necessarily possess sure knowledge of the realities and sublime moral excellence. To learn and act according to the Sharīʿah without certainty or at least profound and sincere belief, without moral excellence and without a well-trained intellect is almost impossible. If one has scant knowledge of the realities or has knowledge of the realities but little virtue, one will never see the point of adhering to the intricacies of living according to the Sharīʿah.

Therefore, although the teaching of jurisprudence is the centre of all the religious institutions, the two more urgent studies also have their place. If students of jurisprudence did not themselves develop their knowledge of the realities and of self-perfection, there simply would not be any students of jurisprudence; the laws of the Sharīʿah would be forgotten and many of the words and commands of God, the Prophet and Imāms would no longer be acted upon because they would no longer be understood.

Notes

1. *faqīhāt* is the feminine plural of *faqīh* and thus means 'female jurisprudents'.
2. The other being Najaf, despite the way it has been weakened and reduced by the Ba'th regime of Iraq.
3. A *dhimmi kāfir* is a *kāfir* (non-Muslim) who lives in peace in the Islamic state in accordance with its laws and subject to the benefits it accords him. No other *kāfir* is allowed to live in an Islamic state.
4. *Iḥrām* is a state to which a person commits himself in which many things become forbidden to the person. During the *ḥajj* and *'umrah* it accompanies the wearing of two plain, white, unsewn pieces of cloth.
5. *Mehr* is like a dowry in reverse, i.e. it is the agreed sum to be paid by the man to the woman as a condition of their marriage.
6. The author has not mentioned that *nadhr* is often made as a promise to do some good deed or deeds in return for a requested favour. In this case, the *nadhr* becomes obligatory only when God has granted that favour.
7. Shrimps, however, are ruled as sea-locusts, and may be eaten, provided, like fish, they are taken from the water live.
8. i.e. half a *mithqāl*, an Eastern measurement.
9. The Ḥakim Sharī'ah is, as we have seen, either a *mujtahid*, who meets the conditions of being just, or his representative, acting on his behalf. The Western equivalent is the role of a magistrate.

PART FIVE

Uṣūl al-Fiqh: Principles of Jurisprudence

Introduction

The subject under consideration here is the *'ilm*, or knowledge of the principles of jurisprudence, *uṣūl al-fiqh*. The two studies of jurisprudence and its principles are interconnected. They are interconnected in the same way as the twin studies of logic and philosophy. The study of the principles is tantamount to a preparation for the study of jurisprudence, and it is for this reason that it has been named the principles of jurisprudence, for the word *uṣūl* means 'roots' or 'principles'.

First, a short definition of these two studies must be given.

The Arabic word *fiqh* essentially means 'profound understanding'. Our information about the affairs and proceedings of this world can be of two types, shallow and superficial or profound. An example from economics will help. We are all aware that products that did not exist years ago are constantly finding their way on to the market, while at the same time numerous products that were previously abundant cannot now be found. Likewise, the prices of certain products increase steadily, while the prices of other goods may be fixed.

This type of information is universally available and is shallow or superficial information. However, some people have profound knowledge of these matters, having progressed from merely experiencing events to a profound understanding of their causes. What this means in this instance is that they understand why a certain article has become available and another article has become unavailable, and why a certain product is expensive and another is inexpensive. They know what causes prices to increase, and they know to what extent these causes are essential, definite and unavoidable, and to what extent they can be controlled.

When a person has a knowledge of economics that surpasses the level of simple experience and attains the level of being able to discern deep-rooted causes and trends, he can be described as one with deep understanding (*mutafaqqih*) in economics.

In the Holy Qur'ān and in Traditions from the Holy Prophet and the Imāms, we are repeatedly commanded towards profound understanding (*tafaqquh*) in religion, and these sources make it abundantly clear that Islam expects Muslims to understand Islam, in all its aspects, profoundly and with thorough insight. Of course, profound understanding in religion, consisting of all facets of Islam, is a great blessing from God. It extends to the principles of Islamic beliefs and the Islamic world view or system of values, to Islamic morals, ethics and upbringing, to all aspects of Islamic society, to Islamic worship, to the civil ordinances of Islam, to individual and social Islamic customs and to much more. However, since the second century of the Hijrah, the word jurisprudence has become a term for a special area of understanding among Muslims that may be called jurisprudence in the commands of religion or jurisprudence in deducing the commands of religion, in other words, 'precise and profound deducing of the Islamic regulations of actions from the relevant sources'.

The commands or regulations of Islam have not been explained by the Qur'ān or by the Prophet and the Imāms in such a way as to deal with each and every particularity. Nor is such a thing possible, for events and situations occur in endlessly different forms. Instead, generalities and precepts have been laid before us in the form of a chain of principles.

A person who wants to explain the law on a certain matter to himself or others must refer to the resources and authentic documents – later we shall clarify the nature of these – and must explain his viewpoint while bearing in mind all the different aspects of those authentic documents. This is what is meant by he statement that jurisprudence is joined to precise and profound understanding of all aspects.

The masters of jurisprudence (*fuqahā*) offer the following definition: Jurisprudence is the study of the secondary commands (i.e. not the principle matters of beliefs and moral perfection, but the commands regulating actions) of the Sharī'ah of Islam gained from the detailed resources and proofs.

The Principles of Jurisprudence

For the study of jurisprudence, it is necessary to prepare by mastering many other branches of learning, as follows.

1. Arabic, namely, syntax, conjugation, vocabulary, semantics, oratory. As the Qur'ān and Traditions are in Arabic, it is not possible to benefit from them without at least a basic knowledge of Arabic language and literature.

2. Commentary upon the Holy Qur'ān (*tafsīr*). Since jurisprudents must use the Qur'ān as a point of reference, some knowledge of the commentaries on the Qur'ān is absolutely essential.

3. Logic, called *mantiq* in Islam. Every branch of learning in which reasoning is used requires the application of logic.

4. The study of the Traditions. A jurisprudent must have a sound knowledge of the Traditions and must be able to distinguish the different types of Traditions. Frequent application of the Traditions is the route to familiarity with their language.

5. The study of the Transmitters (*rijāl*). The study of the Transmitters is the study of the identities and natures of those who make up the chains (*isnād*) of reporters of the Traditions. Later we shall explain how the Traditions existing in the sanctuary of books of Traditions cannot be accepted without examination.

6. The study of the principles of jurisprudence. The most important branch of learning in preparation for jurisprudence is the principles of jurisprudence, a delightful subject and one originated by Muslims.

The principles of jurisprudence is, in reality, 'study of the rules to be used in deducing the Islamic laws' and it teaches us the correct and valid way of deducing from the relevant sources in jurisprudence. Thus, principles, like logic, is a study of instructions, and is more a skill than a branch of knowledge, meaning that in jurisprudence, what is discussed is a chain of things that must be, rather than a chain of things that are.

Bearing in mind that it is possible, in referring to the documents or sources of jurisprudence, to be led to erroneous deductions that are opposed to the real view of the Islamic Sharī'ah, there needs to be a discipline that enables students clearly to discern the correct and valid method of deducing and extracting the laws of Islam from the sources of jurisprudence, by means of the proofs of reasoning and the proofs provided by God through the Prophet and the Imāms. The principles of jurisprudence is that discipline.

From the early days of Islam, another word that is more or less synonymous with *fiqh* (jurisprudence) and that has been in common use among Muslims is the word *ijtihād*. In the Muslim world today, especially the Shī'ite world, the words *faqīh* (jurisprudent) and *mujtahid* are synonymous.

The word *ijtihād* comes from the root *juhd*, which means 'utter striving'. For this reason, a *faqīh* is also called a *mujtahid*, since he must use all his efforts in deducing Islamic laws (*aḥkām*).

The Sources of Jurisprudence

We have seen how the study of the principles of jurisprudence involves reference to the original sources. Now we shall examine what those sources are, and how many they are, and whether all the sects and schools of Islam have the same views about each detail of the sources or whether they hold opposing views. If there are differences, what are those differences? First, we shall discuss the views of Shī'ite jurisprudents on the sources of jurisprudence, with explanations of those sources, as well as the views of the ulamā' of the other Islamic sects. In the view of Shī'ites (with the exception of a small group who are called *akhbāriyyīn*, whose views we shall consider later), there are four sources for jurisprudence:

1. The Book of God, the Qur'ān, to which jurisprudents refer concisely as 'The Book'.
2. 'Sunnah', meaning the words, actions and silent assertions (*taqrīr*) of the Prophet and the Imāms.
3. Consensus, or *ijmā'*.
4. Reasoning, or *'aql*.

These four sources are called the 'four proofs', or the *adillat ul-arba'ah*. The study of jurisprudence is generally centred around these four proofs. Now we shall explain each of these four sources along with the views of the other Islamic sects and those of the *akhbāriyyīn*.

The Qur'ān

There is no doubt that the Holy Qur'ān is the first source of the laws and regulations of Islam. Of course, the *āyah*, or verses, of the Qur'ān are not limited to laws and regulations. In the Qur'ān, hundreds of different types of issues have been introduced, but a part of the Qur'ān, said to consist of about five hundred *āyah*, from a total of six thousand six hundred and sixty, i.e. roughly a thirteenth of the Qur'ān, pertains especially to laws.

From the early days of Islam, Muslims have always used the Qur'ān as the primal point of reference for deducing Islamic laws. However, during the rule of the Safavid dynasty a sect appeared in Iran who maintained that it was forbidden for ordinary people to refer to the Qur'ān and that only the Prophet and the Imāms had this right.

Similarly, this group considered that referral to consensus and reason were impermissible, as consensus had been introduced by the Sunnis and the use of reason is open to error and thus unreliable. In their view the Sunnah was the sole source of reference. For this reason they were called the *akhbāriyyīn*, as *akhbār* means 'tradition'.

This group, by denying the right of referral to the Qur'ān, consensus and reasoning, were essentially denying *ijtihād*, for *ijtihād*, as has been stated, means precise understanding and profound deduction, and it is evident that profound understanding is not possible without making use of reason. This group came to believe that ordinary people, without the medium of a group known as *mujtahids*, must refer to the traditions for guidance in their daily affairs and actions, just as today they refer to the treatises of the *mujtahids*.[1]

The appearance of the *akhbāriyyīn* and the large numbers that were attracted to them in some cities in the south of Iran, islands of the Gulf and in some of the holy cities of Iraq, was the cause of severe decline. Fortunately, however, with the noteworthy and laudable resistance of the *mujtahid*s of the period, their penetration was firmly checked. Today their theories have virtually no support except in a few scattered places.

The Sunnah

The Sunnah signifies the words, actions and assertions of the Holy Prophet and the Imāms. Clearly, if the Holy Prophet verbally explained a certain law, or if it is known how the Prophet performed a certain religious obligation, or if it known that others performed certain religious duties in his presence in a certain way that earnt his blessing and approval – his silence indicating endorsement – this is sufficient proof (*dalīl*) for a jurisprudent to consider the action to be the actual law of Islam.

There is no argument about this definition of Sunnah and its binding (*ḥujjat*) nature, nor does any scholar oppose it. The differences that exist on the subject of the Sunnah concern two points. One is the question as to whether the Sunnah of the Prophet alone is binding or whether the Sunnah related by the pure Imāms is also binding. Our Sunni-Muslim brothers consider the

Sunnah of the Prophet alone as binding, but the Shīʿites also refer to the words, actions and silent approval of the holy Imāms, in accordance with the traditions of the Prophet, which even Sunni Muslims have related and recorded. One of these traditions is the Prophet's instruction, 'I leave behind me two valuable things to which you are to refer, and God forbid that you not refer to them: the Book of God and the people of my House'.

The second point is that the related Sunnah of the Prophet of God and the pure Imāms is sometimes clear and interrelated, i.e. there are different chains of narrators of the same Tradition, and sometimes suspicious, consisting of a Single Report (*khabar al-wāḥid*).

Here views vary excessively. Some, like Abū Ḥanīfa, a jurisprudent of one of the four Sunni schools, paid scant attention to the related Traditions; of all the thousands of Traditions narrated by the Holy Prophet, he considered only seventeen to be reliable.

Others have found confidence even in 'weak', unreliable Traditions. But the Shīʿite ulamā' are of the opinion that reliable traditions only are to be given credence. That is, if the people who make up the chain of narrators, called the *musnad*, are Shīʿite and just, or at least truthful and reliable, then the Tradition itself can be relied upon. So we must know the narrators of the Traditions and must research their conditions and, if it becomes determined that all the narrators of a Tradition were truthful and reliable, we rely upon that Tradition.

Many of the ulamā' of the Sunnis have this same idea, and it is for this reason that the study of the Transmitters exists among them. The *akhbāri* Shīʿites, however, whom we have mentioned, considered the division of Traditions into 'valid' and 'weak' to be uncalled-for and said that all Traditions are reliable, especially those contained in the reliable books. This extreme[2] view is also held by some of the ulamā' of our Sunni brothers.

Consensus

Consensus means the unanimous view of the Muslim ulamā' on a particular issue. In the opinion of the Shīʿite ulamā', consensus is binding because if all Muslims have one view, this is proof that the view has been received from the Holy Prophet.

It would be impossible for all Muslims to share the same view on a matter if it came from themselves, and thus their consensus is proof that the origin of that view is the Sunnah of the Prophet or an Imām.

For example, if it is clear that on one subject all the Muslims of the Prophet's era, with no exceptions, had a certain view and performed a certain type of action, this is proof that they were taught it by the Holy Prophet.

Likewise, if all the companions of one of the pure Imāms who took instructions exclusively from them and the Imāms all took the same view about something, this is proof that they acquired that view from the schooling of their Imām. Therefore, in the Shīʿite view, consensus goes back to the Sunnah of the Prophet.

From the above we learn two things:

First, in the Shīʿite view, the consensus of the ulamā' of the same period as the Prophet or Imāms only is binding. So, if in the present day a consensus occurs about something among all the ulamā', without exception, this is in no way binding for subsequent ulamā'.

Second, in the Shīʿite view, consensus is not genuinely binding in its own right, rather it is binding inasmuch as it is a means of discovering the Sunnah.

In the view of the ulamā' of our Sunni brothers, however, consensus is a proof in its own right. That is, if the ulamā' of Islam, in their view the management of Islam, are all in agreement on a certain point of view about a subject in one period (even our own), their view is definitely correct. They claim that it is possible for some of the nation to err and some not to, but it is not possible for all of them to be in agreement and err.

In the view of our Sunni brothers, complete agreement of all the Muslims in one period is ruled as divine revelation, and thus all the Muslims, at the moment of consensus, are ruled as Prophets, and what is revealed to them is the law of God and cannot be wrong.[3]

Reason

The binding testimony of reason in the Shīʿite view means that if in a set of circumstances reason has a clear rule, then that rule, because it is definite and absolute, is binding.

Here the question arises, whether the laws of the Sharīʿah are in the domain of reason or not We shall answer this question when we discuss the generalities of the principles.

The *akhbāriyyīn* in no way count reason as binding.

Among the ulamā' of our Sunni brothers, Abū Ḥanīfa considered analogy (*qiyās*) to be the fourth proof, and thus in the view of the Ḥanafi sect, there are four sources of jurisprudence: the Book, the Sunnah, consensus and analogy.

The Māliki and Ḥanbali Sunnis, especially the Ḥanbalis, pay no heed whatever to analogy. The Shāfi'i Muslims, following their leader, Muḥammad ibn Idrīs Shāfi'i, pay more attention to Traditions than the Ḥanafis and also more attention to analogy than the Māliki and Ḥanbali Muslims.

The view of the Shīʿite ulamā', however, is that because analogy is pure conjecture and surmise, and because the total of what has been received from the Holy Prophet and the Imāms is sufficient for our responsibility, reference to analogy is strictly forbidden.

A Brief History

A student who wishes to study or gather information about a certain branch of learning must acquaint himself with the origins of that learning, with those who introduced it, with the nature of its development over the centuries, with its notable champions and exponents and with its famous and respected books.

The study of principles is one of the studies that originated and developed in the surroundings of the culture of Islam. It is generally recognized to have been introduced by Muḥammad ibn Idrīs Shāfi'i. Ibn Khaldūn, in his famous *Muqaddamah*, in the section in which he discusses the various sciences and skills, tells us, 'The first person in the study of the principles of jurisprudence to write a book was Shāfi'i, who wrote his famous *Treatise*. In that treatise, he discussed the commands and prohibitions, the Traditions, abrogation and other matters. After him, the Ḥanafi ulamā' wrote similar books and brought extensive research into practice.'

However, as has been pointed out by the late Seyyid Ḥaṣan Ṣadr, may God elevate him,[4] various problems of principles, such as the commands and prohibitions and 'generalities and particularities', had previously been raised by Shīʿite ulamā', who wrote a treatise about each of them. So perhaps it can be said that Shāfi'i was the first person to write one book about all the issues of principles that had been raised by that time.

Likewise, some Orientalists consider that *ijtihād* began among the Shīʿite some two hundred years after it began among the Sunnis; a view they base upon the assumption that during the time of the pure Imāms there was no need among the Shīʿites for *ijtihād* and that, as a result, there was similarly no need for the preparatory studies of *ijtihād*. This view is, however, incorrect.

Ijtihād, in the proper meaning of deducing the consequences (i.e. legislation) of faith from the sources – meaning referring the consequences or legislation to the sources, and applying the sources to the legislation – has existed among Shīʿites ever since the time of the pure Imāms, and the pure Imāms used to command their companions to engage in this practice.

Furthermore, owing to the numerous Traditions about different subjects that have been narrated by the pure Imāms, Shīʿite jurisprudence has naturally been considerably enriched, and thus the struggles of *ijtihād* are somewhat easier. At the same time, however, Shī'ite Islam has never considered itself to be free of the need of *tafaqquh* and *ijtihād*, and the instructions to carry on the struggle of *ijtihād* were especially given by the Imāms to their outstanding companions. In reliable books the following statement from the Imāms is found: 'Upon us are the [general] rules [i.e. the general rules are the responsibility of the Imāms], while upon you is the application [i.e. the application of the rules in all the particular circumstances is your responsibility]'.

Among Shī'ite ulamā', the first outstanding personality to compile books on principles and whose views were discussed in principles for centuries was Seyyid Morteza 'Alam ul Huda. The best-known of his numerous books is *Dhari'ah* ('The Medium').

Seyyid Murtaḍā was the brother of Seyyid Rāḍī, who was the compiler of the famous *Nahj ul-Balāghah*, the book of sermons, letters and sayings of Hazrat 'Alī (rightly called the Way of Eloquence). Seyyid Murtaḍā lived during the late fourth and early fifth centuries AH and died in 436 AH. He had been the student of the famous *mutakallīm*, or master of theology (*kalām*), Shaykh ul-Mufīd (died 413 AH), who in turn had been the pupil of the equally famous Shaykh Ṣadūq (died 381 AH).

Following Seyyid Murtaḍā, a famous and important figure in the study of principles, who wrote a book and whose views were for three or four centuries outstandingly influential, was the great Shaykh Ṭūsī (died 460 AH) who had been the pupil of Seyyid Murtaḍā and who, almost a thousand years ago, founded the scholastic centre of Najaf in Iraq, which is still functioning today.

A later personality in the study of principles was the late Waḥīd Bahbahani (1118–1208 AH), a very important figure in many ways. He brought many of his pupils in jurisprudence and *ijtihād* to a high level of distinction and excellence. He fought vigorously against the previously mentioned *akhbāriyyīn*, who at that time were accumulating extraordinary influence. The success of the system of *ijtihād* over the corrupt system of the *akhbāriyyīn* owes much to his efforts.

Over the past hundred years, without doubt the most important figure in the study of principles is the late Shaykh Murtaḍā Anṣārī (1214–1281 AH), and those who have come after him have all followed his school of thought. Until now no line of thought has emerged to transform or challenge that of Shaykh Anṣārī, although many students of his school have formed views, based on Shaykh Anṣārī's own teachings, that have occasionally abrogated one of his views. His two books, *Farāiḍ ul-uṣūl* and *Makāsib* (on the subject of jurisprudence), are today used as textbooks by students of religion.

Among the pupils of the school of Shaykh Anṣārī the most famous is the late Mullā Khorasāni, who has been recorded in the history books as the man who issued the verdict (*fatwā*) for the constitutional movement in Iran, and who had a major share in the establishment of the constitutional regime.

Among all Islamic studies there is none that is so changeable and variable as the study of principles and even today there exist outstanding figures who have their own (legitimate) views in the field.

The principles of jurisprudence, being concerned with the calculation of knowledge and the mind and involving many minute investigations, is a pleasant and attractive discipline that draws in the seeker of knowledge like a magnet. As an exercise in thought and mental exactitude, it stands alongside logic and philosophy. The students of the ancient sciences owe their precise way of thinking largely to the study of principles.

The Subjects of the Principles

In order to acquaint the respected reader with the issues of the principles of jurisprudence we shall discuss their main outline, not in the order followed by scholars, but in an order that will better suit our purposes.

Earlier, we stated that the study of principles is a study of instructions, meaning that it teaches us the way of correctly and validly deducing the commandments of religion from the original sources. The principles are all related to the four types of sources: the Book, i.e. the Qur'ān, the Sunnah (or both, since both are originally verbal sources), consensus or reason.

Occasionally we may encounter circumstances in which we cannot deduce the necessary Islamic law from the four sources. The Islamic Sharīʿah is not silent on this matter and has established a system of rules and practices from which we can interpret the apparent law.

Acquiring the apparent duty of application (from the requisite rules) after having failed to deduce the actual duty requires that we learn the correct method of benefiting from those rules.

Thus the study of the principles, which is a study of instructions, falls into two parts. One part contains instructions for correct and valid deduction of the actual laws of the Sharīʿah from the relevant sources. The other part is related to the correct and valid way of benefiting from a chain of rules for application after deduction has failed. The first part is called the principles for deducing (*uṣūl al-istinbāṭiyyah*) and the second part is called the principles for application (*uṣūl al-ʿamaliyyah*) (of the special rules when there is no hope of deducing).

Furthermore, since deduction is from one of four sources – the Book, the Sunnah, consensus or reasoning – the issues of the principles of deduction are divided into four parts.

The Binding Testimony of the Qur'ān's Apparent and Accepted Realities (ẓawāhir)

In the principles of jurisprudence there are not many discussions particular to the Qur'ān. The discussions relative to the Qur'ān are basically related both to the Book and to the Sunnah. The only discussion centred solely on the Qur'ān concerns the binding testimony of its apparent realities, that is, whether the apparent laws of the Qur'ān – regardless of whether or not they are qualified, conditioned and explained by existing or authentic traditions – are binding testimonies on which jurisprudents may unconditionally rely.

It may be surprising that the *uṣūliyyīn*, those learned in the principles, should have thought up such a debate. Could the legitimacy of a jurisprudent, relying on the apparent laws of the *āyahs* or verses of the sacred Qur'ān, ever be subject to doubt?

This is a debate that was introduced by the Shī'ite ulamā' of the principles in order to negate the misgivings of the *akhbāriyyīn*, who, as has been shown, believed that, apart from the holy ones (The Prophet, his daughter and the twelve Imāms, peace be upon them all), no one has the right to refer to the Qur'ān or to deduce the Sharī'ah from it. In other words, the eternal benefit that Muslims derive from the Qur'ān must be indirect, must be via the Sunnah of the Ahl Bait, the Prophet and the purified members of his House. The claim of the *akhbāriyyīn* was based upon the Traditions, which forbid interpretation of the Qur'ān in terms of opinion.

The *uṣūliyyīn*, however, have proved that the deduction that Muslims make from the Qur'ān is direct, and that the prohibition on 'interpreting the Qur'ān by opinion' does not mean that people have no right to understand the Qur'ān by their own thoughts and reflections, but that the Qur'ān must not be interpreted according to ambition and inflated ego.

Furthermore, the Holy Prophet and the Imāms are authentically reported to have told us that forged Traditions would appear, and in order to distinguish the true from the false, we must compare all Traditions with the Qur'ān, and any Traditions that disagree with the Qur'ān must be realized to be false and thus be disregarded, being unworthy of any respect. This of course cannot be done without referring to the Qur'ān. What is more, the same Traditions make it clear that, in complete contrast to the claims of the *akhbāriyyīn*, the Sunnah is not the criterion of the Qur'ān, rather the Qur'ān is the criterion of the Sunnah.

The Apparent and Accepted Realities (ẓawāhir) of the Sunnah

Two important subjects are discussed in the study of principles relating to the binding testimony of the Sunnah, that is, the Traditions and narrations that have reiterated the words, actions and silent assertions of the Prophet and the Imāms.

One is the question of the binding testimony of the *khabar al-waḥīd*, the Single Report, and the other is the question of the Traditions that are opposed to the Qur'ān and that must be rejected. These two questions are called, respectively, the Single Report (*khabar al-waḥīd*) and the Unification and Preference (*ta'ādul wa tarājiḥ*).

The Single Report (khabar al-waḥīd)

The Single Report is a Tradition that has been reported from the Imām or Prophet but by one person only, or that is reported by more than one person but on the other hand has not transmitted by so many different people that there is a possibility of the Tradition's being in any way wrong (*tawātur*). Now, can such a Tradition be used as a basis for deducing the Sharī'ah or not?

The *uṣūliyyīn* believe that, provided the transmitters of the Single Report from the first to the last were all just or at least were probably truthful, the Traditions they have narrated can be used to deduce the relevant law. One of the justifications for this claim is the holy *āyah* of the Qur'ān, in which we are told, 'If a wicked man comes to you with news, examine' (49:6). This means that we are to be sceptical of news delivered by a wrongdoer and should research his report and unless we can definitely establish its validity, we must not give it credence or put its recommendations into effect. Similarly, the *āyah* tacitly indicates that if a just person and reliable person gives us a report, we are to put it into effect. The tacit meaning of this *āyah*, therefore, is proof of the binding testimony of the Single Report.[5]

Unification and Preference

Now we come to the issue of opposing Traditions. Often it happens that various Traditions on the same subject are opposed to each other, for example, whether we should recite the *dhikr* (remembrance) of the third and fourth units of prayer (*rak'ats*) – called the *tasbiḥat al-arb'ah* – three times in each unit or whether one time is enough. Some Traditions suggest that it must be said three times, while in another Tradition once is deemed to be enough. Similarly, there are conflicting Traditions about whether it is permissible to sell human manure.

What must be done when we have such varying Traditions? Must we consider that when two contrasting reports exist we are to ignore them both, just as if we had no Traditions on the subject at all? Or do we have the option of acting according to whichever of them we like? Or are we to act with caution and thus to the Tradition that is nearer to caution (which, in relation to our two examples would mean, respectively, reciting the *dhikr* prayer three times, and accepting the prohibition on selling human manure)? Or is there another way of acting?

The ulamā' of the principles have determined, first, that the unified content of all the varying Traditions must as far as possible be implemented and, if this is not possible and neither of the two sides has preference over the other in some way, such as in the reliability of the chain of narrators, in its credibility among earlier ulamā' who may have had some other testimony that we have missed, or in its being clearly not due to *taqiyah*,[6] and the like, we have the option to act according to whichever of them we like.[7]

There are Traditions that themselves contain instructions on what to do in the case of contradicting Traditions. They are called Corrective Reports (*al-akhbar al'ilājiyyah*).

The ulamā' of the principles, on the basis of these Corrective Reports, have expressed their views on the contradicting Traditions. This is the branch of the study of principles that has been named Unification and Preference and which discusses the unification of opposing Traditions and the superiority of some over others.

From what has been said it is clear that the issue of the binding authority of apparent laws is relevant to the Book, whereas the issues of the Single Report and of the contradicting testimonies concern the Sunnah. In the next section we shall look at issues in the principles that are common both to the Book and to the Sunnah.

Issues Common to the Book and the Sunnah

The discussions common to the Book and the Sunnah consist of the following:

- The discussion of imperatives (*awāmir*)
- The discussion of negative imperatives (*nawāhi*)
- The discussion of generalities and particularities (*'ām wa khāṣ*)
- The discussion of unconditional (*muṭlaq*) and conditional (*muqayyad*)

- The discussion of tacit meanings (*mafāhīm*)
- The discussion of the abstract (*mujmal*) and the clear (*mubayyan*)
- The discussion of the abrogator (*nāsīkh*) and the abrogated (*mansūkh*)

We shall look at these briefly in turn.

The Discussion of Imperatives (awāmir)

The Arabic *awāmir* is the plural of the word *amr*, which means 'command'. It also means the type of verb form that in English is called imperative, for example 'listen!' or 'stand!'.

In the Book and the Sunnah, many of the phrases are in the form of the imperative, and it is here that many questions are raised in jurisprudence that must be answered in the study of principles. They include such questions as whether or not the imperative is proof that the action is obligatory (*wājib*) or that it is desirable or neither. Does the imperative signify that the verb is to be done once or a number of times?

For example, the Qur'ān contains the following instruction, 'Take from their property charity, you cleanse them and purify them thereby, and pray for them; your prayer is a soother for them'. (9:103) 'Prayer', in this holy verse, means to supplicate or send a blessing. Here, the first question that is raised concerns the status of the imperative verb form, 'pray'. Does it mean that to supplicate for them or send a blessing upon them is obligatory? In other words, is the imperative here an indication of obligation or not?

The second question is whether or not the imperative is an indication of immediate obligation. Is it obligatory that, straight after taking the divine tax(*zakāt*), prayer is to be offered for it, or is it permissible to leave an interval? Third, is one prayer enough or must it be performed repeatedly?

Such matters are all discussed in detail in the study of jurisprudence and the principles.

The Discussion of Negative Imperatives (nawāhi)

The Arabic word *nawāhi* is the plural of *nahy*, which means to 'stop' or 'prevent', and is the opposite of *amr*, the imperative. If in English we say, 'Do not drink alcohol', this is a negative imperative, which in Arabic becomes a *nahy*. Both in the Book and in the Sunnah there are many phrases that are negative imperatives.

Similar questions arise here to those on the subject of the imperative. Is the negative imperative evidence that the object of the verb is forbidden (*ḥarām*) or that it is not forbidden but merely undesirable (*makrūḥ*)? Likewise, does the negative imperative indicate permanence, i.e. that the action of the verb must never be done or that it is to be refrained from only temporarily?

Discussion of Generalities and Particularities ('ām wa khāṣ)

In the civil and penal laws of human society, a general and common law exists that applies to all, as well as another law related to a group of individuals from that society, a law that is opposed to the common and general law.

In such instances, what is to be done? Must the two laws be interpreted as mutually contradictory? Or, since one of the two laws is general and the other is particular, is the particular law to be received as an exception to the general law?

For example, we are told in the Qur'ān that divorced women must wait after their divorce for three monthly periods before they are free to remarry. In reliable Traditions, however, we are told that if a woman marries a man and divorces before marital relations (i.e. sexual intercourse) occurs between them, it is not necessary for the woman to observe the term.

What are we to do here? Are we to consider this Tradition to be opposed to the Qur'ān and therefore reject it and disregard it, as we have been instructed? Or are we to assume that this Tradition in reality expounds the Qur'ānic *āyah* for us, that it has the rank of an exception in certain of the particular circumstances, and that the Qur'ān is in no way contradicted by it?

It is the second view that is the correct and valid one, of course, for we are used to having a law introduced in the general form and then having the exceptions explained. We are not used to having the exceptions explained before the law is introduced, and the Qur'ān addresses human beings in the terms and language that they understand. In another place the Qur'ān itself deems the Traditions of the Prophet to be reliable. 'What the Prophet gives you, take! And what he has prohibited, avoid!' (59:8). In these types of circumstances, we accept that particularities have the rank of exceptions to generalities.

Unconditional (muṭlaq) and Conditional (muqayyad)

The question of conditional and unconditional is similar to the question of generality and particularity, but generality and particularity are relevant to the applicability of the law, while conditional and unconditional are relevant to the different circumstances and qualities of the law itself. The general and the particular are relevant to the applicability of and the exemptions from the law.

The question of unconditional and conditional, however, is related to the essence and nature of the duty that the dutiful must perform. If the duty has no particular condition attached to it, then it is unconditional, and if it has a particular condition, it is conditional.

In the example we gave above, the Holy Prophet was commanded that, at the time of taking the *zakāt* from the Muslims, he was to supplicate for them. This instruction, as regards whether the Prophet was to supplicate for them loudly or quietly, in company or alone, is unconditional.

If we have no other proof or reason provided by the Qur'ān or reliable Traditions that set conditions, we act according to the unconditional meaning of the *āyah*. That is, we are free to perform the command in whatever fashion we like. If, however, we are provided with an authentic proof, telling us, for example, that the supplication is to be unconditional to the conditional, which means that we are to consider the unconditional sentence to be given a condition by the conditional sentence, we then interpret the unconditional as the conditional.

The Discussion of the Tacit (mafāhīm)

The tacit, in the terminology of the study of principles, is the opposite of spoken. Imagine that someone says, 'Come with me to my house and I will give you such and such a book.' This sentence takes the place of the following two sentences, namely, 'If you come with me to my house I will give you that book' and 'If you do not come with me to my house I will not give you that book'.

So here there are two connections: the affirmative and the negative. The affirmative connection is between accompanying and giving, and exists in the substance of the sentence and it is uttered. For this reason it is called the spoken. The negative connection, on the other hand, is not uttered, but from the sentence it is naturally understood. This is why it is called tacit or, more literally, the understood.

In the discussion on the Single Report we saw how the *uṣūliyyīn* have recognized the binding testimony of the Single Report, when the narrators are all just from the holy *āyah* of the Qur'ān, which tells us, 'If a wicked man comes to you with news, examine'.

This recognition comes from the tacit meaning of the *āyah*. The words of the *āyah* tell us only that we are not to put into effect the news of an unjust person without investigation, while the tacit meaning of the *āyah* is that we are not to put into effect the news he gives us, but we are to put into effect the news given to us by someone who is just.

The Abstract (mujmal) and the Clear (mubayyan)

The discussion of the abstract and the clear has less importance. It simply means that sometimes a phrase in the language of the Holy Prophet is ambiguous for us and its meaning unclear, for example the word *ghinā* (music), while its explanation is to be found in another proof from the Qur'ān or the Sunnah. In such cases the ambiguity of the abstract is cancelled by the clear.

The Abrogator (nāsikh) and the Abrogated (mansūkh)

Sometimes in the Qur'ān and the Sunnah we come across an instruction that was temporary, meaning that after a time a different instruction was given, which has cancelled the first.

For example, the Holy Qur'ān first tells us that if married women commit adultery they are to be confined to their houses until they die or until God establishes some other way for them. Then, the Qur'ān indicates that the way that God establishes for them is the general instruction that if a married man or a married woman commits adultery, the guilty person is to be executed.

Or, for example, a first instruction was given that in the holy month of *Ramaḍān*, men must not have intercourse with their wives, even at night. This rule was then cancelled and permission was given.

It is essential for a jurisprudent to distinguish the abrogator and the abrogated. The study of principles has a wealth of discussion and detail on the issue of abrogation.

Consensus and Reasoning

Consensus

As we saw above, one of the prime sources of jurisprudence is consensus. In the study of principles, the questions of the binding testimony of consensus, the proofs that it is a binding testimony and the pursuance of the method by which proofs are derived from it are all subjects of debate.

One of the topical points related to consensus deals with the binding nature of the proof. The ulamā' of our Sunni brothers claim that the Holy Prophet has told us, 'My nation will not [all] consent to a mistake'. Basing their view on this, they say that if the Muslim nation find the same point of view on an issue, that view is clearly the correct one.

According to this Tradition, the members of the Muslim nation are deemed to have collectively the same status as a Prophet and to be faultlessly free from error. The speech of the whole nation has the same rank as the speech of a Prophet, and the entire nation, as soon as they come to the same view, are faultless, i.e. immaculate.

According to this view, since the whole nation is infallible, whenever such an agreed view occurs, it is as if divine inspiration has been revealed to the Holy Prophet.

Shī'ites, however, in the first place, do not count such a Tradition as coming definitely from the Prophet. Second, they agree that it is impossible for all the members of the whole nation to stray and to err, but the reason for this is that the leader of that nation, the Prophet or Imām, is a person who is infallible and immaculate. That the whole Muslim nation cannot err is because one particular member of the Muslim nation cannot err, not because an infallible is formed from a group of people who are fallible. Third, what is called consensus in the books of jurisprudence and theology (*kalām*) is not the consensus of the whole nation. It is simply the consensus of a group, the group of managers or supervisors – i.e. the ulamā' – of the nation. Furthermore, it is not even the consensus of all the ulamā' of the nation, but the consensus of the ulamā' from one sect of the nation.

Here is where the Shī'ites do not maintain the same principle of consensus as the Sunni ulamā'. Shī'ites maintain the binding testimony of consensus only insofar as it is the means of discovering the Sunnah.

With regard to the Shī'ites, whenever there is no proof in the Book and the Sunnah about a certain subject, but it is known that the general body of the Muslims or a numerous group of the companions of the Prophet or the companions of an Imām who never did anything except in accordance with the divine instructions all used to act in a particular way, then we must assume that in those times an instruction of the Sunnah existed of which we are unaware.

Acquired Consensus and Narrated Consensus

Consensus, whether as accepted by our Sunni brothers or as considered valid by Shī'ites, is of two types, acquired and narrated. Acquired consensus means the consensus of which the *mujtahid* has himself directly acquired knowledge as the result of minute research into history and the views and opinions of the companions of God's Prophet, of the companions of the Imāms or of the people close to the time of the Imāms.[8]

Narrated consensus is the consensus about which the *mujtahid* has no direct information, but which has been related by others. Acquired consensus, of course, is a binding testimony, but narrated consensus, if certitude is not obtained from the narrator, is not to be relied upon. Therefore, the Single Report of consensus does not constitute a binding testimony, even though, as we have seen, the narrated Single Report of the Sunnah does, provided the chain of narrators meets the conditions.

Reasoning

Reasoning is one of the four sources of jurisprudence. This means that, by means of reasoned deduction and logic, we discover that in a certain instance a certain necessary law or prohibitive law of the Sharīʿah exists, or we discover what type of law it is and is not.

The binding testimony of reason is proven by the law of reason ('the sun is shining, hence the proof of the existence of the sun', meaning that with the application of reason no other proof is needed) and also by the confirmation of the Sharīʿah. Essentially we are sure of the Sharīʿah and of the principle of beliefs of religion because of reason. How could it be that in the view of the Sharīʿah reason is not to be considered binding?!

The issues of the principles related to reason are in two parts. One part relates to the inner meaning or philosophy of the commandments. The other part is related to the requirements of the commands.

Let us begin with the first part. One of the obvious elements of Islam, especially in the view of Shīʿites, is that the Sharīʿah of Islam exists in relation to the best and the worst interests of human beings. That is, each command (*amr*) of the Sharīʿah arises from the necessity of meeting the best interests of human beings and each prohibition (*nahy*) of the Sharīʿah arises from the necessity of abstaining from their worst interests, i.e. the things that corrupt them.

Almighty God, in order to inform them as to their best interests, wherein lie their happiness and prosperity, has made a chain of commands obligatory (*wājib*) or desirable (*mustaḥab*) for them. And so as to keep human beings away from all that that corrupts them, He prohibits them from those things. If the best interests and forms of corruption did not exist, neither command nor prohibition would exist. If reasoning human beings had full cognizance of those best interests and those forms of corruption, they would devise the same laws as have been introduced in the Sharīʿah.

This is why the practitioners of the principles and also the *mutakallimīn* consider that, because the laws of the Sharīʿah accord to and are centred on the wisdom of what is best and worst for human beings – and it makes no difference whether those best and worst interests are relevant to the body or the soul, to the individual or the society, to the temporary life or the eternal – wherever laws of reason exist, so the corresponding laws of the Sharīʿah also exist, and wherever no law of reason exists, there exists no law of the Sharīʿah.

Thus, if we suppose that in some case no law of the Sharīʿah has been communicated to us, by narration or otherwise, but reasoning traces with absolute certitude the particular wisdom of the other judgements of the Sharīʿah, then it automatically discovers the law of the Sharīʿah in this case too. In such an instance, reasoning forms a chain of logic. First, in such and such a case, there exists such and such a best interest that must necessarily be met. Second, wherever there exists a best interest that must necessarily be met, the Legislator of Islam is definitely not indifferent, rather He commands that that best interest be met. Third, in such instances, the law of the Sharīʿah is that the best interests be met.

For example, in the time and place of the Holy Prophet there was no opium or addiction to opium, and, in the narrated testimonies of the Qur'ān and the Sunnah and consensus, there is nothing about opium for good or ill, yet human beings have experienced opium addiction and thus have obvious proof of its corruption. Thus, with our reasoning and knowledge, and on the basis of 'a form of corruption that is essentially to be avoided' in the view of the Sharīʿah, we come to the realization that the law about opium is that addiction to opium is forbidden.

Similarly, if it becomes established that smoking tobacco definitely causes cancer, a *mujtahid*, according to the judgement of reasoning, will establish the law that smoking is forbidden according to the Divine Law.

The *uṣūliyyīn* and the *mutakallimīn* call reason and the Sharīʿah inseparable from each other. They say that whatever law is established by reason is also established by the Sharīʿah.

However, this of course is on condition that reasoning traces, in an absolute, certain and indubitable way, those best interests that must be protected and those worst interests or forms of corruption that must be avoided. The word 'reasoning' cannot be applied to opinion, guesswork and conjecture. Analogy falls into the same category and must be discounted, for it is more akin to opinion and imagination than to reasoning and certitude.

On the other hand, when reasoning has played no part in the forming of a particular law and we find that that law has been introduced in the Sharīʿah, we know that our best interests were definitely involved, for otherwise the law would not have been made. Thus, reason realizes the law of the Sharīʿah by realizing the best interests of human beings; and the reverse is also true, namely, that reason realizes the best interests of human beings by realizing the law of the Shari 'ah.

Thus, whatever is a law of reason is a law of the Sharīʿah and equally whatever is a law of the Sharīʿah is a law of reason.

Let us now discuss the second part, the requirements of the commands. We know that a law made by a lawmaker of sanity and intellect naturally entails a chain of essentials that must be judged according to reason, to see if, for example, that law necessitates the drafting of a new law or the abrogation of a an existing law.

For example, if a command is made, such as the *ḥajj* and the form of worship to be performed there – and the *ḥajj* necessitates a chain of preparations, including acquiring a passport, buying a ticket, vaccinations and currency exchange – does the fact that the *ḥajj* is obligatory make these preparations obligatory as well or not?

The same question can apply to the things that are forbidden. Does the prohibition of a thing demand that its preparations also be forbidden?

Another issue is as follows. A person is not able to do two obligatory things at the same time as they must be done separately. For example, it is obligatory to say one's ritual prayers but it is also obligatory to clean the mosque if it has become unclean with blood, urine, etc. So the performing of one of these two duties demands the neglect of the other. Now, does one command necessarily contain the prohibition of the other? Do both the commands include this prohibition?

If two things are obligatory but they cannot both be done at once, it is our duty to perform whichever of the two is more important.

This brings us to another issue. Does our obligation with regard to an important duty lapse altogether with our attention to a more important duty? Suppose two men are in danger of their lives and it is within our means to save only one of them, and one of them is a good Muslim who works for others while the other is a corrupt man who causes only trouble to others, but whose life is nevertheless sacred. Naturally, we must save the Muslim who is good and who helps others and whose life is therefore more valuable to society than the life of the other. That is, to save him is more important; yet it is also important to save the life of the trouble-maker.

In such examples, it is reasoning, with its precise calculations, that clarifies our specific duties. In the study of principles these and similar issues are discussed and the way of properly determining the answers is set out.

From what has been said so far, it should be clear that the issues of principle are all divided into two parts, the 'principles of deducing' and the 'principles of application'. The principles of deducing are in turn divided into two parts, the narrated – which derive from the Book, the Sunnah and consensus – and the reasoned.

The Principles of Application

Jurisprudents, as we have seen, refer to four sources for deducing the laws of the Sharīʿah. Sometimes the jurisprudent is successful in his referrals and sometimes not. That is, sometimes (of course, predominantly) he attains the actual law of the Sharīʿah at the level of certitude or reliable probability, which means a probability that has been divinely endorsed. In such cases, the duty becomes clear and he realizes with certitude or with a strong and permissible probability what it is that the Sharīʿah of Islam demands. Occasionally, however, he is unable to discover the duty and the Divine Law from the four sources, and he remains in doubt and without a defined duty.

What should be done in such cases? Has the Legislator of Islam or reason or both specified a certain duty in the event that the actual duty is out of reach? And if so, what is it?

The answer is, yes, such a duty has been specified. A system of rules and regulations has been specified for such circumstances. Reason too, in certain circumstances, confirms the law of the Sharīʿah, for the independent law of (aware) reasoning is the very same as the law of the Sharīʿah, or in certain instances it is silent, meaning that it has no independent law of its own and accords with the Sharīʿah.

In the part of principles that contains the principles of deducing we learn the correct and valid method of deducing the Sharīʿah and, in the part concerning the principles of application, we learn the correct way of benefiting from the rules that have been introduced for the kind of situation mentioned above, and of putting them into practice.

There are four general principles of application that are used in all the sections of jurisprudence:

- The Principle of Exemption (*barāʾat*)
- The Principle of Caution (*iḥtiyaṭ*)
- The Principle of Option (*takhyyīr*)
- The Principle of Mastery (*istiṣḥāb*)

Each of these four types of principles operates in a special circumstance. Before looking at these, let us first define the four principles themselves.

The Principle of Exemption means that we are released from our obligation and we have no duty. The Principle of Caution means that we must act with caution, i.e. in such a way that if a duty actually exists as a law, we must ensure that we have performed that duty. The Principle of Option means that we have the option to choose whichever one of two things we like, and the Principle of

Mastery means that what existed remains in its original state or has precedence over any doubt about it, and the doubt is ignored. Now we shall consider the circumstances in which these principles apply.

Sometimes a jurisprudent is unable to deduce the law of the Sharī'ah and to trace a particular necessity and thus remains in a state of doubt. This doubt may relate to some existing body of knowledge. For example, it may be doubted whether, in this age of the physical absence of the Imām, the special congregational prayer must be said on Fridays or the normal noon prayer – doubt exists about both the Friday prayer and the noon prayer, in the light of the general information that one of the two is definitely obligatory. Alternatively it may be doubted whether, in the age of the Imāms' absence, the prayer of *'īd-i-fiṭr* in congregation is obligatory. In this second case the doubt is a 'primary doubt' (*shak badwī*) and not a doubt linked to something that is known.

So the doubts of jurisprudents about an obligation are either linked to some general knowledge or are primary doubts. If they are linked to some general knowledge, it is either possible to act in accordance with caution, namely, to perform both possible duties, or it is not possible to act with caution. If caution is possible, one must apply it, and both of the possible duties must be performed. Such an instance calls for the Principle of Caution. Sometimes, however, caution is not possible, because doubt exists between the obligatory and the forbidden. We doubt, for example, in the absence of the Imāms, whether the performance of certain duties is peculiar to the Imām and forbidden to us or whether it is not peculiar to the Imām and is obligatory for us. Here it is self-evident that the way of caution is closed, and instead we must have recourse to the Principle of Option, which means that we may choose to do whichever of the options we please.

Assuming, however, that our doubt is a primary doubt not linked to any general knowledge, the fact is either that we know the previous condition and our doubt relates to whether the previous law stands or has been changed, or that the previous condition not been established. If the previous condition is established, the situation calls for the Principle of Mastery (mastery of the known previous condition over the doubt), and if the previous condition is not established the situation calls for the Principle of Exemption.

A *mujtahid* must, as the effect of frequent application, have great power of discernment in the execution of these four types of principles; discernment that sometimes demands hair-splitting exactitude, failing which he will make mistakes.[9]

Of these four principles, the Principle of Mastery has been uniquely established by the Sharī'ah, and reason is subservient to it, having no independent rule of its own, but the other three principles are principles of reason, which the Sharīʿah has confirmed.

The justification of the Principle of Mastery consists of a number of reliable Traditions which take the form, 'Do not reverse a certitude with a doubt'. From the content of these Traditions and what precedes and follows this sentence it is clear discerned that what is meant is exactly what jurisprudence calls 'mastery'.

On the subject of the Principle of Exemption similarly there exist many Traditions, of which the most famous is the *ḥadīth ur-rafʿi*.

The *ḥadīth ur-rafʿi* is from the Holy Prophet, who told us, 'Nine things have been taken from my nation: what they do not know, what they have not tolerated, what they have been compelled to, what they have found themselves in need of, mistakes, forgetfulness, misfortune, envy (which they have not acted on) and whisperings of doubt in the thoughts of the creation'.

The *uṣūliyyīn* have had numerous discussions about this Tradition and about each of its points, and of course the part that sanctions the Principle of Exemption is the first line, which states that whatever we do not know has been 'taken from' us, thus the obligation is lifted from us.

The *mujtahid*s are not the only ones who may use the four principles as aids to understanding the laws of the Sharīʿah. People who are not *mujtahid*s and who must therefore imitate (*taqlīd*) a *mujtahid* can also benefit from them when they have doubts.

For example, suppose that a baby boy suckles from a woman other than his mother and that when the boy grows up, he wants to marry the daughter of that woman; it is not known whether as a baby he drank so much milk from that woman's breast that he is deemed to be the 'wet-nurse son' of that woman and her husband or not. That is, we doubt whether the boy drank milk from her breast fifteen consecutive times or for a complete day and night or so much that his bones grew from her milk (in which cases the boy is deemed to be her son and the brother of her daughter, whom he is thus forbidden to marry). This instance calls for the Principle of Mastery, because before the boy drank the woman's milk he was not her 'wet-nurse son', yet now we doubt whether or not he is. By the Principle of Mastery, we conclude that there is no question of a wet-nurse relationship.

Similarly, if we have performed the minor ablution obligatory before we say the ritual prayer or are permitted to touch the Qur'ān, and we then doze off and subsequently doubt whether or not we actually fell asleep (in which case the ablution becomes void), by the Principle of Mastery, we conclude that the ablution was valid. In the same way, if we have washed our hands and we then doubt to whether they are still clean or have become *najis* (unclean), by the

Principle of Mastery we conclude them to be clean. If, however, it was *najis* and we doubt whether we have cleaned our hands or not, by the Principle of Mastery we conclude that they are still unclean.

Let us consider some examples of the other principles. Suppose there is a liquid is in front of us and we doubt whether or not it contains alcohol, as some medicines do, the situation calls for the Principle of Exemption, and there is no obstacle to our drinking that liquid. If, however, we have two glasses of medicine and we know that alcohol is present in one of them, the Principle of Caution is called for, and we must not drink either.

Now suppose that we are at the side of a road in the middle of a desert and to follow the road in one direction definitely involves risking our lives, while to follow the road in the other direction means we will find safety; but we do not know in which direction lies safety and in which direction lies the risk to our lives. Here we are presented with two laws. One is the obligation to save life and the other is the prohibition against risking it. In which direction should we travel? This situation calls for the Principle of Option, and we may travel in whichever direction we like, and if we choose the wrong direction, we are blameless.

Notes

1. These treatises (*Risālah*) are works in which the *mujtahid* states his verdicts on almost all the things that can affect daily life.
2. Translator's note: The weakness of this view can be appreciated when it is realized that many of the Traditions recorded in the reliable books, i.e. books compiled by reliable men, contradict each other, which naturally indicates that the only logical way to distinguish the holy words from the false ones is by examining the chain of narrators. It should also be borne in mind that for a number of reasons, such as lack of time for research or of knowledge of transmitters, it may not have been possible for the reliable compilers themselves to make the necessary distinctions.
3. Consensus is discussed further below.
4. His book is called *Ta'sīs ash-shī'ah' ulūm al-islām*.
5. This *āyah* and such 'tacit meanings' (*mafāhīm*) are further discussed in the next section.
6. *Taqiyah* is the legitimate practice of concealing one's faith in times of danger – sometimes by adopting the practices of a different faith – which was often necessary during the times of the Imāms.
7. More light is thrown on this subject under the treatment of the principles of jurisprudence.
8. Translator's note: Of course the Shī'ite view is that the time of the Imāms will last as long as mankind itself; what is referred to here is the era of access to the Imāms.
9. Translator's note: If he were likely to make many mistakes he would naturally not yet be regarded as a *mujtahid* at all.

PART SIX

Islamic Ethics and Morality

Man is a species of animal and thus shares many features with other animals. But many differences distinguish man from animals and grant him a special virtue, an elevation, that leaves him unrivalled. The basic difference between man and the other animals, the touchstone of his humanity, the source of what have come to be known as human civilization and culture, is the presence of insights and beliefs. Animals in general can perceive themselves and the external world and strive to attain their desires and objects in the light of their awareness and cognition. The same holds true of man, but he differs from the rest of the animals in the scope, extent and breadth of his awareness and cognitions and in the level to which his desires and objects rise.

Awareness and Desire in Animals

In the first place, an animal's awareness of the world comes solely through its external senses and is, accordingly, external and superficial; it does not reach into the interiors and internal relationships of things. Second, it is individual and particular; it enjoys nothing of universality and generality. Third, it is localized, limited to the animal's environment. Fourth, it is immediate, confined to the present, divorced from past and future. The animal is not aware of its own history or that of the world and does not consider or relate its endeavours to the future.

The animal is thus confined in a fourfold prison. If it should by any chance emerge, it does so not with awareness, by intelligence and choice, but as a captive to the compulsions of nature, instinctually, without awareness or intelligence.

The level of the animal's desires and objects is also limited. First, it is material, not rising above eating, drinking, sleeping, playing, nesting and copulating. For the animal there is no question of abstract desires and objects, moral values and so on. Second, it is private and individual, related to itself or at most to its mate and offspring. Third, it is localized and related to its environment. Fourth, it is immediate and related to the present. The animal thus lives within certain confines in this respect as well.

If the animal pursues an object or moves towards an aim that is beyond these confines, for instance, if it shows concern for the species rather than the individual or for the future rather than the present, as do such social animals as the honey bee, this behaviour arises unconsciously and instinctually, by the direct command of the power that created it and administers the world.

Awareness and Desire in Man

Whether in the area of awareness, insights and cognitions or desires and objects, the human domain reaches much further and higher than that of the animals. Human awareness and cognition traverse the exterior bounds of objects and phenomena to penetrate into their interiors, their essences and identities, their interrelationships and interdependencies and the necessities governing them. Human awareness does not remain imprisoned within the limits of locale and place, nor does it remain chained to its moment; it journeys through both time and space. Accordingly, man grows aware both of what is beyond his environment and of his own past and future, discovering his own past history and that of the universe – the histories of the earth, the heavens, the mountains, the seas, the planets, plants and other animals – and contemplating the future to the far horizons. Beyond even this, man sends his thoughts racing after things limitless and eternal and gains knowledge of some of them. One who transcends a cognition of the individual and the particular discovers general laws and universal truths that embrace the whole world. Thus, he establishes his dominion over nature.

Man can also attain an elevated level from the standpoint of desires and objects. Man is a being that seeks values and aspires to virtues and ideals that are not material or utilitarian, that are not restricted to self or at most to mate and offspring, that are general and inclusive and embrace the whole of humanity, that are unconfined to a particular environment, locale or time period. Man is so devoted to ideals and beliefs that he may at times place them above all else and put service to others and their comfort ahead of his own comfort. It is as if the thorn that has pierced another's foot has pierced his own foot or even his own eye. He commiserates with others; he rejoices in their joy and grieves at their grief. He may grow so attached to his sacred beliefs and ideals that he readily sacrifices not only his interests but his whole life to them.

The human dimension of civilization, the spirit of civilization, grows out of just such uniquely human feelings and desires.

The Touchstone of Man's Distinctiveness

Man's breadth of insight into the universe stems from humanity's collective efforts amassed and evolved over the centuries. This insight, expressed through special criteria, rules and logical procedures, has come to be known as 'science'. Science in its most general sense means the sum total of human contemplations on the universe (including philosophy), the product of the collective efforts of humanity within a special system of logic.

The elevated and ideal aptitudes of humanity are born of its faith, belief and attachment to certain realities in the universe that are both extra-individual, or general and inclusive, and extra-material, or unrelated to advantage or profit. Such beliefs and attachments are in turn born of certain world views and cosmologies given to humanity by prophets of God or by philosophers who sought to present a kind of thought that would conduce to belief and idealism. As these elevated, ideal, supra-animal aptitudes in man find an ideational and credal infrastructure, they are designated 'faith' (*imān*).

It is therefore my contention that the central difference between man and the other animals, the touchstone of man's humanity, on which humanity depends, is science and faith.

Although some people deny that there is any basic difference between man and other animals, asserting that the difference in awareness and cognition is quantitative or at most qualitative, but not essential, these thinkers have passed over all the wonders and glories that have drawn the great philosophers of East and West to the question of cognition in man. They regard man as an animal entirely, from the standpoint of desires and objects, not differing from the animals in the least in this respect.[1]

Others think that to have a psyche makes the difference; that is, they believe that only man has a psyche, or anima, that other animals have neither feelings nor appetites, know neither pain nor pleasure, that they are soulless machines only resembling animate beings. They think that the true definition of man is 'the animate being'.[2]

Other thinkers who do not consider man the only animate being in the universe but maintain basic distinctions between man and the rest of the animals may be grouped according to which one of man's distinguishing features they have dwelt upon. They have defined man as the reasoning animal, the seeker after the Absolute, the unfinished, the idealist, the seeker after values, the metaphysical animal, the insatiable, the indeterminate, the committed and responsible, the provident, the free and empowered, the rebel, the social animal, the seeker after order, the seeker after beauty, the seeker after justice, the one facing two ways, the lover, the answerable, the conscientious, the one with two hearts, the creator, the solitary, the agitated, the devotee of creeds, the toolmaker, the seeker after the beyond, the visionary, the ideal and the gateway to ideas.

Clearly, each of these distinctions is correct in its way, but if we wish to advance a definition that comprehends all the basic differences, we can do no better than to speak of science and faith and to say that man is distinguished from the other animals by the two features, 'science' and 'faith'.

Relationship between Humanity and Animality

The features that man shares with the animals plus those features that distinguish him from the animals make of him a being with two lives, the animal life and the human life or, in other words, the material life and the life of culture. What relationship exists between man's animality and his humanity, between his animal life and his human life, his material life and his cultural and spiritual life? Is one the basis and the other a reflection of it? Is one the infrastructure and the other the superstructure? Since we are considering this question from a sociological, not a psychological point of view, we may express it thus: among social structures is the economic structure, which is concerned with production and production relations, the principle and the infrastructure? Do the remaining social structures, especially those in which man's humanity is manifested, all constitute something derivative, a superstructure, a reflection of the economic structure? Have science, philosophy, literature, religion, law, morals and art at all times been manifestations of economic realities, having no substantive reality?

This sociological discussion automatically leads to a psychological conclusion and likewise to a philosophical argument that concerns humanity, its objective and substantive realities, the question of what today is called humanism. This conclusion is that man's humanity has no substantive reality, that only his animality has any substantive reality. Thus, any basic distinction between man and animal is rejected.

According to this theory, not only is the substantive reality of human beliefs denied, including the beliefs in truth, goodness, beauty and God, but the substantive reality of the desire to know the reality of the universe from a human viewpoint is denied, in that no viewpoint can be simply a 'viewpoint' and disinterested, but every viewpoint must reflect a particular material tendency. Things cannot be otherwise. Curiously, some schools of thought offer this view and speak of humanity and humanism in the same breath!

The truth is that the course of man's evolution begins with animality and finds its culmination in humanity. This principle holds true for individual and society alike: Man at the outset of his existence is a material body; through an essential evolutionary movement, he is transformed into spirit or a spiritual substance. What is called the human spirit is born in the lap of the body; it is there that it evolves and attains independence. Man's animality amounts to a nest in which man's humanity grows and evolves. It is a property of evolution that the more the organism evolves, the more independent, self-subsistent and governing of its own environment it becomes. The more man's humanity evolves, in the individual or in society, the more it steps toward independence and governance over the other aspects of his being. An evolved human individual has gained a relative ascendancy over his inner and outer environments. The evolved individual is the one who has been freed of dominance by the inner and outer environments, but depends upon belief and faith.

The evolution of society precisely corresponds to the evolution of the spirit in the lap of the body or the evolution of the individual's humanity in the lap of his animality. The germ of human society is economic structures; the cultural and ideal aspects of society amount to the spirit of society. Just as there is an interaction between body and spirit, so there is one between the spirit and the body of society, that is, between its ideal structures and its material ones.[3] Just as the evolution of the individual leads to greater freedom, autonomy and sovereignty of the spirit, so does the evolution of society. That is, the more evolved human society becomes, the greater the autonomy of its cultural life and the sovereignty of that life over its material life. Man of the future is the cultural animal; he is the man of belief, faith and method, not the man of stomach and waistline.

Human society, however, is not moving inexorably and directly to the perfection of human values. Each temporal stage does not necessarily represent a step more advanced than the preceding stage. It is possible for humanity to pass through an era of social life in which, for all its scientific and technical progress, it declines with respect to human ideal values, as is said of humanity in our present time. This idea of human social evolution means rather that humanity is progressing in the sum total of its movements, whether material or ideal, but the movement sometimes twists to the right or left, sometimes stops or occasionally even reverses itself. On the whole, however, it is a progressive, evolutionary movement. Thus, future man is the cultural animal, not the economic animal; future man is the man of belief and faith, not the man of stomach and waistline.

According to this theory, the evolution of the human aspect of man (because of its substantive reality) keeps step with, or rather anticipates the evolution of the tools of production. It gradually reduces his dependence on and susceptibility to the natural and social environments and augments his freedom (which is equivalent to his dependence on belief, ideals, principle and ideology), as well as his influence upon the natural and social environments. In the future, man will attain to ever more perfect spiritual freedom, that is, ever greater independence or ever greater dependence upon faith, belief and ideology. Past man, while enjoying fewer of the blessings of nature and of his own being, was more captive to nature and to his own animality. But future man, while enjoying more of the blessings of nature and of his own being, will be proportionately freer from the captivities of nature and of his own animal potential and be better able to govern himself and nature.

According to this view, the human reality, despite having appeared along with and in the lap of animal and material evolution, is by no means a shadow, reflection or function of these. It is itself an independent, evolving reality. Just as it is influenced by the material aspects of being, it influences them. This, not the evolution of the tools of production, is what determines man's ultimate destiny, and his substantive cultural evolution. The substantive reality of the humanity of man keeps him in motion and evolves the tools of production along with the other concerns of life. The tools of production do not evolve of themselves, and man's humanity is not changed and transformed like the tools defining a system of production, such that it would be spoken of as evolving because it defined an evolving system of production.

Science and Faith

The Relationship between Science and Faith

Now let us see what relationship these two pillars of humanity may bear to each other.

In the Christian world, owing to some textual corruptions in the Old Testament (the Torah), the idea of the opposition of science and faith has become widespread, an idea that has cost both of them dearly.[4] This idea has its roots chiefly in the Book of Genesis. In Genesis 2: 16–17, we find, regarding Adam, paradise and the forbidden tree: '[The LORD GOD] told the man, "You may eat from every tree in the garden, but not from the tree of the knowledge of good and evil; for on the day that you eat from it, you will certainly die"'.[5] In Genesis 3: 1–8, we find:

> The Serpent was more crafty than any wild creature that the Lord God had made. He said to the woman, 'Is it true that God has forbidden you to eat from any tree in the garden?' The woman answered the serpent, 'We may eat the fruit of any tree in the garden, except for the tree in the middle of the garden; God has forbidden us either to eat or to touch the fruit of that; if we do, we shall die.' The serpent said, 'Of course you will not die. God knows that as soon as you eat it, your eyes will be opened and you will be like gods, knowing both good and evil.' When the woman saw that the fruit of the tree was good to eat and that it was pleasing to the eye and tempting to contemplate, she took some of it and ate it. She also gave her husband some and he ate it. Then the eyes of both of them were opened and they discovered that they were naked; so they stitched fig leaves together and made themselves loincloths.

In Genesis 3:23, it is written:

> The LORD God said, 'The man has become like one of us, knowing good and evil; what if he now reaches out his hand and takes fruit from the tree of life also, eats it and lives forever?'

According to this conception of man and God, of consciousness and rebellion, God's command (*din*) is that man must not know good and evil, not grow conscious – the forbidden tree is the tree of consciousness. Man, in his rebellion, his mutiny, against God's command (his balking at the teachings of the revealed laws and prophets), attains consciousness and knowledge and so is driven from God's paradise. All satanic suggestions are the suggestions of consciousness.

To us Muslims, who have studied the Qur'ān, God taught Adam all the names (realities) and then commanded the angels to prostrate themselves before him. Satan was expelled from the court for not prostrating himself before this viceregent of God, conscious of realities. And the Sunnah has taught us that the forbidden tree represented greed or avidity, that is, something connected with the animality of Adam, not with his humanity, that Satan always suggests things contrary to reason but conforming with the passions of the animal ego, and that what manifests Satan within man's being is the ego that incites to evil, not the Adamic reason. For us who are thus schooled, what we see in Genesis is quite astonishing.

It is this conception that divides the last fifteen hundred years of European history into the Age of Faith and the Age of Reason and sets faith and science at odds. But the history of Islamic civilization is divisible into the Age of Flowering, or the Age of Science and Faith, and the Age of Decline, in which science and faith together have declined. We Muslims must eschew the erroneous conception that has inflicted irreparable injuries on science and on faith, indeed on humanity; we must not take this opposition of science and faith for granted.

Let us now try to analyse whether these two aspects of humanity each actually pertain to a certain era. Is man condemned forever to remain half-human, to have only half his humanity in a given era? Is he forever condemned to one of two types of misfortune, the misfortune arising from ignorance and the misfortune arising from absence of faith?

Every faith is inevitably based on a special mode of thought and a special conception of the universe and of being. Many conceptions and interpretations of the universe, although they can serve as bases for faith and devotion, are inconsistent with logical and scientific principles and so necessarily deserve to be rejected. But is there a mode of thought, a kind of conception and interpretation of the universe and of being, that draws support from the region of science, philosophy and logic and can be a firm foundation for a felicitous faith? If such a conception, mode of thought or world view exists, then it will be clear that man is not condemned to the misfortunes arising from either ignorance or lack of faith.

One can address the relationship between science and faith from either of two standpoints. One standpoint is whether an interpretation or conception exists that is both productive of faith and idealism and supported by logic. Are all the ideas that science and philosophy impart to us contrary to faith, devotion, hope and optimism? (This is a question that I will take up later in discussing the idea of a world view.)

The other standpoint is that of the influences on man of science on the one hand and faith on the other. Does science call us to one thing and faith to another, opposed thing? Does science seek to shape us one way and faith another, opposed way? Does science carry us in one direction and faith in another? Or do science and faith fulfil and complement one another? Does science shape half of us and faith the other half, harmoniously?

Science gives us enlightenment and power; faith gives us love, hope and ardour. Science makes instruments; faith constructs purposes. Science gives speed; faith gives direction. Science is power; faith is benevolence. Science shows what is; faith inspires insight into what must be done. Science is the outer revolution; faith is the inner revolution. Science makes the universe the human universe; faith makes the psyche the psyche of humanity. Science expands man's being horizontally; faith conveys him upwards. Science shapes nature; faith shapes man. Both science and faith empower man, but science gives a power of discrimination and faith gives a power of integration. Both science and faith are beauty, but science is the beauty of the reason and faith is the beauty of the spirit. Science is the beauty of thought and faith is the beauty of feeling. Both science and faith give man security but science gives outer security and faith gives inner security. Science gives security against the onslaught of illness, floods, earthquakes, storms; faith, against worry, loneliness, feelings of helplessness, feelings of futility. Science brings the world into greater harmony with man and faith brings man into greater harmony with himself.

Man's need for science and faith together has greatly excited the interest of both religious and non-religious thinkers. 'Allama Muḥammad Iqbal of Lahore has said:

> Humanity needs three things today – a spiritual interpretation of the universe, spiritual emancipation of the individual and basic principles of a universal import directing the evolution of human society on a spiritual basis. Modern Europe has, no doubt, built idealistic systems on these lines, but experience shows that truth revealed through pure reason is incapable of bringing that fire of living conviction which personal revelation alone can bring. This is the reason why pure thought has so little influenced men while religion has always elevated individuals and transformed whole societies. The idealism of Europe never became a living factor in her life and the result is a perverted ego seeking itself through mutually intolerant democracies whose sole function is to exploit the poor in the interest of the rich. Believe me, Europe today is the greatest hindrance in the way of man's ethical achievement. The Muslim, on the other hand, is in possession of these ultimate ideas on the basis of a revelation, which, speaking from the innermost depths of life, internalizes its own apparent externality. With him the spiritual basis of life is a matter of conviction for which even the least enlightened man among us can easily lay down his life.[6]

Will Durant, author of *The History of Civilization*, although not a religious person, says:

> [Lucretius would suggest of our progress in mechanization] that this was a difference of means and not of end. What if all our progress is an improvement in methods, but not in purposes?

He also says:

> Our wealth is a weariness, and our wisdom is a little light that chills; but love warms the heart with unspeakable solace, even more when it is given than when it is received.[7]

Today most people realize that scientism and an unalloyed scientific education are incapable of shaping the whole human being. The product of this education is the raw material of humanity, not the fully shaped humanity. It shapes a humanity with capacity, not one with attainment. It shapes a uniform humanity, not a multiform one. Today most people realize that the age of science-and-nothing-but-science has come to an end. A vacuum in ideals threatens society. Some would fill it with philosophy; others have resorted to literature, the arts and the humanities. In Iran, too, some propose to fill this vacuum with a humanistic culture and especially with the literature of *'irfān*, including such writings as those of Rūmi, Sa'di and Ḥāfiẓ. But they forget that this literature has derived its spirit and attraction from religion. The humanistic spirit of these literatures is that selfsame religious spirit of Islam. Otherwise why are some modern literatures so cold, lifeless and unattractive, for all their humanist affectations? The humane content of our literature of *'irfān* derives from the kind of thought concerning the universe and man that is specifically Islamic. If we take the spirit of Islam away from these literary masterpieces, we are left with nothing more than the dross or a dead form.

Will Durant feels this vacuum and proposes that literature, philosophy and art fill it. He says:

> Our schools and colleges have suffered severely from Spencer's conception of education as the adjustment of the individual to his environment; it was a dead, mechanical definition, drawn from a mechanistic philosophy, and distasteful to every creative spirit. The result has been the conquest of our schools by mechanical and theoretical science, to the comparative exclusion of such 'useless' subjects as literature, history, philosophy and art . . . An education that is purely scientific makes a mere tool of its product; it leaves him a stranger to beauty, and gives him powers that are divorced from wisdom. It would have been better for the world if Spencer had never written on education.[8]

It is remarkable that, although Durant acknowledges that the existing vacuum is, in the first place, a 'vacuum of ideals', a vacuum in the area of objects, ends and aspirations, a vacuum leading to nihilism, although he affirms that it is a vacuum of a kind of thought for and a kind of belief in humane objects and goals, he nonetheless supposes it is remediable through ideal values, even though they may not go beyond the realm of imagination. He supposes that busying oneself with history, art, aesthetics, poetry and music can fill this vacuum that arises from the depths of man's aspiring and idealistic nature.

Non-interchangeability of Science and Faith

Science cannot replace faith as a means of giving, besides illumination and power, love and hope. It cannot raise the level of our desires. Although it can help us attain objects and goals, to follow the road to them, it cannot take from us those objects, aspirations and desires that by nature and instinct turn on individuality and self-interest and give us in their place objects and aspirations that turn on love and on ideal and spiritual bonds. Although it is a tool in our hands, it cannot transform our essence and identity. Likewise, faith cannot replace science, to enable us to understand nature, discover its laws or learn about ourselves.

Historical experiences have shown that the separation of science from faith has brought about irremediable harm. Faith must be known in the light of science; faith must be kept far from superstition in the light of science. When science is removed from faith, faith is deformed into petrification and blind fanaticism; it turns on its own axis and goes nowhere. When there is no science and true knowledge, the faith of an ignorant believer becomes an instrument in the hands of the clever charlatans exemplified in early Islam by the Kharijites and seen in various forms in later times.[9]

Conversely, science without faith is a sword in the hands of a maniac or else a lamp at midnight in the hands of a thief, to enable him to pick out the choicest goods. Thus, the scientifically informed person of today without faith does not differ in the least from the ignoramus without faith of yesterday in the nature and essence of his behaviour. What difference is there between the Churchills, Johnsons, Nixons and Stalins of today and the Ghengises and Attilas of yesterday?

But, it might be said, is science not both light and power? Do the light and power of science not only apply to the external world but also illuminate and reveal to us our inner world and so empower us to change it? If science can shape both the world and man, it can perform both its own function (world shaping) and that of faith (man shaping). The reply is, this is all correct, but the power of science is instrumental, that is, dependent upon man's will and command. In whatever area man wishes to carry out something, he can do it better with the tool of science. Thus, science is man's best aid in attaining the objects he has chosen, in traversing the roads he has decided to follow.

But when man puts the instrument to work, he already has an object in view; instruments are always employed in pursuit of objects. Where has he found these objects? Because man is animal by nature and human by acquisition, that is, because his human potentialities must be gradually nurtured in the light of faith, by nature he moves toward his natural, animal, individual, material, self-interested objects and employs his instruments accordingly. Therefore, man needs a power not among his own instruments and objects but rather that can impel him as an instrument in its own direction. He needs a power that can detonate him from within and activate his hidden potentialities. He needs a power that can produce a revolution in his heart and give him a new direction. This is not accomplished by science, by discovery of the laws governing nature and man. It is born of the sanctification and exaltation of certain values in one's spirit, which values in turn are born of a range of elevated aptitudes in man, which result, further, from a particular conception and way of thinking about the universe and man that one can acquire neither in the laboratory nor from syllogism and deduction.

History shows the consequences of disconnecting science and faith. Where there has been faith and no science, individuals' humanitarian efforts have produced no great effect – at times, no good effect. Sometimes they have given rise to fanaticisms, stagnations and ruinous conflicts. Human history is filled with such events. Where there has been science and no faith, as in some contemporary societies, all the power of science has been expended on selfishness, egoism, acquisitiveness, ambition, exploitation, subjugation, deceit and guile.

One can regard the past two or three centuries as the age of the worship of science and the flight from faith. Many thinkers came to believe that science could solve all man's problems, but experience has proven the contrary. Today no thinker would deny man's need for some kind of faith – if not religious faith, at least faith in something beyond science. Bertrand Russell, although he had materialistic tendencies, admits,

> Work of which the motive is solely pecuniary cannot have this value [of bringing a man into fruitful contact with the outer world], but only work which embodies some kind of devotion, whether to persons, to things, or merely to a vision.[10]

Today materialists are driven to claim they are materialists with respect to philosophy but idealists with respect to morals, that is, they are materialists in theory, but idealists in practice and aims.[11] How it is possible to be a materialist in theory and an idealist in practice is a question for the materialists themselves to answer.

George Sarton describes the inadequacy and incapacity of science to humanize personal relationships and man's urgent need for the power of faith:

> Science has made gigantic progress in certain fields, but in others, e.g., in politics, national and international, we are still fooling ourselves.[12]

He admits that the faith man needs is a religious faith. He says this of man's need for the triad of art, religion and science:

> Art reveals beauty; it is the joy of life. Religion means love; it is the music of life. Science means truth and reason; it is the conscience of mankind. We need all of them – art and religion as well as science. Science is absolutely necessary but it is never sufficient.[13]

Effects and Advantages of Religious Faith

Without ideals, aspirations and faith, man can neither live a sane life nor accomplish anything useful or fruitful for humanity and human civilization. A person who lacks ideals and faith becomes either selfish, never emerging from his shell of private interests, or a wavering, bemused being who does not know his own duty in life, in moral and social questions. Man constantly confronts moral and social questions, and must necessarily respond. If one is attached to a teaching, a belief, a faith, one's duty is clear; but if no teaching or method has clarified one's duty, one lives forever in a state of irresolution, drawn sometimes this way, sometimes that, never in balance. So without any doubt, one must attach oneself to a teaching and an ideal.

Only religious faith, however, can make man truly 'faithful', can make faith, belief and principle dominate selfishness and egoism, can create a kind of devotion and surrender in the individual such that he does not doubt the least point of his faith's teachings, and can render this belief something precious to him, to the extent that life without it is hollow and meaningless and that he will defend it with zeal and fervour.

Aptitudes for religious faith prompt man to struggle against his natural, individual inclinations and sometimes to sacrifice his reputation and very being for the sake of faith. This grows possible when his ideal takes on an aspect of sanctity and comes to rule his being completely. Only the power of religion can sanctify ideals and effect their rule to the fullest over man.

Sometimes individuals make sacrifices and relinquish their fortunes, reputations or lives, not for ideals and religious belief but when driven by obsessions, vindictiveness and vengefulness, in short as a violent reaction to feelings of stress and oppression. We see this sort of thing in various parts of the world. The difference between a religious ideal and a non-religious one is that, when religious belief appears and sanctifies an ideal, sacrifices take place naturally and with complete contentment. There is a difference between an act accomplished in contentment and faith – a kind of choice – and an act accomplished under the impact of obsessions and disturbing internal stresses – a kind of explosion.

If man's world view is a purely materialistic one founded on the restriction of reality to sense objects, any sort of social and humane idealism will prove contrary to the sensible realities through which man then feels related to the world.

What results from a sensual world view is egoism, not idealism. If idealism is founded upon a world view of which it is not the logical consequence, it amounts to nothing more than fantasy. That is, man must figuratively make a separate world of the realities existing within him, from his imagination, and be content with them. But if idealism stems from religion, it rests on a kind of world view whose logical consequence is to live by social ideals and aspirations. Religious faith is a loving bond between man and the universe or, to put it differently, is a harmony between man and the universal ideals of being. Non-religious faith and aspirations, on the other hand, constitute a kind of 'severance' from the universe and an imaginary construction of a world of one's own that is in no way reinforced by the outer world.

Religious faith does more than specify a set of duties for man contrary to his natural propensities; it changes the mien of the universe in man's eyes. It demonstrates the existence of elements in the structure of the universe other than the sensible ones. It transforms a cold, desiccated, mechanical and material universe into one living, intelligent and conscious. Religious faith transforms man's conception of the universe and creation. William James, the American philosopher and psychologist whose life extended into the early part of the twentieth Christian century, says:

> The world interpreted religiously is not the materialistic world over again, with an altered expression; it must have, over and above the altered expression, *a natural constitution* different at some point from that which a materialistic world would have.[14]

Beyond all this, there is an aspiration to sacred truths and realities that can be worshipped innate in every human individual. Man is the focus of a range of potential extra-material aptitudes and capacities waiting to be nurtured. Man's aptitudes are not confined to the material and his ideal aspirations are not solely inculcated and acquired. This is a truth science affirms. William James says:

> So far as our ideal impulses originate in this [mystical or supernatural] region (and most of them do originate in it, for we find them possessing us in a way for which we cannot articulately account), we belong to it in a more intimate way than that in which we belong to the visible world, for we belong in the most intimate sense wherever our ideals belong.[15]

Because these impulses exist, they should be nurtured. If they are not rightly nurtured and rightly profited from, they will deviate and cause unimaginable harm leading to idolatry, anthropolatry, nature worship and a thousand other forms of false worship. Erich Fromm says:

> There is no one without a religious need, a need to have a frame of orientation and an object of devotion . . .
>
> The person may be aware that his system is a religious one, different from systems in the secular realm, or he may think that he has no religion and interpret his devotion to certain allegedly secular aims like power, money or success as nothing but concern for the practical and expedient. The question is not *religion or not* but *which kind of religion.*[16]

What this psychologist means is that man cannot live without worship and a sense of the sacred. If he does not know and worship the One God, he will erect something else as the higher reality and make it the object of his faith and worship.

Therefore, because it is imperative for humanity to have an ideal, an aspiration and a faith and because, on the one hand, religious faith is the only faith that can really penetrate us and, on the other hand, by our nature we seek for something to hold sacred and to worship, the only road open to us is to affirm religious faith.

The Noble Qur'ān was the first book

1. to speak explicitly of religious faith as a kind of harmony with the creation: 'Do they seek for other than God's religion, while all in the heavens and on earth bow to Him?' (3:83)

2. to present religious faith as part of the make-up of human beings: 'So set your face towards religion as one upright – such is the disposition with which God has created man.' (30:30)

Tolstoy, the Russian thinker and writer, says, 'Faith is that by which people live'. Ḥakīm Nāṣir-i Khusraw 'Alavi says to his son,

From the world I turned to religion,
Without which what's the world but my prison?
Son, religion imparts to my heart a kingdom,
That *will* never fall into ruin.[17]

Religious faith has many beneficial effects, including producing cheer and expansiveness, ameliorating social relationships and lessening and remedying inevitable troubles that arise from the structure of the world.

Producing Cheer and Expansiveness

Religious faith creates optimism toward the universe, creation and being. In giving a special form to man's conception of the universe, in representing creation as having an object and the object as goodness, happiness and evolution, religious faith naturally shapes man's view of the universal system of being and its governing laws into an optimistic one.

The conditions of a person who has faith in the 'country' of being resembles the condition of a person who regards as right and just the laws, institutions and regulations of the country in which he lives and believes in its administrators' good intentions. He will inevitably see the way open to progress and elevation for himself and everyone else, and he will believe that only his own laziness and inexperience could hold him back and that the same holds for other responsible beings. Such a person would view himself, not national institutions and regulations, as responsible for his backwardness. He would blame any shortcoming on the failure of himself and his peers to carry out their tasks. This thought would naturally rouse him to zeal and compel him to optimism, hope and action.

A person without faith in the 'country' of being is like a person who regards the laws, institutions and regulations of the country in which he lives as corrupt and oppressive but must endure them. Such a person is always filled with rancour and vindictiveness. He never thinks of reforming himself; rather, he thinks that somehow earth and sky are askew, that all of being is injustice, oppression and wrongness. He thinks, 'What effect can the rightness of a speck like me have?' Such a person never takes pleasure in the world; the world for him is always like a nightmarish prison. Thus, the Noble Qur'ān says, 'For whoever turns away from remembrance of Me, life will be narrow'. (20:124) Faith gives expanse to the life within us and checks pressures on the spiritual agencies.

Religious faith also illuminates the heart. When through religious faith man sees the world illumined with truth and reality, this clairvoyance illumines the spaces of his spirit. It becomes like a lamp illuminating his inward being. By contrast, an individual without faith, who sees the universe as futile and dark, is devoid of perception, insight and light. His heart is dark and oppressed in this dark dwelling he has conceived.

Religious faith provides hope, hope of a good outcome for one's efforts. According to the logic of materialism, the universe regards impartially and indifferently those following the road of verity and those following the road of falsity, those following the road of justice and those following the road of injustice, those following the road of right and those following the road of wrong. The outcome of their work depends only on the level of their effort. But according to the logic of the individual with faith, the system of creation supports people who work in the way of truth and reality, in the way of right, justice and benevolence. 'If you aid God, He will aid you'. (47:7) The reward to those who do good never goes to waste: 'Truly God does not lose the wages of those who do good'. (12:90)

Religious faith gives one peace of mind. Man innately seeks his well-being. He becomes immersed in pleasure at the thought of attaining well-being and he trembles at the thought of a blighted future filled with deprivation. Man's well-being arises from two things, effort and confidence in environmental conditions.

A student's success arises from two things: his own efforts and the appropriateness or supportiveness of the school environment, which includes the encouragement and appreciation of the school authorities. If a hardworking student has no confidence in his study environment or in his teachers who will grade him at the end of the year, if he fears he will be the target of unfairness, he will be filled with apprehension and anxiety every day of the year.

Plainly, one's duty towards oneself does not give rise to anxiety in this area because anxiety arises from doubt and uncertainty. One does not feel doubt or uncertainty in relation to oneself. What does induce such feelings of anxiety is the world and one's relationship with it.

Is there no use in doing good? Are veracity and trustworthiness pointless? Do all our striving and dutifulness lead only to deprivation? Apprehension and anxiety here loom in their most terrible forms.

Religious faith, in relating man, one partner to the transaction, to the universe, the other partner, gives assurance and confidence. It alleviates apprehension and anxiety about the way in which the universe acts upon man and in their place brings peace of mind. Thus, one of the effects of religious faith is peace of mind.

Another effect of religious faith is a greater enjoyment of ideal pleasures. Man knows two kinds of pleasures. Material pleasures are connected with any of the senses and are felt when a relationship is set up between an organ and some external object (the pleasures of the eye in seeing, the ear in hearing, the mouth in tasting, the sense of touch in contact). Ideal pleasures are connected with the depths of the human spirit and conscience, not with any particular organ and not dependent upon a relationship with any external object. Such are the pleasures one feels from beneficence and service, from love and respect or from one's own success or that of one's offspring. These pleasures neither pertain to a particular organ nor arise under the direct influence of an external, material factor.

Ideal pleasures are both stronger and more enduring than material pleasures. For the devotees of truth, the pleasures of worship of God are of this order. When worship is conjoined with presence, humility and absorption, it affords the highest of pleasures, such as are celebrated in the language of religion as 'the relish of faith' and 'the sweetness of faith'. Faith has a sweetness above all sweetnesses. Ideal pleasures are redoubled when such works as scientific study, beneficence, service and success stem from the religious sense and are carried through for the sake of God, when they fall in the domain of worship.

Improving Social Relationships

Like some other animals, man has been created social. The individual alone is incapable of satisfying his needs; life must assume corporate form and all must share in its duties and fruits; a kind of division of labour must exist among individuals. But man differs from the other social animals, such as the honey bee, whose divisions of labour and function take the form of instincts and which are denied any chance to oppose and rebel against these preassigned functions. Man is free and empowered to perform his work freely as a function and duty. Other animals have social needs, but they also have social instincts that govern them.

Man likewise has social needs, but is not governed by social instincts. Man's social instincts consist of a range of demands within him that must be channelled by education.

A sane life for society consists in individuals' respecting the laws, the boundaries and each other's rights; in their regarding justice as sacred; and in their showing kindness to one another. Each should wish for another what he wishes for himself and deem unacceptable for another what he does not accept for himself. All should repose trust and confidence in one another and it should be their spiritual goal to guarantee each other's confidence. Each individual should be committed and responsible to his society and each should be as privately pious and honest as he is publicly. All should act with beneficence to one another with the greatest possible degree of disinterestedness. All should rise against injustice and oppression and leave the oppressors and the corrupt no room to practise their oppression and corruption. All should venerate ethical values. All should unite with and support others as the members of a body.

What honours truth and sanctifies justice, endears hearts to one another, establishes mutual confidence among individuals, causes piety and integrity to penetrate to the depths of the human conscience, invests ethical values with credence, creates courage in the face of oppression and interlinks and unites all individuals like the members of one body is religious faith. Human beings' humane manifestations, shining like stars in the sky of a tumultuous human history, are those manifestations welling forth from religious faith.

Lessening Troubles

Just as human life has its joys, delights, gains and successes, so it also has suffering, disasters, defeats, losses, hardships and disappointments. Many of them can be averted or obviated, albeit after great expenditure of effort. Man is clearly obliged to come to grips with nature, to transform the bitter into the sweet. But some of the vicissitudes of the world, such as old age, cannot be averted or obviated. One advances toward old age and one's life flame dies down. The infirmity and weakness of old age, together with the rest of its adversities, give life a grim face. On top of that, the thought of death and non-being, of closing one's eyes to the world and of entrusting the world to others causes one anguish of another order. Religious faith instils in man the power to resist. It turns bitter to sweet. A person with faith knows that everything in the universe has a fixed value. If he responds to hardships in the proper manner, even though they are irremediable, God Most High will recompense him in another way. As old age ceases to be seen as the end of man's existence and as the individual with faith regularly fills his leisure time with worship and nearness to God, through remembrance of God, life becomes more pleasant in old age than in youth. The visage of death is different in the eyes of one with faith; death is no longer oblivion and nothingness but is a transfer from an ephemeral world to an enduring one, from a smaller world to a greater one. Death is a transfer from the world of labour and sowing to the world of fruition and harvest. Thus, the individual with faith obviates his anxieties about death through efforts in good works, which in the language of religion are called 'acts of devotion'.

According to psychologists, non-religious individuals experience most of the psychological illnesses arising from spiritual turmoil and life's hardships. The stronger and firmer the religious individual's faith, the greater his immunity to such disorders. One of the features of contemporary life arising from the weakening of the faiths is an increase in mental and nervous disorders.

The Teaching: Ideology

Classifications of Actions

What is a teaching, an ideology? How are these concepts defined? By what necessity does one as an individual or as a member of a society follow a school and cleave to, invest faith in, an ideology? Is the existence of an ideology essential for the human individual or society?

Some prefatory remarks are called for here.

Human acts are of two kinds, pleasure-oriented and goal-oriented. People perform pleasure-oriented acts under the direct influence of instinct, nature or habit – which is second nature – to attain some pleasure or avoid some form of pain. For instance, a man grows thirsty and reaches for water, he sees a snake and flees or he feels a craving for a cigarette and lights one. Such acts conform to appetite and have to do directly with pleasure and pain. A pleasurable act attracts and a painful act repels.

One is not drawn to or repelled from goal-oriented acts by instinct and nature. One carries them out or leaves them undone according to reason and volition and with a view to the benefit of either course of action. That is, man's final cause and motive force is benefit, not pleasure. Nature discerns pleasure;

reason discerns benefit. Pleasure excites appetite; benefit mobilizes will. Man takes pleasure in the midst of performing a pleasure-oriented act, but he does not take pleasure in carrying out goal-oriented acts. Rather, he finds satisfaction in conceiving that he has taken a step on an ultimately beneficial course – one leading to a future good, a future attainment, a future pleasure. There is a difference between an act that brings pleasure and happiness and an act that brings neither, that may even bring pain, but that the doer carries through contentedly, bearing even the pain. Because the result is deferred, goal-oriented acts do not result in pleasure and cheer, but they give satisfaction. Man and animal alike experience pleasure and pain, but satisfaction and dissatisfaction are unique to man, as is hope. Satisfaction, dissatisfaction and hope belong to the domain of intelligibles and to the thought per se of man, not to his senses and perceptions.

That goal-oriented acts are performed under the governance of reason means that the evaluative power of the reason sees a good, an attainment or a pleasure from afar, descries the road to it, which may at times be arduous, and plans for the journey to fulfilment. That these acts are performed through the power of the will means that there exists in man a faculty dependent on the faculty of reason that has the function of executing what reason has sanctioned. At times it puts these things that thought has devised and reason has sanctioned into effect in the teeth of all appetites and all natural inclinations. For example, a student's youthful nature calls him to sleep, food, comfort, sensuality and play; but his evaluative reason, which considers, on the one hand, the potentially disastrous outcome of such acts and, on the other, the ultimately happy outcome of working hard, forgoing sleep and abstaining from sensual delights and pleasures impels him, in the name of benefit, to adopt the second alternative. In this instance, man elects the governance of reason, which is benefit, over the governance of nature, which is pleasure. A sick person may loathe his bitter and distasteful medicine and recoil from drinking it. But he drinks it, governed by reason, which heeds benefit, and by willpower, which overrides appetites. The stronger are the reason and the will, the better they impose their command upon nature, despite nature's inclinations.

In his goal-oriented acts, man is continually implementing some plan, some design, some theory. The more he evolves in the area of reason and will, the greater is the ratio of his goal-oriented acts to his pleasure-oriented acts. The nearer he draws to the animal level, the more the reverse is true, because the animal's acts are all pleasure-oriented. Occasionally, animals are observed to act in ways that suggest remote ends and outcomes (nest building, migrations, coatings and reproduction, for example). But none of these is done with awareness, with an end in mind or with thought given to the means that must be chosen to attain that end. Rather, they take place through a kind of irresistible instinctual suggestion from the beyond.

Man has so extended the scope of his goal-oriented acts that it has encompassed his pleasure-oriented acts. That is, the plans he makes on the basis of future benefit may be laid so finely that pleasures are incorporated into them. Each pleasure becomes a component of benefit; and every natural act, answering as it does to a natural need, also complies with the demand of reason. If goal-oriented action covers pleasure-oriented acts, and if pleasure-oriented acts assume a role as part of the general plan and programme of life under a goal-oriented outlook, then nature will accord with reason and appetite will accord with will.

Goal-oriented action, in turning on a range of remote ends and objects, as a matter of course calls for planning, programmes, methods and selections of means to reach these ends. Insofar as this action has an individual aspect (that is, insofar as an individual himself plans for himself), the planner, programmer and theoretician – the one who determines the method and means – is the individual's reason, which, of course, is dependent on the level of the individual's qualifications, information, learning and power of judgement.

Goal-oriented action, even at a hypothetical apogee of perfection, is not sufficient for man's actions to be truly human. Man's goal-oriented action is a necessary condition of humanity in that his reason, science, consciousness and foresight constitute half of his humanity, but it is not a sufficient condition. Human action is truly human when, in addition to being rational and volitional, it serves the more sublime aptitudes of humanity or at the very least does not oppose them. Otherwise, the most criminal of human acts may take shape through projections, ingenuity, forethought, planning and theorizing. The satanic designs of imperialism are the best evidence for this assertion. In Islamic religious terminology, the power of foresight when divorced from human aptitudes and aptitudes for faith and put at the service of material and animal ends is called 'abominable' (*nukrān*) and 'satanism' (*shaytānat*). Goal-oriented acts are not necessarily human; rather, if they turn on animal objects, they become far more dangerous than the pleasure-oriented animal acts themselves. For instance, an animal may tear apart another animal or a person to fill its stomach; but man the planner and evaluator will destroy cities and incinerate alive hundreds of thousands of innocent souls to achieve ends of the same order.

The Insufficiency of Reason

To what extent can reason indicate an individual's best interests? The power of reason, reflection, and thought is certainly indispensable for one's particular and limited plans in life. One is constantly confronted with such problems as choosing friends, a field of study, a spouse, a job, travel, a social circle, entertainment, charitable activities, struggling against fraud and so forth. One needs to think, reflect and plan in all these instances; and the more and better one considers them, the better one will succeed. At times, one will need to call upon others' reflection and experience (the principle of consultation). In all these particular instances, one first prepares a plan and then puts it into effect.

What of questions of a broad and general scope? Can one draft a plan covering all the problems of his personal life, according with his best interests in every respect? Or is the power of the individual mind to plan confined to limited and particular questions? Is it beyond the allotted power of reason to comprehend one's best interests in life as a totality, embracing happiness in all its aspects? We know that some philosophers believe in such self-sufficiency. They claim to have discovered the road from adversity to happiness and to be building their own happiness on the strength of reason and will. But we also know that no two philosophers can be found in the world who are of one mind as to where this road lies. Happiness itself, which is the central and ultimate end and which at first appears self-evident, is one of the most ambiguous of concepts. What is happiness? How is it to be realized? What is wretchedness? What factors go into it? These questions highlight a great gulf in our knowledge because even now man himself, with his potentialities and possibilities, remains unknown. Is it possible, while man himself remains unknown, to know what constitutes his happiness and the means of attaining it?

Moreover, man is a social being. Social life brings about thousands of problems for him, all of which he must solve and vis-à-vis all of which he must define his responsibility. Because man is a social being, his happiness, aspirations, criteria for good and evil, methods and choice of means are interwoven with others' happiness, aspirations, criteria for good and evil, methods and choices of means. One cannot choose one's way independently of others. One must pursue one's happiness on the highway that is leading society to happiness and perfection.

The Need for Ideology Today

If we consider the eternal life of the spirit and the inexperience of reason with respect to the hereafter, the question becomes much more difficult. It is here the need for a teaching, an ideology, becomes apparent – the need for a general theory, a comprehensive, harmonious and concrete design whose central object is to perfect man and secure universal happiness. Along the lines and by the methods it suggests, the musts and must-nots, goods and evils, ends and means, needs, ailments and remedies, responsibilities and duties may be discerned, and every individual may derive a sense of his own responsibility from these.

Ever since his first appearance, or at least since the age when the growth and diffusion of his social life produced a series of differences and disputes, man has needed an ideology – in the language of the Qur'ān, a 'revealed law' (Shari'ah).[18] As time has passed and man has evolved, this need has intensified. In the past, tendencies born of consanguinity, race, ethnicity, tribe and nation governed human societies as a collective spirit. This spirit in turn generated a range of collective (if inhuman) aspirations and gave unity and direction to society. Growth and evolution in reason and science have weakened these ties. An individualistic tendency is an essential property of science. It weakens sympathies and bonds of feeling. What will give unity, direction and shared aspirations to the man of today and, a fortiori, to the man of tomorrow, what will serve as his touchstone of good and evil, of musts and must-nuts, is an elective, conscious, inspirational philosophy of life underpinned by logic – in other words, a comprehensive, perfect ideology. More than the man of yesterday, the man of today needs a philosophy of life that will win him over to realities beyond the individual and his private interests. There is no doubt whatever that a teaching, an ideology, is today among society's most pressing needs.

Designing such an ideology is beyond the power of individual intelligence. But is it within the power of the collective intelligence? Can people design such a thing by using the aggregate of his past and present experiences and learning? If we first assume that man is the greatest of unknowns to himself, knowledge of human society and of what constitutes its happiness would seem to be even more difficult to attain. What is to be done? If we have the correct view of being and creation, if we regard the system of being as a system in equilibrium, if we deny that there is emptiness and futility in being, we shall be obliged to admit that this great system of the creation has not ignored our greatest need, but has marked out the basic lines of the course from a plane above human reason, that is, from the plane of revelation (the principle of prophecy). It is the task of reason and science to move along these basic lines. How beautifully and sublimely Ibn Sīnā wrote in his *Kitāb al-Nājāt* of people's need for a divinely revealed law expressed by human (prophetic) means.

The need for such a man [prophet] to preserve the species of man and to bring it to fruition is much greater than the need for the growth of hair on the eyebrows, the arching of the soles of the feet and other such fine features, which are not essential for man's survival; indeed, most of them do not serve that purpose at all.[19]

How, Ibn Sīnā asks, could this great system of creation, which has not neglected minor and inconsequential needs, neglect the most pressing need of all?

But if we are denied the correct view of being and creation, we must acquiesce in our condemnation to bewilderment and error. Any design, any ideology advanced by this bewildered humanity in this dark edifice of nature will amount to nothing more than a distraction and an entanglement.

Two Types of Ideologies

Ideologies are of two kinds: human and corporate. Human ideologies are addressed to the human species, not to some special nationality, race or class, and their purpose is the salvation of the whole human species. They attract supporters from all strata, groupings, nations and classes. Corporate ideologies are addressed to a certain group, class or stratum and their purpose is the liberation or the hegemony of that group. They thus attract supporters and defenders from that group only.

These two types of ideology are each based on a vision of human. The universal, human type of ideology, exemplified by Islam, embodies a kind of realization of man defined by the concept of primordial nature. According to Islam, in the course of the creation and before historical and social factors came into play, man gained a special existential dimension and lofty capacities that distinguished him from the animals and gave him his identity. According to this view, human beings within creation have gained a kind of species-intelligence and species-consciousness, which in turn have given them a species-individuation, an aptitude to be summoned and addressed and to act. Ideologies issue their summons and engender action by relying on the primordial consciousness that distinguishes the human species.

Another group of ideologies has a different vision of man. According to these, man as a species has no such aptitude to be summoned and be addressed or act because his intelligence, conscience and aptitudes coalesce under the influence of historical factors (in the life of nations and peoples) or social factors (in the class situation of man). Man in the absolute, apart from special historical and social factors, has no intelligence, consciousness or aptitude to be summoned or addressed; he is an abstract being, not an objective one. Marxism and the various nationalistic and ethnic philosophies are based on such a vision. These philosophies arise from class interests, national and racial sentiments or at best from an ethnic culture.

Beyond all doubt, Islamic ideology is human and arises from the primordial nature of man. Thus, Islam is addressed to the *nās*, the people at large, not to a special group or class.[20] Islam in practice has been able to attract supporters from among every group, even from among the very class against whom it has arisen – the class the Qur'ān terms the 'grandees' and the 'affluent' (*mala' wa muṭrāfīn*). To recruit warriors to fight against their own class, to engage members of a group in a struggle against the interests of that group, even to incite an individual to combat his own corruption are things Islam has done in numerous instances throughout its history. Islam, penetrating as it does to the deepest strata of man's existence and resting on primordial human nature, is able to incite the individual to combat his own corruption and to bring about a revolution of self against self known as repentance (*tawba*). The only power for revolution the corporate and class ideologies have is to incite individual against individual or class against class. They are never able to incite a revolution of individual against self, just as they cannot exert control over an individual in his inwardness, at the locus of his essential selfhood.

Islam, in being a religion – in being, of all the revealed religions, the seal of religions – exists to institute social justice.[21] Its goal is to liberate the deprived and oppressed and to struggle against the oppressors. But Islam does not speak to the deprived and oppressed alone, just as it has not attracted supporters from these classes alone. Islam has recruited defenders, even from among the classes against which it has struggled, relying on the power of religion on the one hand and on primordial human nature on the other. Islam is the theory of the victory of humanity over animality, science over ignorance, justice over injustice, equality over discrimination, virtue over iniquity, piety over dissipation, *tawḥīd* over *shirk*.[21] The victory of the downtrodden over the tyrants and the arrogant is one of the manifestations of these other victories.

Cultural Unity or Diversity

Does human culture have a single identity? Does culture have an ethnic, national or class identity, so that what is and always will be are cultures, not culture? These questions, too, relate to whether man has a single and authentic primordial nature, which may bestow a unity on culture, or whether he has no such single primordial nature, with the result that cultures must be the products of historical, ethnic and geographical factors or of profit-oriented class tendencies. Because Islam's world view upholds a single primordial nature, it favours both a single ideology and a single culture.

Only a human ideology, not a corporate ideology, only a unifying ideology, not one based on human division and fragmentation, only a primordial ideology, not a profit-oriented one, can rest on human values and be human in its essence.

Ideological Temporality and Environmental Specificity

Is every ideology tied to a time and a place? Is man condemned to have a particular ideology for each permutation of temporal circumstances and under each set of varying local environmental conditions? Do the principle of variation (according to region and locale) and the principle of abrogation and substitution (according to the time) govern ideology? Or, just as man's ideology is single, not multiple, from the point of view of grouping, is it likewise single, rather than multiple, from the point of view of time and place? In other words, in addition to being general rather than special, is it also absolute rather than relative in terms of time and place?

Whether an ideology is absolute or relative in terms of time and place depends on whether it arises from the specific primordial human nature and has for its object the happiness of the human species, or whether it arises from corporate interests and ethnic and class sensibilities.

In another respect, it depends on what we regard as the essence of social transformation. When a society undergoes transformation, leaving behind an era and embarking on a new era, does that society undergo a change in identity and so come to be governed by a new set of rules, just as, for instance, water, as its temperature rises, finally vaporizes, thereafter to be governed by the gas laws, not the laws governing liquids? Or are the primary laws of social evolution constant? Is the axis on which social change turns itself fixed? Does society undergo changes in stage, but not in the axis, the law, of evolution, just as animals transform and evolve biologically, while the laws of evolution themselves always remain constant?

In a third respect, the question of whether an ideology is absolute or relative from the standpoints of time and place depends on that ideology's world view. Is it scientific, philosophic, or religious? A scientific ideology, being founded on an unstable world view, cannot itself be stable. It thus contrasts with the philosophic world view, founded on first principles and first axioms, and with the religious world view, founded on revelation and prophecy.

Ideological Constancy or Change

Does the principle of constancy or the principle of change govern ideology? Whether ideology varies as time and place vary is a question of the abrogation and substitution of ideologies, but here I speak of a different question – that of the change and transformation of a single ideology. Whether an ideology is general or special in its content, whether it is absolute or relative, is it as a phenomenon constantly transforming and developing, given that this is the nature of phenomena? Is not the character of an ideology at its inception different from its character as it grows and matures? That is, does it not necessarily undergo constant modification, augmentation, deletion and revision at the hands of leaders and ideologues (as current materialistic ideologies do)? Otherwise, will it not soon grow exhausted and outdated and lose its authority? Or can an ideology be so ordered and so set along the primary lines of movement of man and society that it needs no revision or deletion and correction, that the role of the leaders and ideologues is only that of *ijtihād* in tenor and content and that ideological evolution takes place in the realm of these acts *of ijtihād,* not in the substance *of* the ideology?[22] The answer to this question, too, will become clear from the answers to the preceding questions.[23]

The Need for Faith

The individual act of cleaving to an ideology takes its true form when it takes the form of faith, and true faith cannot arise through coercion or with regard to expediency. One may be made to submit or yield to a particular issue or demand, but one cannot yield to an ideology. One must be magnetized by it, one must embrace it. Ideology calls for faith.

An appropriate ideology should, on the one hand, rest on a kind of world view that can convince the reason and nourish the mind and, on the other hand, logically deduce attractive goals from its world view. *At this juncture, love and conviction, the two basic elements of faith, work hand in hand to shape the world.*

Islam: The Comprehensive and All-Encompassing Teaching

Islam, being founded on such a world view, is a comprehensive and realistic teaching. It considers every aspect of human needs, whether this-worldly or otherworldly, physical or spiritual, intellectual or emotional, individual or social. From one point of view, the aggregate of Islamic teachings comprises three areas.

1. Principles of belief, that is, things in which it is the duty of every individual to strive to attain belief. The task that falls to every man comes under the heading of investigation and acquisition of knowledge.
2. Morals, that is, traits that every Muslim must seek to incorporate and use as an adornment of his character and whose opposites he has a duty to shun. The task that falls to every man here comes under the heading of self-control and self-moulding.
3. Decrees, that is, rules that relate to overt and objective acts, including acts with this-worldly and otherworldly ends, and individual and social acts.

According to the Shīʿi school of thought, there are five principles of Islamic belief: *tawḥīd,* justice, prophecy, the imamate, and the hereafter *(maʿād,* the Destination). As regards the principles of belief, which require each individual to acquire the right belief, Islam does not regard imitation and blind submission as sufficient; every individual must freely and independently verify the rightness of this belief. According to Islam, worship is not confined to physical acts of worship, such as alms, *zakāt* and *khums.* There is another kind of worship, and that is mental worship. Mental worship, or contemplation, if directed towards self-reproof, awakening and self-improvement, is superior to years of physical worship.

Where Thought Stumbles

The Glorious Qur'ān, in summoning us to reflect and draw conclusions, in regarding reflection as worship and in regarding acceptance of the principles of belief as flawed without logical reflection, has focused on this basic question: where does human error come from? What is the root of error and straying? If one wishes to think straight and avoid error and deviation, what must one do?

In the Glorious Qur'ān, a series of phenomena are named as the occasions and causes of error: reliance on supposition, subconscious tendencies and desires, haste, traditionalism and obedience to personalities.

Reliance on Supposition Instead of Knowledge and Certainty

The Noble Qur'ān, in numerous verses, stringently opposes action based on supposition instead of knowledge and certainty. It says, 'Do not pursue that of which you have no knowledge' (17:36) and 'The nature of most people is such that if you try to follow them, they will mislead you, because they rely on supposition (not on certainty) and act solely on conjecture and estimation' (paraphrase of 6:116). Modern philosophy has established that this tendency is one of the chief factors in error and confusion. A thousand years after the Qur'ān, Descartes made this recognition the first principle of his logic. He says, 'The first of these [precepts to which I have adhered] was to accept nothing as true that I did not clearly recognize to be so: that is to say, carefully to avoid precipitation and prejudice in judgements, and to accept in them nothing more than what was presented to my mind so clearly and distinctly that I could have no cause to doubt it.'[24]

Subconscious Tendencies and Desires

If one wishes to judge correctly, one must preserve complete impartiality towards the matter under consideration; that is, one must strive to find only reality and submit to reasons and evidence. One must be like a judge considering a case, impartial to the two sides of the dispute. If a judge has a personal bias towards one side, he will unconsciously pay more heed to the reasons adduced for that side's case. Such a bias will cause the judge to err.

If one fails to preserve one's impartiality relative to the right and wrong of an issue, if one's psychic tendencies are weighted towards one side, automatically and subconsciously the compass needle of one's thought will swing to the side of one's subconscious tendencies and desires. Thus, the Qur'ān identifies the desires of the psyche as one reason why the thought may stumble. It says in the *sūra Najm*, 'They follow nothing but supposition and what their own psyches desire'. (53:23)

Haste

Every judgement or expression of opinion demands a certain amount of evidence. Until sufficient evidence has been gathered on a question, any sort of expression of opinion constitutes haste and causes the thought to stumble. The Noble Qur'ān repeatedly alludes to the paucity of man's stock of knowledge and its insufficiency for some major judgements; it regards dogmatic assertions as highly imprudent. For instance, it says, 'Only a little knowledge has been given you', (17:85) which indicates that the amount of knowledge and information we have is insufficient for judgement.

Imām Ṣādiq (peace be upon him) has said:

In two verses of the Qur'ān God has singled out His servants and admonished them: first, they must not affirm a thing until they have attained knowledge of it [haste in affirmation], and second, they must not deny a thing until they have attained knowledge of it – indeed, until they have reached the stage of knowledge and certainty [haste in denial]. God says in one verse, 'Was not the Covenant of the Book [the book of essential disposition or the revealed books] taken from them so that they would not ascribe to God anything but the truth?' (7:169). And in another verse He said, 'But they deny what their knowledge does not encompass'. (10:39)[25]

Traditionalism and Looking to the Past

It is a fact of man's nature that when he sees that a particular thought or belief was accepted by past generations, he automatically accepts it without allowing himself time to consider it. The Qur'ān reminds us not to accede to the accepted notions and beliefs of past generations until we have weighed them on the scales of reason, and recommends independence of thought vis-à-vis the beliefs of past generations. It says in the *sūra Baqara*, verse 170, 'When it is said to them, "Follow what God has sent down," they say, "No, we follow the customs in which our ancestors believed." What? Even though their ancestors were devoid of reason and unguided?'. (2:170)

Obedience to Personalities

Additionally, obedience to personalities may cause the thought to stumble. Great personalities of past and present, thanks to the grandeur they assume in others' minds, may exert an overwhelming influence on others' thoughts and wills. Others think as those personalities think and make decisions as they do. Others give up their independence of thought and will to those personalities.

The Noble Qur'ān summons us to independence of thought and regards blind following of great men and personalities as the way to eternal torment. Accordingly, people who were lost said on the Resurrection, 'Our Lord! We obeyed our leaders and great men, and so they led us to the wrong path'. (33:67)

The Qur'ān, in summoning us to thought and reflection, points out not only the possible stumbling-blocks of thought but also the springs of reflection, that is, the subjects that are suitable for contemplation and as sources of knowledge and information.

In Islam, there has been a general opposition to the expenditure of mental energy on questions that can have no outcome other than mental fatigue (i.e.

which people have no means or tools to investigate) and on questions that, although they can be investigated, offer no benefit to the human condition.

The Most Noble Messenger characterized as pointless a science that brings no benefit and whose absence brings no detriment, but Islam supports and encourages sciences in which investigation can be pursued and that additionally are beneficial. The Noble Qur'ān teaches that three subjects are useful and fruitful to reflect upon.

1. Nature

Throughout the Qur'ān, there are many verses mentioning nature (including earth, sky, stars, sun, moon, clouds, rain, winds, movements of ships upon the sea, plants, animals – in sum, all the sensible phenomena that man sees about him) as something we are to consider closely, for example, 'Say, "Observe all that is in the heavens and on the earth"'. (10:101)

2. History

There are many verses in the Qur'ān that summon us to study peoples of the past and that present such study as a resource for acquiring knowledge. According to the Qur'ān, human history, with its transformations, takes shape in accordance with a range of norms and laws. The exaltations and abasements, victories and defeats, successes and failures, joys and miseries of history are subject to exact and ordered calculations. By studying these calculations and laws, one can gain control of present-day history and employ it to further one's own happiness and that of one's contemporaries. Here is one verse as an example: '[Normative] systems have gone away before you. So travel the earth and observe how things came out for those who practised denial'. (3:137) That is, before your time, norms and laws were actually put into effect. So explore and study the land and the historical legacy of those who have gone before and see how things came out for those who took the truth that God revealed to them to be lies.

3. The Inner Being of Man

The Qur'ān identifies the human heart as a source of a special kind of knowledge. According to the Qur'ān, the whole of creation is a set of signs of God and indications pointing out reality. The Qur'ān terms man's external world 'the horizons' (*afaq*) and his internal world 'the selves' (*anfus*). It thereby underlines the special importance of the inner being of man. This is the source for the terms so frequently met with in Islamic literature.[26]

The German philosopher Kant wrote a universally famous sentence, which is inscribed on his gravestone, 'Two things fill the mind with ever new and increasing admiration and awe, the oftener and more steadily we reflect on them: the starry heavens above me and the moral law within me.'[27]

Notes

1. The English philosopher Hobbes had such a view of man.
2. This is Descartes's theory.
3. The *ḥukamā'* of Islam have a principle for the interrelation of the spirit and the body, expressed thus, 'The soul and the body reflect each other responsively and preparatorily'.

   [Translator's note: The author makes repeated mention of three classes of traditional Islamic scholars in the course of this work. The *falāsifa* (sing. *failāsuf*) are concerned with the theory of knowledge, the structure of language and objective relations. Their field of inquiry is known as *falsafa*. Basically, they are Aristotelians. Ibn Sīnā typifies this class. The terms *falāsifa* and *falsafa* are translated by their English cognates, 'philosophers' and 'philosophy'.

   The *ḥukamā'* (sing. *ḥakīm)* are said to be more concerned with ultimate questions of being, the meaning of life, its end and human responsibility within it. Their field of inquiry is known as *ḥikma* (wisdom, *sagesse).* Ibn Sīnā would also be included in this group in certain respects. More typical representatives would be Mullā Ṣadrā, Mullā Hadi Sabzavarī and Shihāb ad-Dīn Suhravardi. These terms appear untranslated, except in a few instances where the author has used them in non-Islamic contexts or where *ḥikma* is translated as 'wisdom'.

   The *'urafā* (sing. *'ārif*) are the exponents of the theoretical Sufism codified by Ibn 'Arabi and especially influential in Shī'ī thought, known as *'irfān*. These terms, too, appear untranslated.

   The author seems sometimes to treat *falsafa* and *ḥikma* as synonyms, particularly in the section on 'Philosophy'. There he also treats *'irfān* as a synonym for Sufism as such, and many persons familiar in the West as *ṣūfīs* are introduced throughout as *'urafā'*.

   My thanks to Muḥammad Javad Larijani for his help in clarifying these terms. *Trans.*
4. *Tawrāt*: This word is cognate with the word 'Torah', but Muslim commentators hold that the work to which it refers is not to be identified with the existing Jewish scripture. See A. Yusuf 'Alī, translator, *The Holy Qur'ān* (n.p., 1946), pp. 282–85. *Trans.*
5. This and the following quotations are from the New English Bible. *Trans.*
6. Muḥammad Igbal, *The Reconstruction of Religious Thought in Islam* (Lahore, 1962), p. 179.
7. Will Durant, *The Pleasures of Philosophy* (New York, 1953), pp. 240, 114.
8. *Ibid.*, pp. 168–69.
9. The Kharijites were a religio-political sect that rejected the claims to rule of both 'Alī and Mu'awiya, founder of the Umayyad dynasty, as well as evolving certain distinctive theological positions.
10. Bertrand Russell, *Marriage and Morals* (London, 1929), p. 102.
11. See, for instance, Georges Politzer, *Cours de philosophée: 1. Principes élémentaires* (Paris, 1948).
12. George Sarton, Six *Wings: Men of Science in the Renaissance* (London, 1958), p. 218.
13. This quotation is without attribution and the source is unknown. *Trans.*

14. William James, *The Varieties of Religious Experience* (New York, 1929), p. 508.
15. *Ibid.*, p. 506.
16. Erich Fromm, *Psychoanalysis and Religion* (New York, 1950), pp. 25–26.
17. *Divan-i Ash'ar*, ed Naṣrullah Taqavi (Tehran, 1335 Sh./1956), p. 364. Nāṣir-i Khusraw was a famous poet, philosopher and Isma'ili missionary (d. 481/1088). *Trans.*
18. It can be inferred from the noble verses of the Qur'ān taken as a whole that these variations and needs appeared in the time of the prophet Noah. No earlier prophet had been given a revealed law. See 'Allama Sayyid Muḥammad Husayn Tabatabā'i, *Tafsīr al-Mīzān* (hereafter referred to as *Tafsīr al-Mīzān*), the commentary to the blessed *sūra Baqara*, verse 213, 'The people were a single nation, and God sent messengers'. (2:213)
19. Exact place of occurrence not found. *Trans.*
20. Sometimes this word, *nās*, meaning the people at large, is erroneously taken to be synonymous with the masses of the people, as opposed to the privileged classes. Because Islam is addressed to the *nās*, it is claimed that Islam is the religion of the masses, and this is likewise accounted a special feature of Islam. But the real virtue of Islam is that it arose with the support of the masses of the people, not that it is addressed solely to them and so has a corporate or class ideology. What distinguishes Islam even further is that it not only takes hold among the exploited and deprived classes, but also, in resting on primordial human nature, it has at times stirred the conscience of the exploiting classes and capitalists themselves, to the advantage of the exploited.
21. Note Hadid: 25, 'We had sent our apostles with clear signs, and We sent down with them the Book and the Balance, that the people might stand up in equity' (57:25). Note also A'raf: 29, 'Say, "My Lord has commanded equity".' (7:29)
22. *Ijtihād*: used here in a broad and analogical sense; means the deduction of particular applications of law from its principles and ordinances, exercised by a *mujtahid*.
23. In *Khatm-i Nubuvvat* ('Seal of Prophethood') appearing in *Muḥammad, Khatim-i Payambaran*, a publication of the Husayniya-yi Irshad, and later published separately as a pamphlet. I have discussed the universality and absoluteness of Islamic theology along with the role of *ijtihād* in adapting it to cicumstances of different places and changing temporal conditions. I have shown that what is subject to change is *ijtihād*, not Islamic ideology.
24. René Descartes, *Discourse on the Method of Rightly Conducting the Reason*, in 'Philosophical Works' (Cambridge, 1931), vol. 1, p. 92.
25. *Tafsīr al-Mizān* (Arabic Text), vol. 6, p. 319, commentary to A'raf: 169.
26. See *Fussilat*: 53: 'Soon We will show them Our signs on the horizons and in their souls, until it grows clear to them that this is the Truth.' (41:53)
27. Immanuel Kant, *Critique of Pure Reason* (Indianapolis, 1956), conclusion.

Index